W9-DJP-801

PUBLISHED ON THE
FOUNDATION ESTABLISHED IN MEMORY OF
OLIVER BATY CUNNINGHAM
OF THE CLASS OF 1917, YALE COLLEGE

CAPTAIN DREYFUS IN 1894

THE DREYFUS CASE

BY

THE MAN—ALFRED DREYFUS
AND
HIS SON—PIERRE DREYFUS

TRANSLATED AND EDITED
BY DONALD C. McKAY
DEPARTMENT OF HISTORY
HARVARD UNIVERSITY

NEW HAVEN
YALE UNIVERSITY PRESS
1937

THE Great War has passed—leaving desolation in its wake. How many of the principals in that great drama, the Dreyfus Affair—men who had then fought on opposing sides—found themselves united on the field of battle in common love of country! The field of honor claimed Lieutenant-Colonel DU PATY DE CLAM, as it claimed the only sons of Lieutenant-Colonel HENRY, of JOSEPH REINACH, of my uncle, MATHIEU DREYFUS. And there were many others.

But the passions aroused by the Dreyfus Affair have not been extinguished, and lasting peace has yet to settle over that historic struggle. You have but to evoke those years in the mind of a contemporary: his eyes kindle, his voice takes on a sharper note, he shudders at the memory of the violent conflict. The younger generation knows that the Dreyfus Affair shook France to its depths and influenced domestic politics right down to 1914, but that generation rarely concerns itself with the origins of the Affair.

To those splendid men who threw themselves into the battle to defend my father, at the peril of ruining their careers and sacrificing their family life; to my own noble comrades of the War; to the young generation, to whom epic struggles are unknown—I dedicate this book.

PIERRE DREYFUS.

CONTENTS

THE LAST YEARS

BY PIERRE DREYFUS

APPENDICES

ILLUSTRATIONS

Frontispiece

INTRODUCTION

THE Dreyfus Case was the most famous of the nineteenth century *causes célèbres,* and there are probably few educated men today to whom the name of Dreyfus is unknown. To the great public, then and now, the "Affair" has appealed first of all as a "mystery story," with characters and plot to challenge the most fertile author's imagination. An Henry sitting in the shadows of the Intelligence Bureau weaving a web of forgery in which to ensnare his docile and unwary superiors; an Esterhazy trading treason for money to calk the seams of dissipation, at once the tool and the bully of his superiors, daring even to blackmail the President of the Republic—these are figures worthy of the genius of a Conan Doyle.

The Dreyfus Affair, however, had a much wider significance than its casual appeal to the great public would indicate. The arrest of Captain Dreyfus, a Jew, followed in the wake of a wave of anti-Semitism which had swept over France during the previous decade. This movement had affected monarchist and clerical circles above all, and it was these groups which continued to dominate the Army, giving it the character of a caste. Indeed the admission of Dreyfus to the General Staff had caused something of a scandal. Later, when the evidence of Dreyfus' wrongful condemnation began to come to light, the clerico-monarchist forces closed ranks behind the professional Army, which was, in their view, the veritable bulwark of society in an age of high tension in international politics, when only a strong France could play a role worthy of a great power. Hence the honor of the Army must be preserved at all costs. Dreyfus must be guilty, because the military judges had found him guilty. Even if by chance he were innocent, it were better to sacrifice one man than to undermine the prestige of the soldiers. The revival of the Dreyfus Affair would do nothing but discredit the Army. It is interesting to note that this was precisely the view of Count von Bülow, the German Foreign Minister, who wanted to see the Affair "continue to suppurate" and weaken France.

The forces who saw the interests of society, as they conceived them, as superior to those of any individual were faced by the resolute defenders of Dreyfus. These men, of widely differing political opinions, were united in their attachment to the Republic, and were determined to resist all efforts of its foes to undermine it. Imbued with the democratic and individualistic philosophy of the Revolution, they had resolved the eternal problem of the antithesis of individual and society in favor of the former: no society worthy of the name could, in their view, be erected on any base save that of justice for the individual. This struggle between two social ideals soon grew to such magnitude that the figure of Dreyfus receded into the background. The Affair was only the beginning of a prolonged conflict in which the Church and the monarchists presently went down to resounding defeat, culminating in the separation of Church and State in 1905.

The Dreyfus Case thus came to have an ideal value: it acted as a catalytic agent, so to speak, to precipitate a struggle between two social philosophies. This was a conflict which can scarcely have an unfamiliar ring to our own age, when battle is being drawn all along the line between theories of individual rights and social regimentation.

The present book is interesting from many points of view. It includes a long introductory account of the Affair from 1894 to 1899 by Pierre Dreyfus, the son of Captain Dreyfus; the memoirs of Alfred Dreyfus (1899–1906); a considerable number of letters from the correspondence of Captain and Mme. Dreyfus during the Devil's Island period; and a selection of those letters re-

ceived by them from distinguished persons, principally at
the time of the Rennes trial.

No critical, full-length work on the Dreyfus Affair has
yet appeared, nor can it be written until a good deal of
official material is made available and a much deeper
study is made of the period as a whole. But we now know
the Case in its larger lines; and the skillful and stirring
account by Pierre Dreyfus gives us, for the period
1894–99, the first adequate treatment in English, making
use of the latest materials, including the famous posthumous memoirs of the German Military Attaché, Colonel von Schwartzkoppen. The memoirs of Captain Dreyfus are complementary to his *Five Years of My Life,* published in 1901 and which deal with the period from 1894
to 1899. In these recollections Captain Dreyfus resumes
the story after his second condemnation at Rennes; gives
us a vivid picture of his relations with public men such as
Jaurès, Clemenceau, and Combes; describes the tremendous obstacles overcome in the campaign for an appeal;
and carries us down to the final triumph of 1906, when
the decision of the Court-Martial at Rennes was set aside,
and he was restored to the Army.

The correspondence of Dreyfus and Mme. Dreyfus during the Devil's Island imprisonment has always formed
one of the most compelling parts of this dramatic story.
A considerable part of the letters here included have not
before been published. They reveal once again the really
incredible fortitude and endurance of Dreyfus under conditions where a lesser man must surely have been broken.
The letters of Mme. Dreyfus are much more numerous
than those which had previously been published. They offer us an insight into a selfless heroism upon which we
will not presume to comment.

Coming as they do from people well known on both
sides of the Atlantic, the letters to Captain and Mme.
Dreyfus from distinguished personages are of considerable intrinsic interest, and, as a body, they reveal how

deeply moved were people everywhere by the spectacle of the injustice from which Dreyfus suffered and how profoundly aware many of them were of the larger issues involved in the Affair.

Translation itself is at best a difficult, and perhaps a thankless, task. It has been my aim above all to render the French into idiomatic and readable English, without at the same time taking unwarranted liberties with the original. For the translation of numerous French legal terms and for making intelligible the complex legal processes through which the Case passed, I am indebted to my friend and colleague, Professor Sam Bass Warner of the Harvard Law School, who has—quite characteristically— given me generously of time he could ill afford to spare. To the solution of many of my problems Professor André Morize of Harvard has brought his wide and discriminating knowledge of both languages, as well as his unusual acquaintance with recondite aspects of the period. Lieutenant-Colonel Arthur Ringland Harris, U.S.A., has generously permitted me to consult him in connection with the numerous military problems raised. It need scarcely be added that the final responsibility for the translation is entirely mine.

Research assistance was provided by a grant of the Committee for Research in the Social Sciences. A certain number of critical notes and two critical appendices have been included, and in the research for these and for numerous terms in the translation, I have had the energetic and intelligent aid successively of two assistants, Professor Arthur J. Marder of the University of Oregon, and Mr. Lester R. Ott. Mr. John Shea, of the Harvard College Library, has been consistently helpful, now as before, in making the library a useful and pleasant place in which to work.

DONALD C. MCKAY.

John Winthrop House,
  Harvard University,
    February 9, 1937.

DRAMATIS PERSONAE

ANDRÉ, GENERAL LOUIS, 1838–1913. Minister of War (1901–5).

BALLOT-BEAUPRÉ, JULES, 1836–1917. Justice of the Court of Cassation, rapporteur for first appeal of Dreyfus Case (1898–99), Chief Justice of Court of Cassation (1900–1917).

BARRÈS, MAURICE, 1862–1923. French novelist and critic; anti-Dreyfusard; prominent in "nationalist revival" at turn of century.

BASTIAN. Charwoman in German Embassy, in pay of French Intelligence Bureau.

BAUDOUIN, MANUEL. Procureur Général (prosecuting attorney) of Court of Cassation during second appeal of Dreyfus Case (1903–6).

BERTILLON, ALPHONSE, 1853–1914. Chief of the Identification Department of the Judicial Police; inventor of system of criminal finger-printing; summoned as expert on bordereau.

BEXON D'ORMESCHEVILLE, Major A.F.F. Conducted inquiry preceding Court-Martial of 1894.

BILLOT, GENERAL JEAN BAPTISTE, 1828–1907. Minister of War (1882–83, and in 1896).

BRISSON, EUGÈNE HENRI, 1835–1912. Premier (June–October, 1898) after overturn of Méline Ministry, won over as Dreyfus adherent.

BUISSON, FERDINAND, 1841–1932. Deputy, active Dreyfusard.

BUNAU-VARILLA, PHILIPPE, 1860—. Classmate of Dreyfus at École Polytechnique; influenced his brother, editor of *Matin*, to publish bordereau; later Director General of the Interoceanic Panama Company, and appointed representative by the Republic of Panama in 1903 to meet Secretary of State Hay and negotiate to have the United States take over the Panama Canal.

CASIMIR-PÉRIER, JEAN, 1847–1907. Statesman, President of the Republic (1894–95).

CAVAIGNAC, EUGÈNE, 1853–1905. Minister of War in Brisson Cabinet (June–September, 1898); discredited by discovery of Henry forgeries.

CHANOINE, GENERAL CHARLES, 1835–1915. Minister of War (September–November, 1898) in Brisson Cabinet; anti-Dreyfusard.

CHAUMIÉ, JOSEPH. Minister of Justice (January, 1905—March, 1906).

CLAMAGERAN, JEAN, 1827–1903. Senator for life; Chairman of Senate's Amnesty Committee (1900).

CLEMENCEAU, GEORGES, 1841–1929. Journalist, statesman, wartime Premier (November, 1917—January, 1920); vigorously espoused Dreyfus' cause.

CLEMENCEAU, ALBERT, 1861–1927. Brother of Georges; attorney for Zola in 1899.

COMBES, ÉMILE, 1835–1921. Premier (1901–5), anti-clerical, Dreyfusard; influential in initiating final appeal of case.

CUIGNET, CAPTAIN LOUIS. On staff of Cavaignac, Minister of War; discoverer of "Henry forgery"; anti-Dreyfusard.

DE BOISDEFFRE, GENERAL LE MOUTON, 1839–1919. Chief of the General Staff of the French Army (1893–98); anti-Dreyfusard; forced to resign by revelation of Henry forgeries.

DE GALLIFET, GENERAL GASTON, 1830–1909. Won reputation for brutality through sanguinary suppression of Paris Commune (1871); as Minister of War (June, 1899—May, 1900) proposed pardon of Dreyfus and then insisted "incident is closed."

DELCASSÉ, THEOPHILE, 1852–1923. Minister of Foreign Affairs (1898–1905), architect of the Entente Cordiale with Great Britain (1904).

DEMANGE, CHARLES. Attorney for Dreyfus in 1894 and 1899.

DENIEL. Governor of the Salvation Islands.

DE PELLIEUX, GENERAL GEORGES. Charged with preliminary inquiry preceding Esterhazy's trial by Court-Martial (1899); resigned when Henry's suicide revealed he had been dupe of General Staff.

DU PATY DE CLAM, MAJOR MERCIER. Member of Third Bureau of General Staff, one of principals in anti-Dreyfus manoeuvres in Ministry of War.

DUPUY, CHARLES, 1851–1923. Premier (April–December, 1893; May, 1894—January, 1895; November, 1898—June, 1899).

DUTRAIT-CROZON, HENRI. Author of violently prejudiced anti-

Dreyfusard account of the case, *Histoire de l'Affaire Dreyfus* (1905).

ESTERHAZY (MARIE CHARLES FERDINAND WALSIN-ESTERHAZY), 1847–1923. French infantry officer, grandson of illegitimate member of French branch of Austrian House of Esterhazy; in German service as spy; author of bordereau for which Dreyfus was convicted.

FAURE, FÉLIX, 1841–99. President of the French Republic (1895–99); anti-Dreyfusard.

FORZINETTI, MAJOR FERDINAND. Governor of the Cherche-Midi Military Prison; befriended Dreyfus during his imprisonment there (January, 1895).

FRANCE, ANATOLE, 1844–1924. French novelist; vigorous defender of Dreyfus and Zola.

GONSE, GENERAL CHARLES. Deputy Chief of the General Staff; refused to be moved by Picquart's discovery of petit bleu, became one of leading anti-Dreyfusards among the Army officers.

GRIBELIN, FÉLIX. Archivist of the Ministry of War, involved in various anti-Dreyfus manoeuvres.

HANOTAUX, GABRIEL, 1853—. Historian and statesman; member of the French Academy; Minister of Foreign Affairs (May, 1894—January, 1895; November, 1895—June, 1898).

HÉMENT, EDGAR. One of the editors of the *Temps;* intermediary for Premier Combes in communicating with Dreyfus.

HENRY, LIEUTENANT-COLONEL HUBERT JOSEPH, 1846–98. Member of the Statistical Section, later head of the Intelligence Bureau of the General Staff; arch forger of the anti-Dreyfus documents.

JAURÈS, JEAN, 1859–1914. Historian, statesman, most prominent Socialist leader in prewar France; spearhead in Chamber of Deputies of campaign for a review of Dreyfus Case.

JOUAUST, COLONEL ALBERT. President of the Court-Martial at Rennes, 1899.

LABORI, MAÎTRE FERNAND, 1860–1917. Distinguished criminal lawyer, defended Zola (1899), attorney for Dreyfus (1899), defended Madame Caillaux in trial for murder of Gaston Calmette, journalist (1914).

LAUTH, CAPTAIN JULES. Member of Statistical Section of Intelligence Bureau in General Staff; associate of Henry in anti-Dreyfus campaign.

LAZARE, BERNARD, 1866–1903. Critic and journalist; espoused Dreyfus' cause, wrote first pro-Dreyfus pamphlet (*Une erreur judiciaire; la vérité sur l'Affaire Dreyfus,* 1896).

LEBLOIS, MAÎTRE LOUIS, 1854–1928. Attorney; friend of Picquart, who shared secret of petit bleu with him; vigorous Dreyfusard.

LEBON, ANDRÉ, 1859—. Colonial Minister (April, 1896—June, 1898); responsible for placing Dreyfus in "double shackle" (Devil's Island was subject to his jurisdiction).

LEBRUN-RENAULT, CAPTAIN. Receiver of Dreyfus' alleged "confession" on morning of his degradation.

LEMERCIER-PICARD. Pseudonym for Lehmann. Secret agent of Henry, expert in forgery; aided Henry in preparation of forged documents concerning Dreyfus.

LÉPINE, LOUIS, 1846–1933. Prefect of Police (1893–97, 1899–1912).

LOUBET, ÉMILE, 1838–1929. President of French Republic (1899–1906), Dreyfusard successor of anti-Dreyfusard Félix Faure.

MÉLINE, JULES, 1838–1925. Anti-Dreyfusard Premier (1896–98), famous for remark, *"il n'y a pas d'Affaire Dreyfus"* (December 4, 1897).

MERCIER, GENERAL AUGUSTE, 1833–1921. Minister of War (1893–95), responsible for premature arrest of Dreyfus, act which involved him as accomplice in subsequent injustices to Dreyfus.

MICHEL-JAFFARD, ANTOINE. Justice of the Court of Cassation; sometime rapporteur for the Dreyfus appeal in 1903.

MILLERAND, ALEXANDRE, 1859—. Socialist Minister of Commerce and Industry in Waldeck-Rousseau Cabinet (1899–1901), eventually President of the Republic (1920–24).

MONACO, ALBERT, PRINCE OF, 1848–1922. Espoused Dreyfus cause.

MORNARD, MAÎTRE HENRY, 1859—. Distinguished criminal lawyer; Dreyfus attorney in first and second appeals before Court of Cassation.

MÜNSTER, COUNT (later PRINCE) VON, 1820–1902. German Ambassador in Paris (1885–1900).

PAINLEVÉ, PAUL, 1863–1933. Mathematician, statesman, Premier (1917, 1925), Dreyfusard.

PANIZZARDI, COLONEL. Italian Military Attaché in Paris, with whom Dreyfus was also alleged to have had treasonable relations.

PAUFFIN DE SAINT-MOREL, MAJOR. Sometime adjutant to General de Boisdeffre, Minister of War.

PERRENX, A. Editor of the *Aurore,* which published Zola's letter, "J'accuse"; prosecuted with Zola (1899).

PICQUART, LIEUTENANT-COLONEL GEORGES, 1854–1914. As head of Intelligence Bureau of General Staff, discovered petit bleu, established guilt of Esterhazy; prepared way for vindication of Dreyfus; dismissed from Army (1898), reinstated and promoted brigadier general (1906), Minister of War (1906–9).

PRESSENSÉ, FRANCIS DE, 1853–1914. Deputy, Dreyfusard, President of League of Rights of Man.

RANC, ARTHUR, 1831–1908. Senator, early a vigorous supporter of Dreyfus.

REINACH, JOSEPH, 1856–1921. Deputy, writer, historian of Dreyfus case (*Histoire de l'Affaire Dreyfus*), one of zealots in inner circle of Dreyfusards.

SANDHERR, COLONEL. Head of Intelligence Bureau of General Staff when Dreyfus was arrested (October, 1894).

SAUSSIER, GENERAL FÉLIX, 1828–1905. As Governor General of Paris, he issued orders to prosecute Dreyfus (1894) and Esterhazy (1897).

SCHEURER-KESTNER, AUGUSTE, 1833–99. Deputy to National Assembly from Upper Alsace, from the Seine; Senator for life (1875); First Vice-President of Senate (1896); espoused Dreyfus' cause with great vigor and died as a result of his efforts to secure a retrial.

SCHWARTZKOPPEN, LIEUTENANT-COLONEL MAX VON, 1850–1917. German Military Attaché in Paris (1891–97); employed Esterhazy as spy (1894–96); denied repeatedly having had any relations with Dreyfus; his full story told only in posthumous memoirs (*Truth about Dreyfus,* 1930).

SÉVERINE, MME. Pseudonym for Mme. Caroline Rémy Guébhard, 1855–1929. Journalist, Dreyfusard.

SYVETON, GABRIEL, 1864–1904. Nationalist, anti-Dreyfusard; validation of his election as deputy was occasion for Jaurès' famous intervention in the Chamber on behalf of Dreyfus (April 6, 7, 1903).

TRARIEUX, JACQUES, 1840–1904. Senator, ardent Dreyfusard, founder of League of the Rights of Man.

VAL CARLOS, MARQUIS DE. Former attaché in the Spanish Embassy in Paris, onetime spy in the service of the French Intelligence Bureau.

VALLÉE, ERNEST, 1845–1920. Minister of Justice at time of Dreyfus' request for an appeal (November, 1903).

WALDECK-ROUSSEAU, PIERRE MARIE, 1846–1904. Statesman, summoned as Premier (June, 1899) to pacify a France rent by dissensions of the Affair.

ZOLA, ÉMILE, 1840–1902. Novelist; espoused Dreyfus' cause; wrote famous letter, "J'accuse," to President of Republic, denouncing manoeuvres of Army heads; tried and condemned (1898).

ZURLINDEN, GENERAL ÉMILE, 1837–1929. Minister of War (1898), succeeding Cavaignac; unconvinced of Dreyfus' innocence by Henry forgeries; resigned to become Military Governor of Paris, in which office he had Picquart prosecuted.

CHRONOLOGY

1859

Oct. 9. Alfred Dreyfus born at Mulhouse in Alsace.

1880

Dreyfus is graduated from École Polytechnique, appointed second lieutenant.

1882

Dreyfus is made first lieutenant.

1889

Sept. 12. Dreyfus marries Lucie Hadamard.

1892

Dreyfus completes two-year course at École de Guerre.

1893

Jan. 1. Dreyfus assigned to General Staff.

1894

July 20. Esterhazy offers to sell French Army secrets to Schwartzkoppen, German Military Attaché.

Aug. 15–Sept. 6. Esterhazy delivers various documents to Schwartzkoppen, including those enumerated in bordereau; latter arrives at German Embassy between August 16 and September 1, is purloined by Brücker, delivered to Henry (mid-September).

Sept. 15 (ca.)–Oct. 15. Investigation of bordereau by General Staff, leading to

Oct. 15. Arrest and imprisonment of Captain Dreyfus.

Oct. 28. Henry "tips off" *Libre parole,* in order to compromise Mercier and force Dreyfus' prosecution.

Nov. 1. *Libre parole* publishes article on Dreyfus; Cabinet decides on prosecution of Dreyfus.

Nov. 14–29. Bexon d'Ormescheville, rapporteur, conducts preliminary inquiry.

Dec. 3. Report of Bexon d'Ormescheville, known to public only when published by *Siècle*, January 7, 1898.

Dec. 4. Trial of Dreyfus ordered; he is permitted to communicate with family for first time.

Dec. 19–22. Trial by Court-Martial; Dreyfus condemned by unanimous vote.

1895

Jan. 5. Public military degradation of Dreyfus.

Jan. 17–18. Dreyfus taken from Paris to Island of Saint-Martin-de-Ré, concentration point for convicts for French Guiana.

Feb. 21. Dreyfus leaves for Salvation Islands, arriving March 12.

Apr. 13. Dreyfus placed in prison camp, newly constructed for him on Devil's Island.

July 1. Picquart made head of Intelligence Bureau.

1896

Mar. Captain Lauth submits petit bleu to Picquart. Petit bleu presently reveals Esterhazy as author of bordereau.

Sept. 3. *Daily Chronicle* carries false news of Dreyfus' escape. Colonial Minister Lebon orders him to be put in irons each night (the "double shackle"), a punishment lasting from September 6 to October 20.

Aug.–Sept. Picquart makes futile attempts to win his superiors to reparation of wrong done Dreyfus.

Sept. 14. *Éclair* publishes "The Traitor," anonymous history of the Dreyfus Affair, actually written by du Paty de Clam, a fact first established by Walter Littlefield, an American journalist.

Sept.–Nov. Henry "nourishes" Dreyfus dossier with forged documents.

Oct. 27. Picquart ordered to provinces as dangerous, on trumped-up mission, Gonse taking over Intelligence Bureau provisionally.

Nov. 10. *Matin* publishes photograph of bordereau.

Dec.–Jan. (1897). To discredit Picquart, Henry "thickens" Picquart dossier with forged documents.

1897

Jan. Henry constructs forged "ultrasecret" Dreyfus dossier, including "bordereau annoté."

Apr. 2. Picquart prepares a memorandum on Dreyfus Affair, to be given to President of Republic in event of his death.

May 31. Henry attempts to intimidate Picquart by revealing results of investigation of latter's activities as head of the Intelligence Bureau.

June 10. Picquart vigorously denies Henry's charges.

June 21. Picquart reveals Dreyfus' innocence in confidence to his friend and lawyer, Leblois.

July 13. Leblois discloses Picquart's secret to Scheurer-Kestner, Vice-President of Senate, already substantially convinced of Dreyfus' innocence.

July 14. Scheurer confides in fellow officers of Senate his conviction of Dreyfus' innocence.

July–Sept. Scheurer's attempts to inform Dreyfus of his interest fail.

Aug. 17. General Billot rids Army of Esterhazy, retiring him by reason of "temporary infirmity."

Oct. Esterhazy warned by Army chiefs of campaign of Scheurer-Kestner, *et al.*, to "substitute him for Dreyfus."

Oct. 29–Nov. 5. Esterhazy writes three threatening letters to Félix Faure, President of the Republic, demanding protection for his "honor."

Oct. 29. Scheurer talks to President Faure of Dreyfus Affair, but gets no satisfaction.

Nov. 6–12. Mathieu Dreyfus learns that Esterhazy is author of bordereau.

Nov. 15. Mathieu Dreyfus denounces Esterhazy as author of bordereau in open letter to Minister of War.

Nov. 16. Esterhazy asks Minister of War for an investigation of charges.

1898

Jan. 10–11. Esterhazy acquitted by Court-Martial, after sham investigation and trial.

Jan. 13. Zola's famous letter denouncing the authors of the Courts-Martial of 1894 and 1898, "I accuse," appears in *Aurore*.

Feb. 7–23. Zola and Perrenx, editor of *Aurore*, tried for libel and convicted.

Feb. 26. Picquart discharged from Army.

Feb. 28. Mme. Dreyfus requests permission of Colonial Minister Lebon to join her husband, subsequently refused.

July 7. Replying to an interpellation on Dreyfus Case, Cavaignac, Minister of War, reads from tribune of Chamber letters from Schwartzkoppen-Panizzardi correspondence (later proved to be forgeries). Chamber votes by virtual unanimity "posting" of Cavaignac's address.

July 9. Picquart attacks Cavaignac's disclosures.

July 13. Picquart arrested and imprisoned on complaint of Minister of War.

Aug. Cavaignac's own investigation discloses forgeries by Henry.

Aug. 30. Henry confesses forgeries and is imprisoned.

Aug. 31. Henry commits suicide. General de Boisdeffre, Chief of the General Staff, resigns. General de Pellieux resigns.

Sept. 1. Esterhazy flees from France.

Sept. 3. Cavaignac resigns as Minister of War. Mme. Dreyfus submits request for an appeal of her husband's case.

Sept. 26. Cabinet decides to transmit Mme. Dreyfus' request for an appeal to Court of Cassation.

Oct. 29. Criminal Division of Court of Cassation allows Mme. Dreyfus' request for an appeal, and opens investigation of Dreyfus Case.

1899

Feb. 16. Death of President Félix Faure.

June 3. Decision of 1894 condemning Dreyfus set aside by full bench of Court of Cassation; case remanded to Court-Martial at Rennes for retrial.

June 5. Dreyfus informed of decision of Court of Cassation.

June 9. Dreyfus sets sail for France on board Cruiser *Sfax*.

June 22. Formation of Waldeck-Rousseau Ministry to pacify France, rent by struggle of Dreyfus and anti-Dreyfus factions.

July 1. Dreyfus arrives in France; incarcerated in Military Prison at Rennes.

Aug. 7–Sept. 9. Dreyfus' second trial by Court-Martial ends with decision of guilty with "extenuating circumstances," vote of five judges to two; condemned to ten years' imprisonment.

Sept. 19. Government pardons Dreyfus. Death of Scheurer-Kestner.

Sept. 21. Order of the day to the Army from the Minister of War, General de Gallifet: "the incident is closed."

1900

Dec. 27. Passage of Amnesty Law, stifling suits and prosecutions then in progress, arising out of Dreyfus Case.

1901

May 1. Publication of Dreyfus' memoirs, *Five Years of My Life*.

1902

Sept. 29. Death of Zola.

1903

April 6, 7. Jaurès intervenes in Chamber during discussion of election of Syveton to revive the "Affair." General André, Minister of War, states Government is willing to undertake "administrative investigation" of Dreyfus Case.

Apr. Dreyfus submits request for an investigation to Combes Government.

June 4. Captain Targe begins administrative investigation of Case in Ministry of War.

Nov. 22. Results of War Ministry's investigation submitted to Minister of Justice.

Nov. 26. Dreyfus submits to Minister of Justice request for an appeal of Rennes judgment.

Dec. 24. Committee on Appeal of Ministry of Justice adopts unanimous motion in favor of appeal.

1904

Mar. 3. Proceedings open before Criminal Division of Court of Cassation.

Mar. 5. Criminal Division allows request for an appeal.

Nov. 28. Criminal Division renders final decision, allowing Dreyfus' appeal (which now goes before full bench of Court of Cassation).

1906

June 15–July 12. Sessions of full bench of Court of Cassation.

July 9. By unanimous vote, Court sets aside Rennes judgment.

July 11. Court votes, 31 to 18, to set aside the judgment of Rennes without remand.

July 12. Judgment proclaiming Dreyfus' innocence read.

July 13. Senate and Chamber of Deputies adopt bills reinstating Dreyfus and Picquart, promoting former major and latter brigadier general.

July 20. Dreyfus made chevalier of Legion of Honor. His stripes restored in ceremony at École Militaire.

Oct. 15. Dreyfus resumes military duties at Fort of Vincennes.

1907

July 26. Dreyfus applies for retirement from Army.

1908

June 4. Dreyfus wounded by journalist at ceremonies accompanying translation of Zola's ashes to Pantheon.

1914

Aug. 2. Dreyfus returns to active service.

1918

Jan. Dreyfus sent to rear upon reaching age limit; appointed to command of artillery park at Orleans.

Sept. 5. Dreyfus made lieutenant-colonel; promoted officer of Legion of Honor.

1935

July 11. Death of Dreyfus.

A HISTORY OF "THE AFFAIR"
(1894–1899)
BY PIERRE DREYFUS

PREFACE

ON the evening of the day we bore my father to his final rest, I took from the shelves of my library that remarkable book *Five Years of My Life* and the admirable *Histoire de l'Affaire* by Joseph Reinach. I read again long chapters from both. I had witnessed my father's last moments, outwardly unmoved. I had controlled my feelings all through the heartbreaking final rites. But as I read those pages in which the story of his long and terrible suffering lived again, I wept like a child. What, I asked myself, underlies human motives? Why should men, respectable by conviction and reputation, torture year after year a victim whom they knew to be innocent? Why did they refuse to grant him those elementary rights which the law gives even to the guilty? Why, for no reason, did they aggravate and prolong his suffering? Were these men, most of whom are now dead, completely heartless? Were they, like Schwartzkoppen, smitten with remorse at the end? And did those of them who had religious convictions reflect that they would one day be summoned to account for their misdeeds?

.   .   .   .

AT the time of my father's arrest in October, 1894, I was three years old, my sister Jeanne eighteen months. And so the event which convulsed the lives of our parents and was later to attract world interest left no trace in our minds. Indeed, my mother did everything in her power to keep from us a sorrow which we had no way of understanding. Her love for us was such that she succeeded in concealing her own suffering. She contrived to shelter us from street demonstrations and to keep newspapers from us when we learned to read. But in the evening, when she came to tuck us in our beds, she taught us to pray God to send back soon the father who had left us to go on a long journey. By speaking of him often she kept our memory of him fresh. And so that he might have a message from us by each mail, she would have us write him little notes, herself guiding our childish hands.

My earliest memory of the Affair dates from the presidential election of February, 1899, when I was eight years old. As I learned later, the partisans of truth[1] ardently desired the election of Loubet. I knew nothing about the matter except that that would please my mother. One of my aunts took me for a walk along the Boulevards as far as the offices of the *Matin* in order to read its election bulletins. As soon as we learned that Méline had been defeated, we ran to our home in the Rue de Châteaudun, and I burst into the parlor to announce the good news. But when some-one asked me why the election of Loubet pleased me so much, I had nothing to reply and burst into tears.

My second distinct recollection is that of our journey to Carpentras seven months later. My sister and I were taken there by our grandparents to meet father and mother, after father had been given his freedom as a result of the trial at Rennes. I can still see clearly the scene of our arrival—mother greeting us and, standing at her side, a gentleman with hair nearly white, gaunt features, an air of weariness, his clothes ill fitting his emaciated form. But there was so much tenderness in his kindly blue eyes, and he embraced us so warmly, that we returned his embraces and accepted him at once as our father.

Some time afterward, as I became conscious of the fact that there was a sort of mystery in the life of my parents, I questioned them. And they described for me the more important elements of the Affair and showed me an Épinal print, illustrating the principal episodes of the case. Henceforth, they talked more freely in front of me, but I was still so young that the significance of these events lay beyond my comprehension, and the abnormal quality in our family life continued to elude me. I had become accustomed to seeing my father eternally seated at his desk going through documents and covering large sheets of foolscap in his fine hand; accustomed to seeing him receive frequent visits from serious and preoccupied gentlemen who discussed questions I did not understand. But not once did I have the feeling that I was living in an unusual environment. Moreover, my parents were always at great pains to prevent their cares from disturbing my youth; they sought above all to assure me the normal life of other youngsters of my age. To be sure laughter and gayety were not the rule in our home. My father's steady and intense preoccupation (until 1906 he was obsessed by a single idea—to win official

1. i.e., the supporters of Dreyfus.

recognition of his innocence) weighed upon us all and lent a certain austerity to our family life. But aside from that I enjoyed a
youth substantially the same as that of my school companions at
the *lycée* where I was sent to pursue my studies.

My father was naturally reserved. Five years of solitude and of
suffering had made him even more so. He lived an intense inner
life, but he scarcely knew any longer how to communicate his
emotions to others: he had simply lost the habit of expressing
them. He was averse, moreover, to complaint and to any public
manifestation of his suffering. And so he seemed very cold and
very distant to those who knew him slightly. Joseph Reinach, one
of the most courageous and understanding of his defenders, tells
how he went to Carpentras at the end of the year 1899 to meet my
father for the first time. My father, who was fully aware of all he
owed to Reinach and who was profoundly grateful to him, stood
awaiting him at the gate of my Aunt Valabrègue's estate (where
we were staying). When Reinach arrived, my father held out his
hand and said to him simply, "Merci." Reinach continues: "And
that was all, that single word by way of salutation, and I was
proud to believe it equally worthy of him and of me. But many
of his supporters, to whom he expressed his gratitude with no
more show of feeling, were offended. . . . To the minds of most
men simplicity is the least accessible of spiritual beauties. . . .
It was generally held that Dreyfus continued to play his role badly
precisely because he played no role at all but simply remained
himself. His shyness was mistaken for coldness. His full heart was
thought to be empty because it did not overflow."

Maître Mornard, who was Dreyfus' lawyer[2] and who defended
him ably and devotedly before the Court of Cassation,[3] said in his
plea of July 5, 1906: "How are we to blame him who for years
was tracked like a wild beast and tortured like a martyr, how are
we to blame him if he has so completely withdrawn into himself
that he can no longer reveal his feelings—if he is possessed by what
we might call the shyness of suffering?"

2. *Maître* is the title given in France to all members of the legal profession:
the *avocat*, or barrister, who pleads cases; the *avoué*, or solicitor, who deals
with clients and prepares cases; the *notaire*, who receives and draws up con-
tracts, deeds, etc., to give them authenticity.
3. The Supreme Court of France; on the French Judicial System, *see* Appendix II.

In the days following the trial at Rennes, my father found himself literally exhausted as a result of the terrible suffering, physical and spiritual, which he had undergone. When he came to Carpentras, September 20, 1899, he could with difficulty walk a few hundred yards. He was prey to terrible nightmares, and it was nearly two years before he regained his balance. His most bitter memory—one which never ceased to haunt him—was that of the double shackle.[4] Even during his last years he would sometimes awake with a terrible cry, believing himself fastened in iron rings bolted to his bed. He was without hatred, but to the end he cherished a profound resentment toward the Colonial Minister, André Lebon, who was influenced by sordid political prejudice to inflict upon him this abominable torment. Dreyfus could understand (although he could not forgive) the mistakes, even the treachery, of certain Army officers, influenced by religious hatred or *esprit de caste*. But he could not excuse a man who had no good reason for wishing him ill—whose acts indeed, by very reason of his office, should have reflected a scrupulous conscience—and yet who had taken it upon himself to aggravate my father's suffering, contrary both to the regulations and to the most elementary rules of justice.

As soon as he was sufficiently strong, my father set to work. With obvious amazement he rapidly mastered the multiple aspects of the great drama of which he had been the center during the five years when man's injustice had cut him off from the society of his fellows. It was for him painful to learn of the ignominy of his superior officers, and difficult to believe the existence of all the villainy and treacherous prejudice which were revealed. On the other hand, the heroic stand of those who undertook his defense filled his heart with boundless gratitude. Shortly before his death, on one of those peaceful days reserved to him by the solicitude and affection of his family (for he scarcely went out at all any more), he could still write:

"I know no bitterness and have always risen above narrow prejudice. I have tried to understand how those who did me such great wrong—unwilling in their pride to admit their error—turned first to untruth and then to treachery. But before all else, my thoughts return to those noble men whose courage was on a

4. *See* p. 74.

plane with their moral integrity and whose conscience prescribed their duty to them. It is they who are my solace. It is they whose memory I evoke with pleasure during my long hours of meditation.''

But even his best friends complicated my father's task when, beginning in 1900, divergent views among them became evident. The verdict of the Court-Martial at Rennes had amazed and shocked them. Most of them were convinced that, after the unanimous decision of the Court of Cassation, this new trial would be a pure formality, and that acquittal was the only possible outcome. Their disappointment was great. All their hopes fell to the ground, and they were faced with the prospect of beginning anew. The Government, stirred itself by the scandalous judgment and by unanimous protest the world over, offered my father a pardon. And for the moment this brought comfort to us all.

The Affair, however, now entered the realm of politics, and various parties seized upon it. Everyone wanted to guide my father in accordance with his own views. There were even those who went so far as to regret that he was no longer in prison, believing that as a free man he had lost his martyr's halo, and that as a result the campaign which they considered essential to force the Government to resubmit the case to the Court of Cassation had been compromised.

And there were others, influenced by temperamental considerations or by personal ambition, who wished my father to follow their advice and seize upon the first element of new evidence (whatever its weight might be) as the basis for requesting a review of the case. But he was opposed to committing himself to such a course until he should be adequately prepared from every point of view. My father had a clear and precise mind, and was opposed to all unnecessary agitation. He wanted the case to remain henceforth in the hands of the courts. He felt that he could never rest satisfied until his innocence should have been established— convincingly, completely, irrefutably—by the highest court of the land. For six long years he pursued unswervingly the task he had set himself, and his memoirs reveal with what consistency, logic, and courage he accomplished it.

There were those, however, who did not share his wish to keep the Affair on the judicial plane, who found themselves opposed by his inflexible will, and who were quite visibly chafed. They insisted that he failed to understand the Affair because he did not understand it as they did. They accused him of coldness because his gratitude did not take the form of blindly following their advice, even when he considered that advice fatal. Certain acts of friends, toward whom he felt the deepest gratitude, caused him much pain. Although my father relates these incidents in a spirit of great moderation in his recollections, I considered that I should be more faithful to his memory if I omitted them. I feel that no useful end is served by emphasizing the petty weaknesses of unselfish men.

My father proved to be completely right. Thanks to his perseverance he won on July 12, 1906, what he had so much desired—final recognition of his innocence by the Court of Cassation which, in a magnificent decision, destroyed every element in the accusation.

. . . .

The historical truth is established today beyond any shadow of doubt, and the present book is in no sense intended to make a new contribution to that truth. My aim is quite other. For those who have attributed mysterious origins to the Affair and have devised singularly complicated explanations for it, I wish to bring out its very simple and quite human psychology, to set forth the salient facts, to describe the principal persons concerned as I believe they are to be understood. But above all it is my most ardent wish that, by revealing the essential aspects of the Affair, by publishing some of my father's and mother's splendid correspondence and a part of my father's memoirs, I may render the homage of a son to the man who will remain for future generations one of the noblest heroes in the history of our beloved France.

THE DREYFUS AFFAIR

CHAPTER I

ON THE THRESHOLD OF THE DRAMA

ON October 15, 1894, Captain Alfred Dreyfus of the General Staff of the French Army left his home on the Avenue du Trocadéro on his way to the Ministry of War, Rue Saint-Dominique, where he had been summoned to appear at nine o'clock. The morning was cool, harbinger of one of those splendid autumn days when Paris is at its best—with a faint blue sky lightly obscured by haze. As Dreyfus made his way rapidly along the quays of the Seine he was thinking how richly life had bestowed her favors on him. He was in the fulness of his powers, profoundly happy, possessed of all that a man could ask—a family united in affection, children whom he adored, a fortune well invested in the prosperous industry in Mulhouse which his brothers managed. Finally, thanks to his brilliant career at the École de Guerre,[1] he had realized the most cherished of his boyhood dreams—admission to the General Staff.

This gratifying picture, which Dreyfus evoked with such warmth, was marred in one respect—by the resurgence of anti-Semitism which was then sweeping over the country, and evidences of which he had noticed for some time among his colleagues. He attached no exaggerated importance to this development, although he had already suffered its consequences at the time of his graduation from the École de Guerre. General de Bonnefond, whose function it was to offer a general estimate of the candidate, supplementary to his examination grades, had given Dreyfus a zero, his excuse being that he wanted no Jews on the General Staff. The result was that Dreyfus was dropped from third to ninth place among the candidates, but suffered no other penalty. His colleagues of the General Staff often ostentatiously showed him copies of the *Libre parole*, which published violent articles by

1. The *École Supérieure de Guerre*, the staff college at Paris which prepared selected captains and lieutenants for General Staff work.

Drumont, leader of the anti-Semitic movement.[2] But Dreyfus was very reserved, even proud, and attributed little importance to these stupidities.

And so on this Monday morning in October Dreyfus was reporting to the Ministry of War to undergo a general inspection. He was in mufti, in accordance with instructions of the official letter which had reached him Saturday. The wording of the summons had at first somewhat surprised him, but he had not bothered to seek further for a reason. Habitually punctual, he had set out for the Ministry in time for his appointment.

Upon his arrival Major Picquart of the General Staff, who appeared to be awaiting him, conducted Dreyfus immediately to the office of General de Boisdeffre, Chief of the General Staff. There, to his amazement, he found himself in the presence not only of an officer belonging to the Third Bureau,[3] Major du Paty de Clam, but also of three civilians who seemed to be keeping themselves in the background. Major du Paty de Clam asked him to fill out the formal descriptive part of his inspection blank. Then, indicating his thumb which he had put in a sling for the occasion, he continued: "The General will be here shortly. I have a bad thumb and will appreciate your writing a letter for me while we are waiting." Although both the request and the setting of the whole scene were bizarre, Dreyfus acceded.

Du Paty took a seat near him and began to dictate the famous letter whose text was precisely that of the document later known as the *bordereau*. Suddenly du Paty brutally interrupted: "You're trembling, Captain!" Dreyfus was not trembling, but his hands were chilled. He said so calmly in so many words. This was not at all to the liking of du Paty, who was obviously trying to intimidate

2. The anti-Semitic movement had its beginnings in the 'eighties with a group of journalists of clerical sympathies, who identified the Jews with the abuses of high finance and all the evils of the bourgeois Republic. The Jewish aspects of the Panama Scandal gave a fresh impulse to anti-Semitism, a formidable clerical-royalist movement by 1894.

3. The General Staff (*État-Major de l'Armée*) had its functions divided as follows: Personnel Section; Materiel and Finance Section; the First Bureau (organization and mobilization); Second Bureau (intelligence); Third Bureau (military operations and training); and Fourth Bureau (communications and transport); the African Section; and the famous Historical Section. The General Staff studied questions relating to general territorial defense and the preparation of war plans.

him. And so he added harshly: "Watch yourself, this is a serious matter."

A few lines further on du Paty rose, struck a theatrical pose, laid his hand on Dreyfus' shoulder and exclaimed in a loud voice: "Captain Dreyfus, I arrest you in the name of the law. You are accused of the crime of high treason." As if moved by a spring, Dreyfus leaped to his feet, coloring violently under the insult. But the blow was so unexpected, the accusation so heinous that his head swam and he could only stammer incoherently. Then gaining control of himself, he protested with all his strength against the terrible error of which he was the victim. The civilian witnesses now drew near—M. Gribelin, Archivist of the Ministry of War; M. Cochefert, representative of the police;[4] and the latter's secretary.

For two terrible hours Dreyfus fought like a madman. He was ignorant of the fact that his fate had already been decided, incapable of believing that his questioners sought anything but the truth. And so he strove to convince du Paty de Clam, and then Cochefert, that there was nothing either in his official or in his private life which could justify the slightest suspicion. It was of no avail. His heartbreaking protests, his requests for the documents on which the accusation was based, his reiterated professions of innocence—all these succeeded only in exasperating the narrow and bigoted minds of these men. What they wanted was a confession. And when they were unable to get it, they were incensed. Dreyfus was searched like a criminal, and just as in every orthodox scenario of this type, a revolver was placed within his reach so that he might himself do the work of justice. Finally du Paty de Clam realized that he would get no results that day. He ordered Major Henry to conduct Dreyfus to the Cherche-Midi Military Prison where that very morning a cell had been reserved by order of General Mercier.[5]

Captain Dreyfus was placed in solitary confinement. His calvary had begun.

4. *Commissaire aux Délégations.* For the function of the police in treason cases, *see* Appendix II.

5. Minister of War; for the identification of participants in the Affair, *see* "Dramatis Personæ," pp. xiii–xviii.

CHAPTER II

THE CRIME

THE Intelligence Bureau of the Ministry of War,[1] under the direction of Colonel Sandherr, included a special branch, the so-called "Statistical Section," which was concerned above all with counterespionage. One of its members was Major Henry. In the middle of September, 1894, Major Henry received from one of his regular agents, Brücker by name, a letter which the latter had purloined from the *loge* of the *concierge* in the German Embassy. The letter was addressed to the German Military Attaché, Lieutenant-Colonel von Schwartzkoppen, and ran as follows:

ALTHOUGH I have had no word indicating that you wish to see me, I am sending you, Monsieur, certain interesting items of information:

(1) A note on the hydraulic brake of the 120[2] and on the action of this gun;
(2) A note on the covering troops[3] (some changes will be made under the new plan);
(3) A note on a change in artillery formation;
(4) A note on Madagascar;

1. The Commander-in-Chief of all the armed forces is the President of the Republic, but the practical direction of affairs lies in the hands of the Minister of War, who is assisted by the *Conseil Supérieur de la Guerre*, a body of senior generals, including the Chief of the General Staff. The Ministry of War is divided into branches for infantry, cavalry, etc., and special services, such as those for explosives, health, etc. The General Staff is a department of the War Ministry, placed under the direct orders of the Chief of the General Staff, who is dependent on the Minister of War in time of peace.

2. A field artillery gun (howitzer) of medium caliber (120 millimeters or 4.72 inches), which was just being developed at this time, and to which a hydraulic brake, similar to that used on the "75," was being applied. This was a significant experiment, since the "75" brake had proved eminently successful. The "120" was the principal medium-sized field piece used during the World War.

3. Troops along a frontier, garrisoning frontier towns, hence covering mobilization.

(5) The draft of the Field Artillery Manual of Fire (March 14, 1894) ;[4]

This last-named document is very difficult to secure and I can have the use of it only for a very few days; the Ministry of War sent a fixed number of copies to the various corps concerned, and these corps are responsible for them. Each officer who has one must return it after manoeuvres.

Hence, if you will be good enough to copy anything that interests you and keep the original for me, I will call for it—unless you prefer that I copy it *in extenso* and send you the copy.

I am about to leave for manoeuvres.

This letter, known later as the bordereau, betrayed the treason of its author. For Henry, its revelation was the presage of catastrophe. He recognized the handwriting of his friend, Major Esterhazy, and his first reaction was to destroy the letter. But Brücker, proud of his fine catch, refused to see things that way, and Henry was obliged to paste together the torn pieces of the letter and take it to his superiors. Henry's fright is comprehensible in the light of his character and history.

Henry had risen from the ranks, had fought in the War of 1870, and had then languished in the lower grades of the hierarchy. He had been aide-de-camp to General de Miribel, and subsequently served for ten years in Africa in a regiment of Zouaves. On his return to France he managed to attract the favorable attention of General de Boisdeffre, and the latter's influence secured him a place in the Second Bureau of the General Staff. Henry was intelligent and crafty, but uncultivated. He was not unlike a cunning peasant, who all his life has coveted a field to round out his farm and who has stopped at nothing—not even crime—to achieve his end. Henry had attained the rank of major through an unhoped-for piece of good luck, and now he had ambitions to be head of the Second Bureau. If, however, it had been learned in high places that he had been the friend, perhaps the accomplice, of a traitor, his career would have been ruined.

And so when Henry was obliged to submit the letter in ques-

4. Artillery range tables, which give the possibilities and limitations of the various field artillery pieces then in use, hence of great interest to the enemy.

tion to his superiors, he was apparently animated by only one desire—that they should not discover the author and that the case should be shelved. It was the latter result he hoped for in the beginning, despite the fact that the document had greatly disturbed his colleagues and superiors. The investigation yielded no result until Colonel Fabre, Chief of the Fourth Bureau, discussed it on October 6 with his assistant, Lieutenant-Colonel d'Aboville. The latter had just been appointed to this position, and asked nothing better than to begin his new career with a master stroke. D'Aboville came to the conclusion that the letter in question could only have been written by an artillery officer who was at the same time a probationer on the General Staff. On the list of the probationers his attention was immediately drawn to the name of the only Jew who appeared on it—Dreyfus. As luck would have it, the handwriting of Dreyfus had on casual examination a certain similarity with that of the bordereau. In any event presumption quickly became conviction. Colonel Fabre; Colonel Sandherr, Chief of the Second Bureau; General Gonse, Deputy Chief of the General Staff; General de Boisdeffre; and finally General Mercier, Minister of War, were informed. The virus of anti-Semitism had done its work well: these gentlemen were ready to be swept along on the wave of conviction.

In the background was Henry. He was delighted with the discovery of a scapegoat by the General Staff and felt instinctively that, having discovered the detested Jew, they would never let him slip away. Henry now began to spread rumors which insinuated themselves into the minds of his colleagues and gradually strengthened the conviction of Dreyfus' guilt. Mercier, however, had discussed the question with certain of his colleagues of the Ministry of War, and had been advised not to commit himself until he possessed irrefutable proof. Dreyfus' military record had been excellent. His career promised to be brilliant. He was rich, married, the father of a family. A motive for treason was difficult to find.

The first examination of the bordereau was confided to Gobert, an expert of the Bank of France. His conclusion, favorable to Dreyfus, was that the differences in handwriting were so considerable that the anonymous letter might well be that of a person other than the suspect. The next opinion solicited was that of a man in no sense qualified—Alphonse Bertillon, Chief of the Identification Department of the Judicial Police.[5] As a matter of fact the General Staff did not ask Bertillon for his expert opinion. They told him instead that they were certain of Dreyfus' guilt, and urged him to corroborate their conviction. Bertillon had no reason to doubt the word of officers of the General Staff. Moreover, he was not an expert in handwriting. Hence he began with the notion that the problem was already solved and that his function was to find a theory which would permit him to prove what the General Staff already believed. He devised a demonstration whose absurdity was easily established later on, but which nonetheless he had the fatuity to defend against the greatest French authorities, even after the latter had demonstrated its complete inadequacy. Fortified by Bertillon's demonstration, however, Mercier decided to have Dreyfus arrested, and directed du Paty de Clam to act as arresting officer.

Du Paty, who had something of the soul of a medieval inquisitor but who had not the least conception of justice, felt called upon to play an heroic role. It was he who had devised the scenario played out at the Ministry of War. He now improved on that. In the Cherche-Midi cell where he had had Dreyfus lodged, he now devoted himself, at the expense of his prisoner, to the most despicable and degrading of judicial comedies. He who had passed in a few hours from supreme happiness to unrelieved despair understood nothing of what had happened to him. Ignorant of the reasons for his arrest and conscious only that it was a hideous injustice, Dreyfus threw himself against the walls and filled his cell with cries of frenzied grief.

For three days he was left in complete solitude—without news of his family, writhing in that empty cell on the verge of madness. For three days and three nights, deprived of all human contact, without paper on which to write, without books, sick with dread and despair, Dreyfus was—in a tradition revived from another age—''buried alive.'' Instead of physical torture, he was left to the spiritual torture of his own thoughts, which it was hoped would unhinge the mind of this man who never

5. The Judicial Police was a bureau of detectives charged with the apprehension of criminals and the collection of evidence for their trial. It formed an element in the Prefecture of Police.

ceased protesting his innocence, and wring from him a confession of guilt. Finally, when he believed his prisoner was "ripe," du Paty came to the Cherche-Midi Prison and proceeded to an initial "performance." Major Forzinetti, Governor of the Cherche-Midi Prison, gave the following details of this procedure in his testimony of December 24, 1898, before the Court of Cassation:

DURING the evening of the 18th, Major du Paty presented himself at the prison with an order from the Minister of War directing me to permit him to go freely to the prisoner's cell.

He asked me to have the door to Dreyfus' cell opened as quietly as possible. He also asked me if I did not have some projector lamps, with which he could surprise and "unhinge" Dreyfus. I replied that the premises did not lend themselves to such an act; further, that I had no such lamps; and that finally, even if all this were feasible, I would not accommodate him, because I was opposed to any such proceedings.

It was under these conditions that the performances—one could scarcely call them inquiries—took place, roughly every other day, and generally in the evening. Du Paty, who had a fertile imagination, invented new ordeals for each occasion. He cut up photographs of letters of Dreyfus and of the bordereau, mixed them together in his cap, and made the prisoner select fragments of words and identify the handwriting. Dreyfus never once failed. Du Paty posed the most insidious and absurd questions, meanwhile refusing steadily to tell Dreyfus the exact reason for the arrest, although assuring him that there were numerous incriminating documents at the Ministry of War.

Then du Paty ceased his visits, and Dreyfus passed through a terrible period. His mind worked unceasingly, day and night, searching futilely for some solid basis on which to construct a solution. He tried to plumb the abominable plot of which he was the victim, and, by turning aimlessly in the void of his own ignorance, he nearly lost his mind. But through all his anguish he felt that he must live; that if he died or went mad, men would consider him guilty, and the honor of his children's name would be forever stained. In his affliction Dreyfus found a friend in Major Forzinetti, Governor of the Prison. This loyal and upright officer, who without the least doubt in the world shared the prejudices and suspicions of his colleagues, had from the very beginning a presentiment that an error had been committed. In order to satisfy his conscience, he went out of his way to mitigate his prisoner's tragic lot. In view of the circumstances, his compassion and humanity revealed rare courage. It is not too much to say that, during these sinister days at the beginning of his imprisonment, it was the solace which Forzinetti offered him which saved Dreyfus from suicide or madness. It should always be remembered that Forzinetti was, without any exaggeration, the first of the *Dreyfusards*.[6]

It was only on October 29, two weeks after the arrest, that du Paty showed Dreyfus the bordereau. This act lifted a great weight from Dreyfus' mind. After two weeks of uncertainty and of suffering, he finally learned the inanity of the accusation, and realized that he would have no difficulty in proving himself innocent.

Meanwhile du Paty was continuing his investigations elsewhere. On the very day of the arrest, about noon, he went with Cochefert to see Mme. Dreyfus:

"MADAME, I have a very sad mission to fulfill."
  "My husband is dead?"
  "No, worse than that."
  "A fall from a horse?"
  "No, madame, he is in prison."

Then he searched the whole apartment—but found nothing. Before leaving, however, he forbade Mme. Dreyfus to inform her family:

"A WORD, a single word from you, and your husband is irretrievably lost. The sole means of saving him is—silence."

Subsequently he returned every two or three days to see the distracted Mme. Dreyfus, who begged him to let her see her husband, even with witnesses, and to allow her to write him. Du Paty put on his most charming airs, but at the same time declared his conviction of Dreyfus' guilt. He tried to get information from Mme. Dreyfus, but knowing nothing she could say nothing, ex-

6. Those who supported Dreyfus and sought his vindication, as contrasted with his opponents, the *Anti-Dreyfusards*.

cept that she was convinced that there was a mistake—perhaps some similarity in names. And while her husband was crying out his innocence to the four walls of his prison, Mme. Dreyfus, who had not yet reached her twenty-fifth year, swore to the man who was torturing them both her conviction, her absolute faith, that her husband had not committed the crime with which he was charged. Thus these two noble souls, separated by a cruel stroke of fate, with no way to communicate their thoughts, protested with the same vehemence against this hideous accusation. And later it was the confidence of his wife and her deep and unshaken love which saved Dreyfus.

During this period the Prefect of Police had, upon the order of the Minister of Justice, appointed three experts.[7] The decision of one of them, Pelletier, was categorically negative: he refused to attribute the bordereau to the suspect. A second, Teysonières, whose conduct was at that very time being investigated and whom the Tribunal de la Seine[8] a few days later removed from its list of experts by reason of acts of a most serious nature, went to see Bertillon. Under the latter's influence, he found Dreyfus guilty. Finally, there was Charavay, who hesitated, but who was of the opinion that the incriminating document was in the same hand as those it was being compared with, although he pointed out the possibility of "twin hands." Later, however, Charavay was to make formal admission of his error.

Meanwhile du Paty was getting nowhere. He wrote the Minister of War, asking whether he should release Dreyfus for lack of proof or continue the investigation. Mercier hesitated. He had recently suffered a series of resounding defeats in the Chamber, and he felt his position shaken. By having Dreyfus arrested too quickly, he had exceeded his rights. As a matter of fact, it was the function of the Governor-General of Paris to determine whether prosecution should be instituted and to sign the order of imprisonment. But General Saussier[9] and the Government were both opposed to an arrest without formal proofs. Impulsive and headstrong, Mercier, who was very much under the influence of

7. On the relation of the Prefect of Police to treason cases, *see* Appendix II.

8. A Court of first instance for the Department of the Seine.

9. Governor-General of Paris.

his staff, had acted heedlessly. Should he disavow his acts at this stage?

Henry was watching in the shadows. His prey must not escape. It was a matter of his official position (for Henry just as it was for Mercier), and he well knew the weak point in the latter's armor. Henry saw only one way to triumph over the hesitations of Mercier: to "tip off" the newspapers, who were still in ignorance of the arrest. In the face of publicity, the Minister would be forced to see the thing through. On the evening of October 28, Papillaud, editor of the *Libre parole*,[10] received the following letter:

My dear friend:

As I have already told you, it is Captain Dreyfus who lives at 6, avenue du Trocadéro, who was arrested on the fifteenth as a spy and who is now in the Cherche-Midi Prison. The story is that he is traveling, but that is a lie told because they want to stifle the affair. All Israel is stirring.

Yours,

HENRY.

Have my little investigation finished as soon as possible.

On the next day, October 29, the *Libre parole* published a brief note, asking if it were true that an important arrest had taken place by order of military authorities; the article gave no name. Mercier, who did not feel himself on firm ground and who would have preferred to see the Dreyfus investigation continue in silence, was much irritated by the indiscretion which had been committed. On the thirtieth he sent a note to the Havas Agency, indicating that the officer arrested was "suspected of having delivered to foreigners certain documents, which were confidential but of minor importance, and that the case would soon be solved."

On November 1, following a fresh communication from Henry, the *Libre parole* published a headline: "High treason. Arrest of Jewish officer, A. Dreyfus." Mercier was compromised. He could no longer find Dreyfus innocent without being accused by public opinion either of being in the pay of the Jews or of having acted with precipitation. Moreover, his colleagues would not forgive

10. Leading anti-Semitic newspaper.

him for having disregarded their prudent advice. If Dreyfus were freed, Mercier would be forced to resign as minister—it would be the end of his political career. Ambition, the love of power, stifled the man's conscience. He did not understand that to admit a mistake is not to debase, but to exalt oneself, in the esteem of one's fellow men. For Mercier the problem was summed up in this dilemma: "Dreyfus or I?" He fought to the end against Dreyfus.

At the meeting of the Cabinet, hastily summoned for this same November 1, Mercier's answer was affirmative.[11] No one doubted his word, and the trial of Dreyfus was unanimously decided. On November 3, General Saussier, Governor of Paris, appointed Major Bexon d'Ormescheville to conduct the Army's case as *rapporteur* for the first Court-Martial.[12]

Henry had won the first hand. He had compromised the Minister of War and had made him, all unsuspecting, an accomplice. Now he must see Dreyfus condemned, for once he should be deported to a distant land, from which he would probably never return, the risk of discovery of the author of the bordereau would be eliminated once and for all. And Henry would see all his most cherished ambitions realized.

Meanwhile du Paty, who had read the *Libre parole* of October 29, could no longer keep his secret, and so he authorized Mme. Dreyfus to inform her family. She telegraphed to her brothers-in-law. One of them, Mathieu, who with his brothers managed the family's cotton-spinning and weaving factory at Mulhouse, took the first train, and arrived in Paris on the morning of November 1. He learned from the newspapers of the arrest of his brother. Not for an instant did he hesitate, any more than had Mme. Dreyfus: his brother was the victim of a blunder. These level heads, these loyal and profoundly patriotic hearts, were not for a moment ruffled by the suspicion that one of their family had betrayed France. Neither Mathieu Dreyfus nor Mme. Dreyfus even suspected an indiscretion. It was all the result of some confusion whose origin they had no means of knowing. They would investigate it and quickly secure the liberation of the prisoner,

11. i.e., that the evidence justified trial of Dreyfus.
12. The *rapporteur* corresponds to the judge advocate in American court-martial procedure.

who was completely innocent of the preposterous crime of which he was accused.

.   .   .   .

The press had seized upon the Affair, and the family, finally informed, were now in a position to take steps to learn the exact cause of the arrest. But Dreyfus himself was still held incommunicado, being permitted no contact even with his family. On November 14, Major Bexon d'Ormescheville began his official examinations, twelve in number, which ended November 29. Dreyfus replied with clearness and precision. Since he now knew the basis of the accusation, he was certain that its emptiness would be quickly recognized. The statements of Dreyfus, moreover, were easy to verify, but d'Ormescheville did not even trouble himself to do that. He put himself under du Paty's wing and repeatedly interrupted the examinations to consult him.

During the first examination Dreyfus requested d'Ormescheville that he be permitted to see the Minister of War, and said:

My honor I prize above all else in this world; I challenge any man to take it from me. For six weeks I have been kept incommunicado, suffering the most terrible agony an innocent man could endure. I am an Alsatian; my family opted for France;[13] I gave up an assured position in Alsace so that I might serve my country. I am just as worthy today as I was yesterday to lead my men into battle.

D'Ormescheville submitted his report on December 3. On the fourth, General Saussier ordered the trial of Dreyfus. He was no longer to be held incommunicado, and was permitted to receive an attorney. For the defense of his brother, Mathieu Dreyfus turned during the entire Affair to the leading lawyers of the period, not to those who had acquired a reputation by defending malodorous causes, but to men of distinguished clientele, whose names were above all suspicion. The extraordinary feature of the situation was that, as soon as the different lawyers examined the dossier, they invariably became rabid partisans of their client, and later his friends.

13. By the Treaty of Frankfort following the War of 1870, citizens of the parts of Alsace and Lorraine annexed by Germany were permitted to elect French citizenship and emigrate to France by September 30, 1872.

When Mathieu Dreyfus approached Demange, the latter, a fervent Catholic and a warm admirer of the Army, at first refused to take the case. And then, when his petitioner became insistent, Demange agreed to examine the dossier, but declared that, if his conscience forbade him to defend Mathieu's brother, he would return it to him publicly—which would be Dreyfus' first condemnation. And so on December 5 Demange went to the Cherche-Midi Prison, posed his conditions to Dreyfus, and said: "I will be your first judge." Dreyfus accepted his conditions without hesitation. Demange at once began the study of the dossier. He was dumbfounded by the flimsiness of the charges, by the hatred which characterized the incoherent report of d'Ormescheville, whose first duty was impartiality. Demange realized that the case had been perverted by religious hatred. Convinced of the innocence of his client, he returned to the Cherche-Midi Prison to say that he accepted the task of defending him.

THE rights of the accused in such instances are perfectly definite, but in Dreyfus' case they were not respected. Mercier refused to let him see his family, and only on December 5, seven weeks after his arrest, was he permitted for the first time to communicate with his wife—by letter.

THE Court-Martial opened its sessions on Wednesday, December 19, at the Hôtel du Cherche-Midi. In spite of the objections of Demange, the Court decided to hold its sessions *in camera*. In the courtroom there remained only the seven military judges; the Prefect of Police, Lépine; Major Picquart, appointed by the Minister of War to represent him at the trial; the accused; and his attorney. The witnesses were heard. Despite the malignant testimony of certain of them, the charges were obviously falling to the ground. Picquart advised Mercier "that the case was going pretty badly." Henry was frantic. For the latter, as well as for the Minister of War, a judgment of guilty was imperative. Henry asked to be allowed to testify anew, and declared to the Court that in March, 1894, a personage of unquestioned integrity had informed the Intelligence Service that there was a treasonable officer in the Ministry of War, and that in June this same person had specifically stated to Henry himself that the traitor belonged to the Second Bureau. Henry concluded his testimony, and turning toward Dreyfus shouted: "And there is the traitor!"

Dreyfus and his lawyer sprang to their feet. They demanded the name of the informer, and that he be summoned to testify before the Court. Henry refused with a theatrical gesture: "There are secrets in an officer's head which even his *képi* must not know." The President of the Court interposed: "We do not insist upon his name, but will you swear on your honor that this person said to you that the treasonable officer was a member of the Second Bureau, and was in fact Captain Dreyfus?" Henry raised his hand toward the crucifix: "I swear it."

This testimony shook the Court, but did not convince it. Something more was needed for conviction. Before the beginning of the pleas preceding the judgment, du Paty placed in the hands of the President of the Court a sealed envelope from Colonel Sandherr, and directed him in the name of General Mercier to read its contents to the judges. This envelope contained the following documents:

(1) A rough pencil draft of a document, the pieces of which had been found by the charwoman, Bastian, in a wastebasket of the German Embassy (January, 1894) and which had been reconstructed to read as follows:

DOUBT . . . proof . . . Officer's commission . . . dangerous situation for me, with a French officer . . . don't conduct negotiations personally . . . bring what there is . . . absolute . . . Intelligence Bureau . . . no report . . . corps of troops . . . important only . . . leaving the Ministry; already somewhere else.

(2) A letter dated January, 1894, from Panizzardi, the Italian Military Attaché, to Schwartzkoppen, the German Military Attaché, received in the same way and including the following:

I HAVE written once again to Colonel Davignon and for that reason urge that, if you have an opportunity to take up this question with your friend, you use discretion, so that Davignon will learn nothing of it. In any event, he would not reply, for it must never appear that one at . . . [attaché] has dealings with another.

(3) Another letter from one of the two Military Attachés to

his colleague, undated, but believed to have reached the Second Bureau in 1892 (according to some) or 1893 (according to others), and which ran as follows:

I AM indeed sorry not to have seen you before my departure. I shall, however, be back in a week. I enclose twelve key maps of Nice, which that scoundrel of a D—— gave me for you. I told him you had no intention of resuming relations with him. He claims that there was a misunderstanding, and that he will do everything in his power to meet your requirements. He says that he was obstinate, and that you will have nothing to do with him. I told him he was mad, and that I did not believe you would renew relations with him.

These various documents are not of great importance in themselves. At the very most, the one in which is mentioned ''that scoundrel of a D——'' might at first sight suggest that it referred to Dreyfus. But on reflection it was difficult to imagine why Dreyfus should be interested in selling key maps of Nice for a few francs apiece. Moreover, it was proved later on (and this was confirmed by Schwartzkoppen in his memoirs[14]) that these maps were handed over by a subordinate named Dubois, from whom they were purchased for ten francs each.

So that the Court would miss nothing of the force of these documents, du Paty drew up a commentary to reveal the connection among them and to show that all applied to Dreyfus. Du Paty managed later to retrieve the original of this commentary, and submitted it to the Court of Cassation, March 26, 1904. But it was not du Paty's commentary which accompanied these secret documents. It was a longer document attributing to Dreyfus a whole series of leakages that had taken place in the course of the preceding years at the École de Pyrotechnie at Bourges, or at the École de Guerre when he was a student there.

Neither the exact wording of this document nor the identity of its author has ever been disclosed. But it was the result of the cooperation of General Mercier, General de Boisdeffre, and Colonel Sandherr. As soon as the President of the Court had returned the dossier of secret documents to Major du Paty (after having communicated its contents to the military judges, in accordance with

14. Max von Schwartzkoppen, *Die Wahrheit über Dreyfus* (Berlin, 1930); English translation, *The Truth About Dreyfus from the Schwartzkoppen Papers* (London and New York, 1931).

the Minister's directions), General Mercier gave orders to distribute the documents and destroy the commentary. When General Mercier learned, in 1897, that there was still a copy of the commentary in the Ministry of War, he asked General Gonse to bring it to him, and burned it in his presence, just as he had previously done, in 1894, with the original. In the course of his testimony before the Court of Cassation, March 26, 1904, General Mercier explained his act in the following dialogue:

Procureur général:[15] How could you burn a document which was official?

General Mercier: No, it was not official . . .

Procureur général: It was official in so far as it emanated from you.

General Mercier: On the contrary, it did not emanate from me—it was drawn up for me.

Procureur général: You are quibbling, General. It was drawn up for you—so far so good. But once it had been drawn up for you, it was sent by you to the Court, and consequently was an official document.

General Mercier: It was not official, because it was not part of the proceedings. On the contrary, it was sent to the Court unofficially.

Procureur général: It was not sent unofficially, but officially, because, if I am not mistaken, it was not M. Mercier who directed it to M. Maurel, but General Mercier, Minister of War, who wrote to the Colonel presiding over the Court-Martial, submitting to him the documents, so that he would examine them. That was what took place, was it not?

General Mercier: Yes.

Procureur général: Very well then, and you were of the opinion that you, as Minister of War, had the right to destroy a document of that character, under those conditions?

General Mercier: That is my belief.

Procureur général: Very well, we shall see about that. On this point, I can follow you, and I am of the opinion that you have committed an act of the utmost gravity. . . .

The attitude of General Mercier aroused the indignation of Procureur Général Baudoin to such a point that, in his summing up before the Court of Cassation (June, 1906), he used the following language:

15. There was one *procureur général* attached to each of the permanent official staffs of the Courts of Appeal, the Court of Cassation, and the *Cour des Comptes* (charged with the review of the public accounts). He was in each case prosecuting attorney for the government.

IT was indispensable to preserve from the outset all documents upon the basis of which the judgment had been reached—documents which would be fundamental to any fresh examination of the case, and whose destruction would compromise, perhaps utterly destroy, the exercise of a right which the law guarantees.

And that was precisely General Mercier's object, when he burned the original and the copy of the commentary. This is no conjecture on our part: General Mercier himself admits it.

This commentary, said Maître Demange to the General during the hearing on August 15, 1899, would have been very helpful to us in to-day's discussion. Why did General Mercier destroy it? Was there some special reason why he wished to do away with it?

General Mercier: There was no special reason, except that at that time the campaign for an appeal of the case had begun, and I felt that we ought not to furnish any pretext which would precipitate such action.

That was exactly it: *Habemus confitentum reum!*

Yes, at the moment when he destroyed the copy, after having already destroyed the original, General Mercier had no illusions about the extreme gravity of the act which he was committing! The law granted the condemned the right of rehabilitation in the light of the error of which he had been the victim. General Mercier wanted deliberately to deprive him of all means of exercising this right. He did everything in his power to foil the request for an appeal, a request only too well justified, but one whose success required as a fundamental condition a clear statement of the crime of which he had been found guilty.

And so, to his first offense—the communication of the commentary to the Court, General Mercier added a second—its destruction.

.   .   .   .

The members of the Court-Martial were not lawyers. They did not grasp the irregularity involved in the communication to them of secret documents. It did not occur to any of them that the primary right of the accused is to be informed of all documents upon which the charges are based. The Minister of War swore to Dreyfus' guilt and gave his word that the documents submitted could refer to no one else. Why should the military judges doubt the word of their superior?

On December 22, 1894, they rendered a unanimous judgment of guilty.

CHAPTER III

ALFRED DREYFUS

ALFRED DREYFUS was born at Mulhouse, October 9, 1859. His family was of Jewish origin. Alsatian for centuries, it was passionately attached to France. From modest beginnings his father had built up a small cotton-spinning mill to which he had subsequently added a weave shed. Industry and scrupulous honesty won him success and eventually a comfortable fortune. He had that integrity which is traditional among certain Alsatians who look upon their plighted word as of the same value as the most meticulously drawn contract.

Pleasantly situated in the wide plain watered by the River Ill, Mulhouse was already at that time an important city with a population of more than 50,000. With a world-wide reputation for prints and calicoes, it had also among its industries a number of cotton- and wool-spinning plants, and calico, muslin, cambric and sheet factories. It was the cradle of numerous great industrial families, who have richly contributed to the prosperity of their *petite patrie*, and who likewise have been characterized by wide philanthropic interests. Mulhouse was a French town of ancient and patriotic tradition.

In 1869 the Dreyfus family, whose situation was steadily improving, moved from its little apartment in the Rue du Sauvage into more commodious quarters in the Rue de la Sinne. The youngest of seven children (three girls and four boys), Alfred grew up in an affectionate and charming family atmosphere, and, being the youngest, he was spoiled both by his parents and by his elder brothers and sisters. The War of 1870 broke out when he was only eleven years old and exercised a decisive influence upon his choice of a career. He witnessed the cuirassiers marching off beneath his window to their glorious fate at Reischoffen,[1] a vision which never left him. Then followed the entry of the German

1. Where, on August 6, 1870, they covered themselves with glory by a memorable, though futile, charge in a battle won by the numerically superior Germans.

troops into Mulhouse, which made him weep with despair and humiliation, and which left upon his youthful mind an ineradicable impression. From that moment he determined to become an officer and to serve with all his strength that France left mutilate by the War.

The Treaty of Frankfort of 1871, which sanctioned the annexation of Alsace by Germany, permitted its inhabitants to opt for France on the express condition that they leave Alsace. Alfred's father, Raphael Dreyfus, did not hesitate: he was one of those Alsatian patriots who preferred exile to German rule. And so, although he owned large factories, he opted for himself and for those of his children who were under age. On October 1, 1872, he left the cherished town of his birth and established a residence temporarily at Basle, Switzerland, whose proximity to Mulhouse allowed him to continue to manage his business with the aid of his son. The latter, Jacques Dreyfus, had served France in the Alsace-Lorraine Legion during the entire period of the War. But now, obeying a feeling of duty to his family, he agreed not to opt for France; at the same time he promised himself that, if he should have sons, they should be French. In fact German law permitted a father to secure an emigration permit for a son who had reached the age of seventeen; the son then lost his German nationality and could not reënter the country before he was forty-five years of age. Subsequently Jacques Dreyfus had six sons and sent them one after another to France. In 1897, in the midst of the agitation over his brother, Jacques Dreyfus himself, unwilling to remain any longer beyond the borders of France, had the courage to transfer part of his factories to Belfort and to claim citizenship in his native land once again.

For a time young Alfred, whom his father had taken with him to Basle, studied at the Realschule, but he was handicapped by the fact that the instruction was given in German. At the beginning of 1873 he was sent to Paris to continue his education. But he was a sensitive boy, accustomed to an affectionate home environment. He could not endure the rigors of boarding-school life at the Collège Sainte-Barbe, and presently returned to his family. After an adequate rest, he went back to Paris to continue his studies at the Collège Chaptal, where he completed the bacca-

*Young Dreyfus at the Collège
Sainte-Barbe.*

laureate.[2] He then returned to Sainte-Barbe to prepare for the entrance examinations to the École Polytechnique.[3]

At this point his brothers urged him insistently to join them in their father's business, and emphasized the splendid position which he could make for himself. But his mind was more than ever fixed upon his chosen career. He was possessed by the thought—the expression is his own—"of Alsace trembling beneath the foreign yoke; of those whose hearts were French and yet who suffered tyranny." And so he held unswervingly to his youthful resolve. He was accepted for the École Polytechnique the first time he took the examinations, at the age of nineteen. He graduated in 1880, and as second lieutenant entered the École d'Application at Fontainebleau.[4] At the expiration of his term of training there he was made a lieutenant (1882) and attached, first, to the Thirty-First Regiment of Artillery at Le Mans, then a year later to the mounted battery of the First Cavalry Division in Paris.

While he was quartered in the capital, he decided to prepare for the examinations for admission to the École Supérieure de Guerre. He was promoted to a captaincy on September 12, 1889, and sent as adjutant to the École Centrale de Pyrotechnie Militaire[5] at Bourges. Shortly after that he became engaged to Mademoiselle Lucie Hadamard, daughter of a diamond merchant and granddaughter of Captain Hatzfeld, former student at the École Polytechnique (class of 1835). On the eve of his marriage (April

2. The degree in France which marks completion of work in the secondary school, variously termed *collège* or *lycée*; the degree is usually attained about the age of eighteen.

3. The École Polytechnique is a school primarily of higher mathematical culture, preparing students for careers in engineering, etc. The course is two years, following which the best graduates pass to various state schools (Mines, Naval Architecture, Roads and Bridges, etc.); others become second lieutenants in the engineering and artillery corps.

4. The École d'Application gives supplementary technical instruction to second lieutenants leaving the École Polytechnique and Saint-Cyr (specifically the École Spéciale Militaire at Saint-Cyr-l'École), the famous school, established 1802, in which officers for the cavalry and infantry are trained (likewise today for the air force). It corresponds to the American West Point, the English Sandhurst.

5. This is a center for the manufacture of war supplies, and includes a school for the instruction of selected artillery officers in the manufacture and use of munitions.

20, 1890), Alfred Dreyfus was deeply gratified to learn that he
had been accepted at the École de Guerre. He entered at the beginning of the autumn, completed the course in 1892 among the
first twelve in his class, and won, as his reward, an assignment to
the General Staff of the Army.

All his dreams were coming true. A splendid career was opening before him. Of his happy marriage, two children were born—
a son, Pierre, in 1891, and a daughter, Jeanne, in 1893. His fe-
licity lacked nothing for completeness. Then came the thunderbolt which shattered his life. He was arrested for a crime he had
not committed. He was held incommunicado from October 15 till
December 5, 1894. For seven weeks he was denied the right to
communicate with a single member of his family or to receive any
news whatever. Only on December 5 was he permitted to write to
his wife, swearing to her his innocence, asking himself if he were
not really the sport of a horrible nightmare. From the correspondence of Dreyfus and his wife (daily from then on) we have
selected the following letters.

Cherche-Midi Prison,
Thursday morning, December 6, 1894.

I AM waiting impatiently for a letter from you. You are my hope
and my consolation. But for you my life would no longer be
worth living. I shudder when I think that they could accuse me
of a crime so horrible, so monstrous. My whole being revolts
against it. To have labored all my life with but a single object,
revenge against the infamous despoiler of our cherished Alsace,
and to be accused of treason—no, my beloved, that my poor mind
cannot understand. Do you remember my telling you that, when
I was in Mulhouse some ten years ago in September, I heard
passing under my window a German band celebrating the anniversary of Sedan? I experienced such anguish that I swore to devote all my strength and ability to the service of my country
against the enemy who thus outraged the feelings of Alsatians.

No, no, I won't go on, for I shall become mad, and I must keep
my reason. My life has henceforth but one aim: to find the wretch
who betrayed his country, to find the traitor for whom there is
no punishment too severe. . . . Never has a man gone through

the torture I endure. No physical suffering can be compared to the spiritual anguish I feel when my thoughts go back to that accusation. Were it not for my honor—honor I must defend—I swear to you I had rather be dead—death at least would be oblivion. . . .

ALFRED.

Cherche-Midi Prison,
Tuesday, December 18, 1894.

Ma bonne chérie:

At last I am approaching the end of my sufferings, the end of my torture. Tomorrow I shall appear before my judges, my head high, my soul at peace.

The trials that I have undergone, terrible as they have been, have purified my heart. I shall come back to you a nobler man. My only wish is to devote what remains of my life to you, to my children, to our dear families.

I told you that I have been through frightful attacks of hysteria. The thought of an accusation of such enormity has brought upon me attacks of raging madness.

I am ready to stand before my fellow soldiers as a soldier who has nothing for which to reproach himself. My innocence they will see in my face, read in my eyes; they will be convinced of it, as all those who know me have been convinced.

I have devoted all my strength and ability to the service of my country, and I have nothing to fear.

You may sleep peacefully, my dear, you need have no anxiety. Think only of our joy at being soon in one another's arms again, forgetful of these sad and melancholy days. . . .

ALFRED.

Cherche-Midi Prison,
December 23, 1894.

My dearest :[6]

I suffer much, but I pity you more than myself. I know how much you love me. Your heart must bleed. For my part, my be-

6. This letter follows the conviction of Dreyfus by the Court-Martial, December 22.

loved, my thoughts have always been of you, by night and by day.

To be innocent, to have lived a stainless life, and yet to be convicted of the most heinous crime a soldier can commit—what could be more terrible than this! At times it seems to me that I am the sport of some horrible nightmare.

It is for you alone that I have borne up until today. It is for you alone, my beloved, that I have endured this long torture. Will my strength endure until the end? I do not know. Only you can give me courage. It is your love alone that can give me strength. . . .

I have signed my request for a review of the case.

I dare not speak to you of the children. The memory of them is breaking my heart. . . .

My sorrow is so great, my heart so bitter that, but for the memory of you and the fear of adding to your grief, I should already have taken my life. . . .

What you must do before all else, no matter what becomes of me, is to move heaven and earth to discover the truth, to vindicate my name which has been dragged in the mire—even if it be necessary to spend every cent of our fortune. We must wipe out that unmerited stain, whatever the cost.

I have no courage to write you more now. . . .

Mille et mille baisers.

ALFRED.

Try to get permission to see me. I should think they could no longer refuse it to you.

Cherche-Midi Prison,
Friday noon, December 28, 1894.

Your letter of Thursday evening has come, as well as the amusing little note from Pierrot. Kiss the little darling for me, and Jeanne as well. I must live. I must marshal all my strength to wash away the stain on the name of my children. I should be a coward if I deserted my post. I *will* live—that I am determined.

Je t'embrasse,

ALFRED.

Sunday, December 30, 1894.

Mon trésor chéri:

Your letters bring me such joy. They come as a ray of happiness lighting up the dark recesses of my grief. I gain the feeling that you are better—brave and resigned—and that cheers me. You must be strong and resolute, my dear. You must never be disheartened. Don't think of the humiliation which is coming. Think only of the future—your vindication, your deliverance.

We are busy every moment with the investigation. We are moving heaven and earth to get a definite result. Our minds are filled with nothing else. We talk of nothing but that. But to achieve our ends we must move very, very cautiously; one false step will ruin everything.

You must not torture yourself, my dear. We are all of us concentrating our efforts, our intelligence, all our abilities on this one thing. You can rely completely on our devotion. As for myself, you have long known, and I need not tell you again, that my very life is yours.

This evening is the anniversary of the death of your father, and we are all going to the temple. Poor grandfather, in dying he little realized his happiness. . . .

LUCIE.

December 31, evening.

Mon bon chéri:

I have been deeply touched by the expressions of affection for me, and esteem and sympathy for you, which I have had on every side. Both our intimate and our casual friends are indignant at the proceedings of which you are the victim. They admire your courage and your splendid spirit.

Our children are terribly spoiled. It rains toys and candy. . . . I have a cupboard full. If you could only see how delighted they are with the dolls, the animals, and the mechanical toys! Pierrot is remarkably dexterous. He uses his ten little fingers nimbly and cunningly. Jeanne sits herself solidly down on the floor amidst her dolls and utters cries of joy and happiness. How happy the darlings are!

I have given up our apartment with a heavy heart. I have been so happy there with you, that I was consoled by the joy which these memories brought, even in the midst of my grief. But my family was very anxious that I should not leave them, or at least that I should live somewhere near them until your departure. And so I yielded to their wish.

I think I told you that Virginia is for the time being with Mathieu's family. That splendid girl is so fond of us that she doesn't want to leave, and she told Suzanne that, if we would agree, she would go down there[7] with us. The nurse feels just the same. So you see, my dear, there are still fine people on this earth. . . .

LUCIE.

Wednesday evening, January 2, 1895.

Mon bon chéri:

At last we have had the meeting we had so longed for. At last we have seen and talked to each other. Such happiness it was to look into your eyes again, to hear your voice. But how terrible it was, too, to be so close to each other and yet to be separated by those frightful bars. I was terribly shaken by seeing you. I wanted to say so many things. I wanted to give you courage, to comfort you. But I hadn't the strength to say what I felt—I couldn't even find words to tell you my admiration, my gratitude for the great sacrifice you have made. Courage?—it is *you* who have given *me* courage. You have been magnificent.

After I left you, I went to see General Tyssère to ask him for a permanent pass and the right to see you without bars between us and without witnesses. I only hope he may prove human, and I am awaiting his reply with the greatest impatience. . . .

YOUR LUCIE.

Cherche-Midi Prison,
Thursday noon, January 3.

Ma chérie:

I am told that my supreme humiliation[8] is to take place day after tomorrow. I expected this news and was prepared for it. Nonetheless it was a terrible blow. I will bear up—I promised

7. Mme. Dreyfus expected to accompany her husband when he was deported.

8. The public military degradation of Dreyfus.

you I would. I will find the strength that I need in your love, in the affection of all of you, in the memory of our dear children, in the high hope that some day the truth will be known. But I must feel the warmth of your affection. I must feel that you are fighting with me, that you are searching always and unceasingly for the truth. . . .

ALFRED.

Friday evening, January 4, 1895.

Mon Fred chéri:

By the time you receive this letter the frightful ceremony will be over. I only hope that you bore it with all the dignity, the courage, the heroism which you have shown thus far. You have been magnificent, *mon pauvre martyr.* Bear unflinchingly your torment, for you have terrible days before you. But one day God will richly reward you for all your suffering. You have promised me to fight to the end for me and for the children. For that I am profoundly grateful. I wish that we were already in New Caledonia;[9] you would be less wretched there than in these dingy prisons. I shall be with you and shall try to restore your strength. There we shall be as happy as possible, while we wait for the day of your vindication. Fear nothing, my dearest, that will not be long. There is no case where the innocence of an unjustly condemned man was not recognized sooner or later.

Our poor children are well. . . . Pierrot is becoming very gentle. When I cried this morning as I thought of you, he asked me what was the matter. I told him that I was sad because I missed you so. "Don't cry now, mamma," he said, "when I grow up, I shall take you with me to hunt papa. We will kiss him many times, and he will come back with us." He has a tender heart, the dear little fellow, and I hope he will resemble you. Have courage, my dearest ! . . .

YOUR LUCIE.

.   .   .   .

9. It was to New Caledonia, where the regular penal colony was located, that Dreyfus was originally to have been sent, and there his wife was to have accompanied him. But a law of February 9, 1895, passed without debate, permitted the use of the Salvation Islands (including Devil's Island) for imprisonment for crimes of the type of that for which Dreyfus had been condemned (*see* p. 72).

In accordance with the judgment of the Court-Martial, Dreyfus was degraded on January 5, at nine o'clock in the morning, in the courtyard of the École Militaire. He underwent the cruel ceremony with heroic courage, repeatedly shouting out his innocence to the hostile crowd which surrounded him. If he was able to stand erect, his head high in the face of the howling mob, it was because he felt himself strong in the love and confidence of his wife, and because he had the unshakeable determination to vindicate that honor of which he had been unjustly deprived.

. . . .

Santé Prison,
Saturday, January 5, 1895.

My dearest:

I have not the heart to tell you what I have gone through today. That would only add to your own suffering, already so bitter.

When I promised you to live, when I promised to bear up until my name had been vindicated, I made the greatest sacrifice possible for a man of feeling and integrity, whose honor has been shorn from him. Pray God that my physical strength will not desert me! My spiritual strength is unimpaired, my conscience is clear and sustains me, but I am reaching the end of my endurance and my physical powers are ebbing. . . .

Leave no stone unturned, my dearest, to find the real culprit; don't slacken your efforts for a single instant. This is my only hope in the midst of this horrible tragedy of which I am the victim. . . .

ALFRED.

January 12, 1895.

Mon Fred chéri:

I have just received your good letter of yesterday. It has made me happy, for in it I see that you are brave and resigned. This is the only course open to us for the present, my dearest—to have patience, to bear our torture bravely, and to await your vindication without flinching. You will realize that he who is guilty of this infamy, he who has betrayed his country under cover of your name, cannot be discovered from one day to the next. Only through strength of will, industry, perseverance, will we finally discover the key to this mystery. I understand your suffering. I share it. This inactivity, this impotence, this mental torture is maddening.

You must not praise me, my dearest. What I do is only natural. I am influenced neither by sentiments of duty nor of self-sacrifice. I am inspired simply by my deep feeling of respect, by my profound love for you. My course of action is clear. I will never desert you. I can and will live only for you.

As you see, my dearest husband, I am strong. Thank God, my health is good—I am well armed for the fight. I will go with you into exile, and there I will be your companion and your solace until France shall recognize her error and call us back to her. What a splendid day that will be for us, when we arrive once more in our own beloved country, honored and happy with our children and our families. That is the future we must look forward to, my dearest. It is that hope which will comfort and sustain us in the midst of all our suffering. . . .

Come then, my darling, be strong, be brave. . . .

LUCIE.

About ten o'clock on the night of January 17, Dreyfus was rudely awakened. Shortly afterward he set out on the journey to Rochefort and the Island of Saint-Martin-de-Ré, first stage on the road to his exile.

CHAPTER IV

SCHWARTZKOPPEN AND PANIZZARDI

FOLLOWING the Boutonnet incident in 1890,[1] and as a result of representations by the French Government, Count von Münster, the German Ambassador, had ordered his staff to renounce all espionage. Nevertheless, about three o'clock on the afternoon of July 20, 1894, Major Esterhazy of the French infantry appeared at the German Embassy and offered his services to the Military Attaché, Lieutenant-Colonel von Schwartzkoppen. In his posthumous memoirs, the latter roundly states that he tried to induce Esterhazy to renounce his intention and that in the end he dismissed him. On the following day, July 21, Schwartzkoppen received a letter from Esterhazy repeating his offer. In the face of this persistence, Schwartzkoppen communicated directly with the Intelligence Service in Berlin, taking care to say nothing of the matter to his Ambassador. On the twenty-sixth, he received a formal order to negotiate with Esterhazy. The latter continued his visits and was remunerated accordingly. On August 15, notably, he brought the artillery mobilization plan, which had just been brought up to date. On September 1, toward the end of the afternoon, he had a long talk with Schwartzkoppen, in the course of which he told him an expedition to Madagascar had just been decided upon. At the same time he gave him the following documents:

(1) The list of covering troops.
(2) The description of the "120" howitzer.
(3) The draft of the Field Artillery Manual of Fire.[2]

Finally, on September 5, he gave to Schwartzkoppen certain observations which he had made during the manoeuvres at Sissonne, and the next day sent him by letter a report on the projected Madagascar expedition. But the famous bordereau, which

1. Boutonnet was a member of the civilian staff of the Technical Artillery Committee attached to the Ministry of War. He was sentenced to five years' imprisonment for delivering documents to the German Embassy in Paris.
2. These were three of the items enumerated in the bordereau (see pp. 12–13).

announced the submission of these documents, never reached its destination, and Schwartzkoppen learned of its existence only in 1896, when the facsimile of the bordereau was published in *Le Matin*. Esterhazy himself, not knowing that the dangerous missive had been purloined by the Secret Agent Brücker from the *loge* of the *concierge* at the German Embassy, believed that it was safely in the hands of the Military Attaché. Accordingly he continued his visits about every two weeks, handing over documents whose exact character Schwartzkoppen does not indicate in his memoirs, but of which he notes the increasing importance. The relations between the two lasted until March, 1896. Up to the present, however, no light has been thrown on the question as to how Esterhazy, who was only a major of infantry, secured so many important documents, or who it was who provided them for him.

Schwartzkoppen was a friend of Lieutenant-Colonel Panizzardi, the Italian Military Attaché, and was in the habit of exchanging with him documents of mutual interest, which one or the other had secured.[3] When the note of October 29 appeared in the *Libre parole*,[4] Schwartzkoppen was considerably disturbed. For if he were found to be involved in any way in this espionage affair, it would mean a sharp rebuke from his superior, the German Ambassador. But as soon as the name of Dreyfus appeared, November 1, he could breathe more easily, and declared to his Italian colleague: "That's not my man." Panizzardi, however, suggested the hypothesis that Dreyfus might have carried on relations directly with the Italian General Staff. He immediately posed that question at Rome, at the same time being careful to point out that he did not know Dreyfus at all. On the following day, November 2, moved by newspaper attacks on his country, Panizzardi dispatched a code message to the Italian General Staff: "If Captain Dreyfus has had no relations with you, it would be helpful if you would have the Ambassador directed to publish an official denial, in order to avoid press comment." On

3. This is not surprising, in light of the fact that Italy and Germany were members of the Triple Alliance, and had thus a large community of military interest.

4. *See* p. 19.

that same day, General Marselli, second in command of the General Staff, replied: "Neither the Italian General Staff, nor any one of the services connected with it, has ever had any relations, direct or indirect, with Captain Dreyfus."

Panizzardi had occasion to confirm these facts in 1899, when General Roget was testifying at the retrial of Dreyfus at Rennes. When Roget declared that the Italian Military Attaché had at that time[5] submitted to his Ambassador a report, in which he said that Dreyfus had been a spy in the pay of Germany, Panizzardi with great loyalty telegraphed, on August 17:[6] "I never made any such report, nor any such declaration. . . . I learned the name of the French Captain only at the time of his arrest, a fact which, moreover, I stated officially and in writing, on my honor as a soldier and a gentleman."

The German Ambassador had also been aimed at by French newspaper articles. Count von Münster inserted in the *Figaro* of November 10, 1894, a very precise declaration, to the effect that neither Schwartzkoppen nor the Embassy had ever had any relations, direct or indirect, with Captain Dreyfus. Finally, at Rome in the *Italia* of November 12, and at Paris in the *Figaro* of November 14, the Italian and Austrian Governments likewise published formal denials.

And yet, despite these clarifications, the press attacks on Germany were only aggravated. Count von Münster then protested to the French Government, which was annoyed by this situation, and which had several official notes published to the effect that "allegations which continue to appear in various newspaper articles on espionage, indicating that foreign Embassies and Legations are concerned in this affair, are entirely without foundation." But this phraseology appeared inadequate to the German Government. Count von Münster returned to the charge, and flatly declared that no document affecting the trial of Captain Dreyfus could have been taken from the German Embassy, since no one there knew Dreyfus. The second part of this statement was correct, but not the first. For, without the Ambassador's knowledge and contrary to his orders, the Military Attaché had

5. i.e., in November, 1894.
6. This telegram was sent to the President of the Court-Martial at Rennes, August 17, 1899.

continued his espionage activities with the consent of his superiors on the German General Staff. And when, after the conviction of Dreyfus, Count von Münster called on Dupuy, the French Premier, to renew his protests in perfectly good faith, it is probable that Dupuy was not seriously impressed.

Nevertheless, Schwartzkoppen, who had left for Berlin, December 27, had occasion to discuss the Dreyfus Affair with the Emperor and the Chancellor. Following these interviews, Count von Münster received from Chancellor von Hohenlohe the following dispatch:

His Majesty the Emperor, reposing complete confidence in the loyalty of the President and Government of the Republic, requests Your Excellency to say to Monsieur Casimir-Périer that, if it is proved that the German Embassy has never been implicated in the Dreyfus Affair, His Majesty hopes that the Government of the Republic will not hesitate to make a declaration to this effect.

Without a formal declaration, the legends, which the press has not ceased to broadcast at the expense of the German Embassy, would continue, and would compromise the position of the Emperor's Representative.

Nevertheless, the ambiguous situation was allowed to continue. For, if Dreyfus were innocent, others were guilty. At his own request, Count von Münster was received on January 6 by M. Casimir-Périer, President of the Republic, in the presence of the Premier, M. Dupuy. Both Governments wished to find a friendly solution for the problem. And so, after an exchange of views, it was decided to send to the Havas Agency a new note, confirming that which had already appeared on November 30, 1894. And with that, the incident was considered to be closed.

CHAPTER V

PICQUART

THE Statistical Section[1] of the Ministry of War continued to receive from Bastian, the charwoman, containers filled with the papers which she collected each day from the wastebaskets of the German Embassy. During the absence of Major Henry, who had been called away by the illness of his mother, Captain Lauth was intrusted with the reconstruction of Bastian's documents. In March, 1896, Lauth submitted to Lieutenant-Colonel Picquart (who had succeeded Colonel Sandherr as head of the Second Bureau in July, 1895) an unstamped *carte pneumatique*[2] which had been torn in small pieces.[3] When reconstructed this card read as follows:

Major Esterhazy,
27, rue de la Bienfaisance,
Paris.

Monsieur:

I am awaiting above all a more detailed explanation than that which you gave me the other day, concerning the question which is in abeyance. Hence, I beg you to give it to me in writing, so that I may be able to decide whether or not I can continue my relations with the House of R.

(*signed*) C.

Picquart was greatly disturbed by this discovery. He had, however, deplored the premature commotion caused in connection with the Dreyfus Affair (although he believed Dreyfus guilty), and so he considered it wiser to make a careful investigation before he referred the matter to his superiors. Alsatian by

1. *See* p. 12.
2. The *cartes pneumatiques* were postal forms printed on light paper for use in the Paris system of pneumatic tubes, which were particularly useful for rapid communication before the telephone became general, but which are still in use today.
3. According to Schwartzkoppen, the card had been dropped in a letter box, and must have been recovered from the post (*Truth about Dreyfus*, pp. 79–80).

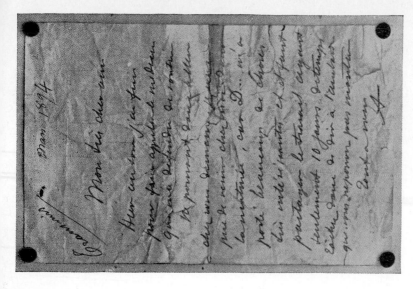

*Letter from Schwartzkoppen to Panizzardi,
altered by Henry to implicate Dreyfus.*

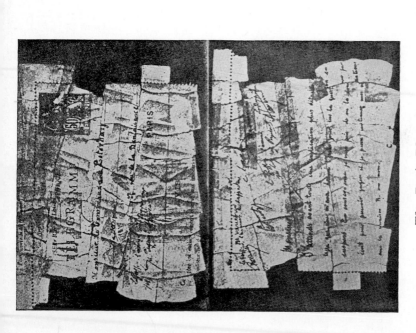

*The Petit Bleu.
Reconstruction of the letter from Schwartzkoppen to Esterhazy, which enabled Picquart to identify the latter as the traitor.*

birth, Picquart was a man of self-confidence and integrity. He had an orderly mind, and could pride himself on a very brilliant career. He had graduated fifth in his class at Saint-Cyr, second in his class at the École de Guerre; he had been captain at twenty-four, major and chevalier of the Legion of Honor at thirty-three. He had fought in Tonkin and in China, and upon his return to France had been appointed Professor at the École de Guerre. General de Boisdeffre had made him head of the Second Bureau for the purpose of reorganizing that department.

Despite the efforts of Picquart, however, leakages had continued, and various clues had been followed without success. But once he had in his hands the card addressed to Major Esterhazy (the card known later as the *petit bleu*), Picquart made inquiries concerning that officer's reputation, and received the most damaging kind of information. Some time later, in the month of June, while on a General Staff mission with General de Boisdeffre, Picquart was given a letter from Colonel de Foucault, Military Attaché at Berlin, by Major Pauffin de Saint-Morel, the General's adjutant. Colonel de Foucault declared that he had received a visit from a man by the name of Cuers (a spy formerly in the pay of the German Intelligence Service), who wanted an interview with a representative of the French General Staff. De Foucault came to Paris a little later, and personally gave Picquart further interesting details. In particular he told him that the German General Staff was still asking itself with whom Dreyfus could have had relations, since they had never had anything to do with him. On the other hand, Schwartzkoppen regularly received documents from a major in the French infantry. This information had been given him by Cuers, who declared himself ready to supplement these revelations. Picquart arranged a rendezvous at Basle, to which he sent Lauth, who asked to have Henry accompany him. Upon their return, the two officers declared that Cuers had only repeated what he had already said to Colonel de Foucault.

Meanwhile, Esterhazy, who had been a member of the Intelligence Bureau as a translator of German in 1876, and who had there met Henry, whose friend he had remained, redoubled his efforts to enter that service once again. Not only did he attempt to use political influence, but he wrote directly to one of the adjutants of the Minister of War, as well as to the head of the latter's Civil Department, who transmitted these letters to Picquart.

Thus Picquart now had two specimens of Esterhazy's handwriting, and was immediately struck by its familiarity. He compared it to that of the bordereau, photographs of which had remained in various files of the Intelligence Bureau, and was astonished, not by the mere resemblance of the two, but by their complete identity. He then had the letters photographed, was careful to suppress the address and signature, and showed them to du Paty de Clam, who replied, "That is Mathieu Dreyfus' hand"; then to Bertillon, who said, "That is the writing in the bordereau." When Picquart went on to say that these specimens were from a recent correspondence, Bertillon replied without batting an eyelash: "Then the Jews have trained someone in the past year to imitate that hand, and they have succeeded in producing one identical with it."

Picquart had too much good sense to be deterred by such a crazy theory as this. He was convinced that the bordereau was, beyond peradventure of a doubt, in Esterhazy's hand. And he began to wonder if Esterhazy had not been an accomplice of Dreyfus. He then recalled that when Colonel Sandherr had turned over to him the direction of the Intelligence Bureau, he had confided in him that the secret dossier submitted to the judges of the Court-Martial in 1894 had been placed in a kind of strongbox which Major Henry kept in his desk. For Picquart, Dreyfus' guilt was beyond doubt, and he had been no more surprised by the illegal submission of secret documents to the judges than had his colleagues. Hence, he had never had the curiosity to consult this secret dossier. But he now directed the Archivist, Gribelin, to bring it to him. He expected to find in it crushing proofs of Dreyfus' guilt. When he examined the various documents, he was astounded to discover that none of them could be made to refer to Dreyfus. As to the draft of du Paty de Clam's commentary, Picquart was shocked that an officer charged with so responsible a duty could have been guilty of such treachery and deceit.

In a flash he saw the truth, and he had the painful feeling that he had in a measure contributed to the conviction of Dreyfus—by representing the Ministry of War in all the sessions of the Court-Martial, by bringing to its Presiding Judge (at least so he believed) General Mercier's envelope containing the secret dossier. He was deeply moved when he thought of the innocent victim, tortured these eighteen months. The whole night through he could not rid his mind of this picture. On the morning of September 1, he drew up in brief form the charges against Esterhazy. And then, armed with this document, the petit bleu, and the bordereau, he hastened to the office of Boisdeffre to lay before him his discovery. Boisdeffre, however, was obviously annoyed, and directed him to submit the question to his colleague, General Gonse, Deputy Chief of the General Staff.

Picquart went to his superiors, conscious that he was doing his duty and certain of their support. An error had been committed. He brought to them the irrefutable proof of that error. Hence there could be no doubt of the result: measures would be taken immediately to rectify that wrong. On September 3, he visited Gonse, then on leave in the country, and submitted the documents to him. The General examined them, and was struck by the importance of the discovery. But, in answer to direct question of his subordinate, Gonse told him to deal separately with the Dreyfus Affair and with that concerning Esterhazy. This point of view was presently given the support of Boisdeffre—all of which greatly disturbed Picquart. Henceforth he had the impression that his superiors were averse to the idea of making so grave a decision as that of publicly recognizing the error which had been committed. Nevertheless, he did not doubt their sense of justice, and refused to believe that they would knowingly keep an innocent man in prison.

Picquart was a soldier. He respected the military hierarchy and its essential discipline. But this feeling did not extend to the point of servility, and, outside the service, he considered himself justified in exercising independent judgment. He continued his investigation and submitted the results to General Gonse, who had been designated by General de Boisdeffre to supervise the inquiry.

Meanwhile an English newspaper published a false report of the escape of Dreyfus, which was at once seized upon by the French press. An official denial followed shortly, but newspaper polemics would not be downed at once, and a Deputy, Castelin, went so far as to seek an interpellation on the subject. For the first time in nearly two years, the attention of the public was fastened on the fate of Dreyfus. General Billot, Minister of War, had learned nothing as yet of the discoveries of the Chief of the Intelligence Bureau. Not without difficulty, Picquart finally obtained General de Boisdeffre's authorization to inform General Billot of the situation. This he did with complete frankness, showing him the relevant documents. Billot was impressed, but Boisdeffre was on guard. He visited Billot, and then indicated to Picquart that he had explained to the General in detail the origins of the Affair.

By now Picquart was well aware of the hesitations of his superiors. At the same time, he was practically certain that the re-awakening of public interest in the Affair was the work of the Dreyfus family. Under these conditions, he considered it very much to be desired that the truth should be made known, not through the intervention of friends of the condemned, but through the initiative of those who, in all good faith, had committed the error. Indeed, if the honor of the Army were to be saved, no further vacillation was permissible. Accordingly, on September 8, Picquart wrote to General Gonse as follows: "I think that I have done all that I could to justify our taking the initiative. If we lose too much time, the initiative will come from another source, which, even if we ignore considerations of a higher order, will deprive us of a magnanimous role." On the tenth Gonse replied, advising prudence and indicating that he would return on the fifteenth. But on the fourteenth there came a bolt from the blue, when the newspaper, *L'Éclair,* published an article entitled "The Traitor," a veritable history of the Affair which could only have been inspired by one close to the General Staff. Among other things, it was stated that there existed in the Ministry of War a photograph of a letter exchanged by the German and Italian Military Attachés, in which the name of Dreyfus appeared in so many letters. The article, which was embellished with details unknown to the public, caused a tremendous stir, above all at the Ministry of War, where it was asked who could have committed so unfortunate an indiscretion. Picquart referred the matter to Gonse, requesting an investigation and punishment. But the latter replied that he wished to talk the matter over with Boisdeffre, who had left for manoeuvres on September 12. Taking advantage of this interview, Picquart then brought the discussion around to the judicial wrong and the moral obligation to rectify it. But Gonse would hear nothing of it, and there then followed the historic dialogue:

"WHAT is it to *you*, if that Jew stays on Devil's Island?"

"But, General, he is innocent."

"It is a case we can't reopen. General Mercier and General Saussier are involved in it."

"But since he's innocent!"

"If you say nothing, no one will be the wiser."

"What you have just said is an abomination, General! I don't know what I shall do, but in any event I will not carry this secret to my grave."

.   .   .   .

At last Picquart understood. Boisdeffre and Gonse knew that Dreyfus was innocent, and they had known it from the beginning. But for reasons which they considered to be of a higher order, they refused to make amends for the injustice done. In short, the whole Affair had resulted from Mercier's initial blunder in having signed too precipitately the order for Dreyfus' arrest. Indiscretions followed. The anti-Semitic press immediately made the question of Dreyfus' guilt one of politics, instead of one of justice. And the heads of the Army were forced to intervene to insure a conviction. Apparently they hesitated, and felt some twinges of conscience in the beginning. But pretty soon they managed to convince themselves that the life of one man was of little value when weighed in the balance with reasons of state and the honor of the Army. The latter must not in any case be sullied—a result which, they held, would follow if they should admit the commission of such a blunder. There were other considerations also—these of a more immediate nature—which influenced their attitude. They realized that if the innocence of Dreyfus should be acknowledged, the duplicity of the General Staff would stand revealed. This would mean ruined careers, forced retirement, and disgrace.

Henceforth, Picquart was convinced that Boisdeffre and Gonse were too deeply compromised to alter their policy: he had the feeling that he was driving against a stone wall. Nonetheless, he persisted in his attempts to win over his military superiors to the cause of justice. He once again interviewed Gonse, then Bois-deffre, finally the Minister of War. The last named, who had been deceived by his subordinates, now became alarmed. Clearly Picquart was becoming a source of embarrassment; it was desirable to remove him from the scene. Under the pretext that Picquart had been "hypnotized" by the Dreyfus Affair and was neglecting his duties, Boisdeffre suggested to General Billot that he be sent to Tonkin, where he had previously made a distinguished record. The Minister of War, however, had a high regard for Picquart, whom he considered an admirable officer, and refused to visit such a disgrace upon him. In Billot's view, the only criticism which could be made of Picquart was that of possessing too scrupulous a conscience. But Boisdeffre continued to press the matter and finally won over Billot, who was easily influenced: Picquart was not to be sent to the Far East, but was to be given a special mission, the inspection of the Intelligence and War Espionage Services on the eastern and southeastern frontiers. During his absence General Gonse was to be given the provisional direction of the Intelligence Bureau at the Ministry of War.

The order providing for Picquart's mission was signed on October 27. On October 30 Gonse demanded that Picquart deliver to him the secret Dreyfus dossier, although Picquart was not to leave until November 14. Picquart began his mock circuit of the frontiers. When he submitted his reports on the eastern frontier, Gonse ordered him to inspect also the Sixth Province, then the Seventh, the Fourteenth, the Fifteenth. When he reached Marseilles he was informed that the Minister of War had decided to enlarge his mission to include the organization of Intelligence Services in Algeria and Tunis.

Picquart had left Paris with only a valise, believing that he was to be absent for just a few days. He now suddenly realized that his superiors, uneasy about their own safety, wanted to banish him for good from General Staff headquarters. But what he did not yet know, and what he learned in the course of his stay overseas, was that his mere banishment soon appeared quite inadequate to his superiors. They then attempted to discredit him, to misrepresent his official acts as head of the Second Bureau. He began to fear that these uneasy spirits would not hesitate, if need arose, to engineer a convenient accident. And so he added a long codicil to his will, which he wrote at Susa,[4] on April 2, 1897, and enclosed in a sealed envelope bearing the following words: ''In the event of the death of the undersigned, place this envelope in the hands of the President of the Republic, who alone is authorized to read it.''

Picquart had kept his word to General Gonse that he would not carry the secret to his grave.

4. French ''Sousse,'' city in northern Tunis.

CHAPTER VI

THE LABORATORY

LET us go back a year, to a period some six months after the verdict of the Court-Martial. What was the attitude toward the Dreyfus Affair then prevailing in high Army circles? That attitude is nicely indicated by the order Boisdeffre then gave to Picquart (newly appointed head of the Second Bureau), directing him to investigate the motives of the Dreyfus crime and to "nourish" the dossier. The unremitting and tireless affirmations by Dreyfus of his innocence, his pathetic letters, his unvarying replies to the questions of du Paty de Clam, his protestations of innocence to Forzinetti, his frank and impassioned attempt to shake the conviction of Captain Lebrun-Renault who led him to the place of his degradation—all these facts had disturbed the General Staff.

Picquart accordingly pursued his investigation. Might Dreyfus' motives have been gambling or women? Picquart was obliged to admit in all sincerity that he could find nothing of any importance on this score. With the scrupulous honesty which he brought to his task, Picquart eliminated one after another the prejudiced reports submitted to him. But meanwhile Henry, to whom it was of vital interest that the treason of Dreyfus should be unquestioned, undertook to "nourish" the dossier himself, without the knowledge of his superior.

. . . .

The dispatch of the Italian Military Attaché to the Chief of the General Staff in Rome,[1] dated November 2, 1894, had been [intercepted but] incorrectly decoded. Although the correct wording had been arrived at some days later, the original version had been preserved. In the correct version were the words "if Captain Dreyfus has had no relations with you, it would be helpful if you would have the Ambassador directed to publish an official denial, in order to avoid press comment"; whereas, in the incor-

1. *See* p. 39.

rect version, the last six words had been translated, "our agent has been warned." Later this document formed part of the secret dossier, which, with its accompanying commentary, was submitted to the judges of the Court-Martial, in contravention of every principle of justice.

. . . .

In October, 1895, Dreyfus received on Devil's Island a letter signed "your old cousin Blenheim." Since he had no relative of that name, he considered it of no importance and put the envelope in a drawer. It was only after his return to France that Dreyfus, in arranging his papers, noticed that the following message, written in sympathetic ink, had appeared between the lines: "Wire broken. Try to repair it. Our two attempts have failed. We must be careful. They very nearly discovered all. Let me know where 2249 was hidden. They know about the affair of Jura 34." Apparently the author hoped that the writing in sympathetic ink would appear during the passage to Devil's Island; that the Director of the Penal Administration, who regularly read the letters addressed to Dreyfus, would discover it; and that the General Staff, duly informed, would conclude that an accomplice of the traitor continued to correspond with him in code.

Although this experiment failed, it was tried again about a year later. On September 4, 1896, another letter of the same type was sent to Dreyfus. But on this occasion, it was mailed in a Paris post office, and was read in the Colonial Ministry before being sent on. The letter was signed by one Weill, Weiss or Weyler, announced the marriage of his daughter at Basle, and contained little of intrinsic interest. But under the action of the light, the following compromising words appeared between the lines: "Impossible to decipher last communication. Give me precise information as to where the documents of interest are—also the combination for the strongbox. Agent ready to act at once."

This document surprised and greatly disturbed the Colonial Minister, Lebon. He at once informed his colleague, General Billot, Minister of War, and the latter sent the Archivist, Gribelin, to look into the matter. The latter informed Picquart, who sent word in turn to Boisdeffre. Now, by a strange coincidence, this letter arrived to confirm the treason of Dreyfus shortly after

Picquart had discovered the judicial wrong committed, and had submitted the proof of it to his superiors. It at once occurred to Picquart that it was the work of Mathieu Dreyfus, desiring to focus attention on the terrible fate of his brother at any cost. He confided this theory to the *Chef du cabinet* of the Prefect of Police, who replied: "Yes, unless this document is a forgery." These words were a shaft of light for Picquart. Since Henry was on leave when the letter was intercepted, it did not occur to him that he could be the author. Instead, he mistakenly attributed it to the man who, in the light of his invidious role in 1894, was interested in causing the attempted vindication to miscarry. In the eyes of Picquart the forger could only be du Paty de Clam.

Upon the suggestion of Bertillon, and with the object of putting Dreyfus to the proof, a facsimile of the letter was forwarded to Devil's Island. It had no result whatever. As in the preceding case, Dreyfus indifferently filed it away among his papers.

His vacation at an end, Henry returned to his post more determined than ever to "thicken" the famous dossier, to crush beneath indubitable proofs anyone who might appear to question Dreyfus' guilt. He had scarcely settled down to work, when, without mentioning the matter to Picquart, he submitted to Gonse a document which had arrived in the paper containers forwarded by the charwoman Bastian. In the present instance, it was a letter from Schwartzkoppen to Panizzardi, which read:

LAST evening I was obliged to call the doctor, who forbade me to go out.

Since I can't come to see you tomorrow, please do look in on me during the morning, for D—— has brought me numerous things of interest, and, with only ten days' time, we shall have to share the work.

So do make a point of telling the Embassy that you can't be there.

The truth is that Schwartzkoppen named in his note the person to whom he owed these "things of interest." But that did not hinder Henry. He simply erased the name and replaced it with the initial "D." And, when it occurred to him that it would be a bit crude to accuse Dreyfus of having given information to the German Military Attaché in September, 1896, he discreetly dated the letter March, 1894.

Even if one admits the good faith of Boisdeffre and Gonse up to this point, one is surprised by the astonishing readiness with which these generals accepted, without discussion, the documents which Henry submitted to them. This is even more disturbing when it is recalled that at the very time when Schwartzkoppen's letter arrived, Picquart, proofs in hand, was trying to convince them of the wrong which had been committed. It was only too apparent that Henry's "discoveries" were in harmony with the inmost desires of his superiors.

At a later date, du Paty de Clam declared, in the course of testimony before the Court of Cassation, that on October 31, 1896, he had said to Boisdeffre, referring to press polemics caused by the article in the *Éclair:*[2] "Suppose we are mistaken or have been deceived (neither of which I believe). It is bad enough to commit an error, but it is worse to persevere in it." And he elicited this reply from the Chief of the General Staff: "Set your mind at rest, there are proofs unknown to you which do not permit even the slightest doubt."

Henry, however, encouraged by the sympathy of his colleagues, was of the opinion that the dossier was not yet sufficiently "nourished." At his request, Gonse returned to him the secret dossier, which he now proceeded to "thicken" with unassailable documents. Toward the end of October, the fragments of a letter of Panizzardi to Schwartzkoppen were found, along with the relevant envelope, in the containers of the charwoman Bastian. With these fragments, and the aid of one of his secret agents, known by the name of Lemercier-Picard, an expert in forgery, Henry obtained these two convincing documents:

I HAVE read that a deputy is going to make an interpellation concerning Dreyfus. If they demand fresh explanations in Rome, I will say that I never had any traffic with this Jew.

That's understood. If you are asked, say the same thing, because what went on with him must never be known.

Second letter:

HERE is the manual; I have paid your share (180) as we arranged. Agreed for Wednesday at eight in the evening at Laurent's. I have invited three members of the Embassy, of whom one is a Jew. Don't fail us.

This second letter was dated June 14, 1894.

2. *See* p. 46.

This sinister business was accomplished on November 1, 1896, in the following manner: For the first letter Henry used fragments recently received; for the second, a message of Panizzardi taken from the secret dossier. He cleverly interspersed a certain number of words actually written by the Italian Attaché with others, which he devised and which were inserted by Lemercier-Picard, using the blank spaces in the two letters. But what Henry failed to notice at the time was the fact that Panizzardi's two letters were written on *quadrillé* paper,[3] and that the rulings in the two cases differed slightly in size and color. It was in fact necessary to hold them up to the light to perceive the difference. Some days later Henry, to round out his handiwork, fabricated two replies of Schwartzkoppen to the first letter, one a mere acknowledgment, the second longer and noting the reasons why Deputy Castelin's interpellation did not in the least disturb him. It was this collection of letters which produced such a profound impression upon the Chamber when the Minister of War, Cavaignac, read them from the tribune in 1898 to prove Dreyfus' guilt definitively.

Henry submitted to Gonse on November 2 the two forged letters, said to be those of Panizzardi. The General showed no surprise whatever at their timeliness, or at the curious style attributed to the Italian Military Attaché. Nor did Gonse betray any astonishment at this fortunate corroboration of the new theory adopted by the Army heads, to the effect that, contrary to what had been hitherto believed, Dreyfus had never had any direct relations with Schwartzkoppen, but had acted through Panizzardi as intermediary. That same day, with the permission of Gonse, Henry submitted to Boisdeffre the forgery relating to Castelin's interpellation, and had him compare the writing with that in the forgery dated June, 1894. Boisdeffre unhesitatingly accepted the two documents as authentic and agreed with his subordinates that it was preferable not to mention them to Picquart, who, they felt, was already too deeply interested in the Dreyfus Affair. On the other hand, Boisdeffre did take them to General Billot, who was disturbed by the acrimony of the public controversies over Dreyfus, and who asked nothing better than to be convinced once and for all.

3. Ruled in almost invisible squares.

Henry was triumphant: his superiors were convinced, or pretended to be; Picquart had been exiled in disgrace; while he, Henry, found himself at the head of the Intelligence Bureau, under the nominal direction of Gonse. And yet his mind was not entirely at peace. There was still something which disturbed him—the shadow of Picquart. He realized that, as long as there was a possibility of a renewed attack by his former chief, he could never rest easily. What was he to do? He did not long hesitate. His own security demanded that he disgrace Picquart.

Picquart was obliged by the nature of his mission to move constantly from place to place. And so he had his mail addressed to the Ministry of War, whence the Archivist, Gribelin, had it forwarded to him. Henry took advantage of this situation to read Picquart's mail. One fine day, taking the phraseology of one of the letters to Picquart as a model, he forged the following letter in its entirety:

PARIS, 12:35 A.M. I am just leaving home. Our friends are in a state of consternation. Your unfortunate departure has thrown everything into confusion. Hasten your return here! Hasten with all possible speed! The holiday season is very favorable for our cause, and we are counting on you for the twentieth. *She* is ready, but *she* cannot and will not act until she has talked with you. When the demigod has spoken, we can act.

In this way proof was offered that Picquart was in the service of the defenders of Dreyfus, the "treason syndicate." This forgery was submitted by Henry to General Gonse on December 15, 1896. Gonse knew only too well the integrity of Picquart, who wrote him regularly with assurances of his (very real) affection. But notwithstanding this fact, Gonse accepted this document without the slightest objection. Naturally the letter was not forwarded to the addressee, but was duly filed in the Picquart dossier, which now was likewise in need of being "nourished."

During this same period, Henry undertook a still more delicate task. On the petit bleu, which had been reconstructed by Captain Lauth and which had originally convinced Picquart of Dreyfus' innocence, he erased the name of Esterhazy, and then rewrote it in a hand differing from that of the rest of the message. It would thus become a simple matter to accuse Picquart, when the time should come, of having suppressed the name of the real addressee of Schwartzkoppen's card and of having substituted that of Esterhazy. But Henry had forgotten about the photographic negatives made of the original document, and so neglected to destroy them.

Finally, in order to prove that the Picquart plot was not of recent date, Henry clipped from a newspaper an obituary notice of the Marquis de Nettancourt, father-in-law of Esterhazy, who died on January 4, 1897. Henry dated the clipping in red pencil "January 5, 1896," and filed it at the beginning of the Esterhazy dossier, which had been turned over to Gonse by Picquart when the latter placed the Intelligence Bureau in his hands. It could thus be shown that Picquart, who claimed that he learned of Esterhazy's name for the first time when he read the petit bleu, had already for some time been interested in Esterhazy.

With this problem settled, Henry, carried away by his imagination and enthusiasm, set about the construction of an "ultra-secret dossier." By the very gravity of the documents which this file would be supposed to include, it could not under any circumstances be made public. The revelation of such documents might lead to serious international complications. Its principal purpose would be to reinforce the conviction of successive Ministers of War and of their Chiefs of the General Staff. This mysterious dossier, concerning which so much ink has been spilled, was composed of two parts, each with its own history:

(1) The photographs of eight letters, seven addressed by Dreyfus to the German Emperor, and one from the latter to his Ambassador in Paris, Count von Münster. These letters had, so to speak, been purloined from the Embassy, and subsequently returned, as the result of a peremptory summons from the Government at Berlin.

(2) Various photographs of the real bordereau, on heavy paper, annotated by William II. In the latter connection, the implication was that the document (which included, opposite the individual items offered by the traitor, the prices demanded) had been submitted by Schwartzkoppen to the Emperor. William II had then returned it to Count von Münster with this annotation in his own hand: "This scoundrel of a Dreyfus is becoming very demanding; however, we must have the documents mentioned as quickly as possible." This original bordereau, which had also

been taken from the German Embassy, had perforce to be returned to avoid a serious controversy. But this was done only after a certain number of photographic negatives of the document had been taken, and after Colonel Sandherr (then head of the Second Bureau) had had an opportunity to have it copied by Esterhazy, whom he sometimes made use of by reason of the latter's knowledge of foreign languages. It was this copy, on transparent paper, without the Emperor's annotation and without the prices, which was alleged to have been submitted to the judges of the Court-Martial, and to have convinced them.

Henry had thus provided his superiors with arguments calculated to satisfy the most exacting consciences and to convince the most stubborn minds. No one, except the authorities, knew precisely what this ultrasecret dossier contained. But the rumor was cleverly circulated among the public that documents of an absolutely decisive character existed, and that only the safety of the State prevented their publication.

. . . .

Meanwhile the Affair, which had passed through a period of quiet, entered on an active phase once more. Scheurer-Kestner, Vice-President of the Senate, became interested in it. Whence, it was asked, came the information which convinced him? From the General Staff, it was affirmed without hesitation. Picquart was the guilty man, and it was imperative that his activity be stopped once and for all. Once more Henry stepped into the breach. With the approval of Boisdeffre and of Gonse, he wrote Picquart on May 31, 1897, that an investigation had just revealed that, during 1896, the following three developments had taken place in the Statistical Section:

(1) Initiation of a correspondence, unconnected with the Intelligence Bureau, and with an object which no one here has been able to understand.

(2) Proposals made to two members of the Staff of the Statistical Section, asking them to testify, if need be, that a certain document in their official files had been seized in the mail, and had come from a person whose identity was known.

(3) Opening of a secret dossier and examination of the documents therein contained, an act which had been followed by indiscretions, whose object was contrary to the best interest of the service.

Henry hoped that he could terrify Picquart, as he had succeeded in terrifying so many others—and that he would thus seal his lips. But Henry had misjudged Picquart. The latter received Henry's message at Gabès, June 7. He replied on the tenth with a withering denial of the charges. He then secured a leave from his corps commander, and arrived in Paris on June 20. The next day he went to see his very old friend, the lawyer, Leblois. Picquart told Leblois his story and declared that Dreyfus was innocent, without, however, telling him upon what documents his conviction was based, or mentioning to him the petit bleu. He then asked Leblois to take charge of his interests. But he forbade Leblois to take any step, except to inform the Government—and that only in case it were essential for the purpose of frustrating the sinister plots with which he felt himself menaced. He added that he would consider the slightest indiscretion as an abuse of confidence. On June 30 Picquart set out again for Susa.

CHAPTER VII

ESTERHAZY AND THE GENERAL STAFF

MARIE CHARLES FERDINAND WALSIN-ESTER-HAZY was born in Paris, December 16, 1847. He was a descendant of an illegitimate member of the French branch of the Austrian House of Esterhazy,[1] but that noble and illustrious family was never willing to acknowledge him as one of their members. Left an orphan at the age of eighteen, he lived for a time on a small inheritance from his mother, and then, in May, 1869, enlisted in the Roman Legion.[2] He resigned from that service in March, 1870, and returned to France, where his uncle, General Walsin, had him join the Foreign Legion with the rank of second lieutenant. After the fourth of September,[3] Esterhazy was naturalized and took part, as a Frenchman, in the Campaign of the Loire. During the years following the War he was for a time adjutant to General Grenier in Africa, and was then appointed lieutenant of the Fifty-first Regiment of the Line at Beauvais. In 1876 he succeeded in being assigned to the Intelligence Bureau of the Ministry of War as translator of German, and it was there that he met and formed an intimate friendship with Henry. Later Esterhazy claimed that he had even lent Henry money at the time of his marriage, and that he had never been repaid.

In any event, it is a fact that henceforth Esterhazy himself was steadily in need of money. His salary was inadequate for the satisfaction of the increasing demands made on it. He played the Stock Exchange, frequented gambling houses, and borrowed money from women—with whom his enterprising manner and unfailing gift for small talk assured him considerable success. This dissolute life, however, did not prevent him from winning the favor of his superiors and even the support of important

1. His grandfather was an illegitimate member of the French house of Esterhazy, which had emigrated from Austria in the eighteenth century.
2. Or Papal Zouaves, the force raised by the Pope, and enlisting Catholics of various nationalities, for the protection of papal territories.
3. September 4, 1870, date of the proclamation of the Third French Republic.

politicians. He was made captain in 1880, and chevalier of the Legion of Honor in 1882. In short, although he had risen from the ranks, Esterhazy had forged for himself a splendid career. And yet he was dissatisfied. To his mistress, Madame de Boulancy, he wrote letters brimming with insults to the Army and its leaders, to whom, however, he owed everything:

IF this evening I were to be told that tomorrow, as Captain of Uhlans, I should die cutting the French to pieces with my sword, I would be perfectly happy.

I wouldn't do a puppy the least harm in the world, but I would kill a hundred thousand Frenchmen with pleasure. . . . Ah! these filthy fellows with their cowardly and anonymous gossip, who go from woman to woman retailing their savoury bits from brothels—and always finding listeners. What a sad figure they would make in the red sun of battle, with Paris taken by assault and delivered over to the pillage of a hundred thousand drunken soldiers.

> That's a fête to dream of.
> And may it come to pass!

And elsewhere:

ALL these grotesque generals still wear the mark of the Prussian boot on their behinds. . . . All these great leaders, cowards and ignoramuses that they are, will be miserably discomfited, and will once more fill the German prisons, which again will prove too small to hold them all. . . . All the pranks of these charlatans will avail little in the face of the magnificent and well-commanded Prussian regiments. . . . The Germans will put all these fellows in their place before long. . . .

But all this insubordination and all this questionable activity did not keep the process servers from his heels. He was hounded by his creditors and at the end of his resources, when, in 1886, he managed to marry a young lady of fine family, Mademoiselle de Nettancourt-Vaubécourt, who had been dazzled by his conversation. After her family obliged her to divorce Esterhazy she retained for him a touching affection, in spite of all his faults. The dowry of 200,000 francs was soon dissipated. To save the remainder of her fortune, his wife, in 1888, asked for separate maintenance. And Esterhazy, once more in debt, returned to his premarital habits.

He was made a major on July 10, 1892, and assigned to Dunkirk, much to his irritation since he wanted to remain in Paris. Even by using his influence, the best he could do was to be transferred to Rouen at the end of December. His need of money continued to increase, and his speculations on the Stock Exchange turned out badly. It was under these conditions that he decided to offer his services to Lieutenant-Colonel von Schwartzkoppen, the German Military Attaché.

.   .   .   .

Henry's mind had been completely at ease until the petit bleu fell into Picquart's hands, and the name of Esterhazy, unknown hitherto, sprang into untimely prominence. A new phase of the Dreyfus Affair was thus opened, and Henry had perforce to take counsel for the future. Dreyfus must be crushed beneath proofs of guilt. Picquart must be overwhelmed by the fear of scandal. Above all, Esterhazy must be controlled to prevent him from committing new indiscretions; at the same time plans must be laid for his defense, if that should become necessary. Esterhazy was accordingly told of Picquart's discovery, and of the fact that he was being watched. Esterhazy's reply was boldly to seek a place once again in the Intelligence Bureau. But his request was refused by General Billot. Meanwhile, a striking event took place: on November 10, 1896, the *Matin* published a photograph of the bordereau, which had remained in the hands of one of the experts, Teysonnières. Esterhazy thought he was lost. But, as if by a miracle, Schwartzkoppen alone recognized Esterhazy's handwriting, and silence descended once more upon the Dreyfus Affair.

.   .   .   .

General Billot had sacrificed Picquart to the demands of Boisdeffre and Gonse. But he entertained no doubt as to the criminal character of the acts of Esterhazy, and decided, although somewhat tardily, to place him where he could do no harm. He dared not arrest him, which was clearly his duty, since he feared the reaction of public opinion and the violence of the press. Instead, Billot invited him to request his retirement for reasons of health, and signed the relevant order on August 17, 1897.

Meanwhile Scheurer-Kestner, Vice-President of the Senate,

was making more pressing representations. He had recently become convinced of Dreyfus' innocence, and had determined to devote himself to the cause of vindicating him. On several occasions he called on his old friend, Billot, and stated officially his conviction of Dreyfus' innocence. All of which greatly disturbed the General Staff.

About the middle of October, Gonse summoned Henry, Lauth, and du Paty de Clam for a conference. Du Paty had had nothing to do with the Dreyfus Affair for a long time. Gonse told him about the campaign to substitute Esterhazy for Dreyfus, which had begun eighteen months earlier. He explained to him that Esterhazy had a doubtful reputation and that the Jews, taking advantage of his failings, had chosen to saddle Esterhazy with the crime of their coreligionist. He added that a careful inquiry had revealed the falsity of the accusation, but that, if he were denounced by Scheurer-Kestner, Esterhazy might lose his head and commit suicide or flee the country. Such a move would be equivalent to a confession of guilt and would constitute a triumph for the friends of Dreyfus. The honor of the Army demanded that such a scandal be avoided at all costs. Esterhazy must be warned and prevented from losing his head.

To accelerate the action, Henry turned to his usual methods. On October 19, as if by chance, General Billot received an anonymous letter calling upon him to take steps against Scheurer and Picquart as the authors of a plot to substitute Esterhazy for Dreyfus. The Minister of War gave the letter to Gonse, who hastened to show it to Henry and du Paty de Clam. It was decided that Esterhazy should be warned at once. Du Paty prepared an anonymous letter for this purpose, but the Minister of War would not permit it to be sent. Henry then had another letter drafted by one of his agents, and had it delivered personally to Esterhazy, who subsequently testified that it had come by mail, although he was never able to produce the envelope. This message, in which the proper names had been purposely altered, was signed *Espérance,* and its paternity has been ascribed to du Paty.

General de Boisdeffre likewise summoned du Paty de Clam. He declared to him that Esterhazy was innocent, and that he was absolutely convinced of Dreyfus' guilt. The attempt to substitute another officer for Dreyfus stirred Boisdeffre's indignation, and he indicated that he was agreeable to the plan of making contact with Esterhazy. He appealed to the patriotism of du Paty, who yielded out of respect for his superior and accepted the mission. Henry then drafted another anonymous letter for Esterhazy and gave it to Gribelin, who, anxious lest he be recognized, disguised himself before delivering it. A meeting was arranged for five o'clock in the afternoon of October 23 in the Montsouris Park. Du Paty, Henry and Gribelin all went, but Henry remained hidden. Du Paty explained the plot of the Jews to Esterhazy, and assured him that he could count on resolute defenders if he was ready to obey the instructions which would be given him.

On the following day, du Paty met Esterhazy again, in the Montmartre Cemetery, and advised him to seek an interview with the Minister of War, "guardian of the honor of his officers." But Billot, who knew nothing of the *pourparlers* which had been initiated, refused to receive him and directed him to General Millet, Director of Infantry. After Millet had listened to his story, he induced him to draw up a detailed account for the Minister of War. That same day, with the consent of General de Boisdeffre, Esterhazy submitted a long report which concluded:

My life I value as less than nothing. But I have a glorious heritage to defend. If necessary, I shall address myself to the Emperor of Germany.[4] He is an enemy, but he is a soldier. He knows what the name I bear represents, and I have no reason to doubt that he would authorize his aide-de-camp to protest against the infamy of which I am the victim.

And so this pitiful farce continued. Gonse and Boisdeffre realized that they were irremediably compromised, and sought to mitigate the consequences of their blunders by taking the real traitor under their protection. In order to make sure of Esterhazy they had devised a way to use him. He was not perhaps dishonest at heart, but he was both naïve and dissolute. They had readily convinced him of the exalted national mission with which he was intrusted. All of which did not prevent them from shamelessly deserting him later on: when the criminal traffic of du Paty and Esterhazy came to the attention of the public, they

4. The Emperor of Germany remained the feudal suzerain of the house of Esterhazy. Hence appeals in questions of honor lay to him (*see* p. 64).

permitted the latter to be retired for "serious misconduct in the service."[5]

On his part, Esterhazy played the game, now worried, now threatening; hugely enjoying all these manoeuvres; judging at their correct value these pitiful generals, whose weakness disgusted him, and whom he made dance to his own tune under the threat of revelation. He, who cared nothing for his own honor, found it amusing to see a man like Boisdeffre posing as the incarnation of the honor of the French Army.

.   .   .   .

About this time it began to be realized that these conferences between Esterhazy and officers of the General Staff were not without danger—that some unfortunate chance encounter was always possible. Gonse prudently suggested to Esterhazy that he name an intermediary. The latter suggested his mistress, the Pays girl, who was accepted without discussion. Du Paty de Clam received her in his own home in the presence of his wife. The latter agreed to carry the letters herself to Esterhazy, for whom she waited, veiled, in a cab, at a meeting place arranged the day previous.

Meanwhile Scheurer-Kestner had returned to Paris. He considered it desirable that justice come from above. And so he decided to request an interview with President Félix Faure. As a matter of courtesy, he informed Billot of his intention, and the latter hastened to warn Boisdeffre. Esterhazy was told of the intended move, and du Paty de Clam sketched for him the rough draft of a letter to the President of the Republic. In this letter, which Félix Faure received on October 29, after stating that he had addressed himself to the Minister of War in vain, Esterhazy declared:

I AM addressing myself, therefore, to the Commander in Chief of the Army, to the President of the Republic, and I ask that he put a stop to this scandal, as he can and should do. . . . If I have the misfortune not to be heard by the Sovereign Chief of my own country, I have taken steps to insure my appeal reaching my Heraldic Chief, Suzerain of the Esterhazy family, the Emperor of Germany.

When Félix Faure received Scheurer-Kestner a few hours

5. *"Fautes graves dans le service."*

later, he refused to listen to his explanations and promised at most a benevolent neutrality. Scheurer-Kestner turned once more to Billot. The latter asked for two weeks in which to make a personal inquiry, it being understood that they both agreed to say nothing of the matter meanwhile. But the secret was short-lived. An hour after the interview Esterhazy was given private reassurances, and on the following day the newspapers announced that Scheurer had furnished the Minister of War with no proof. Scheurer-Kestner was deeply offended by this breach of faith. He wrote Billot, November 1, warmly urging him to permit no one to intervene in his investigation. And he added:

THE Army, which I love even as you do, only stands to lose by such proceedings. The Army can still save itself with honor. Tomorrow perhaps it will be too late.

I implore you, in the name of this sacred trust, to cast aside every secondary consideration. This is worthy of you. . . .

In what way could it affect the Army, if the Generals themselves should admit that perhaps a judicial wrong had been committed? The present Generals would be exalted—and General Mercier and the others as well. Public opinion would be with them, be quite sure of that.

If, on the other hand, they succeed in suppressing what ought not to be suppressed in this country of ours (unless they are willing to be overwhelmed later by the truth), then, General, you must be prepared for disaster, not only to yourself, but to this Army to which we so freely give our admiration and affection.

We must join forces to prevent so great a calamity. And, as you well know, I stand ready to aid in this task with my whole heart.

Do but listen to me then, my old friend!

The General Staff, however, was on the watch. To stifle this new enemy, they brought into play the press, which, oiled by monies from the secret funds and the Jesuit treasury, took up this task with enthusiasm. At the same time the legend of Dreyfus' confession was revived, and Gonse secured from Lebrun-Renault, who had previously denied the fact, a written and signed confirmation. Certain newspapers, such as the *Temps*, the *Figaro*, the *Radical*, abstained from the press campaign. In the recently founded *Aurore*, Clemenceau, who did not as yet believe in the innocence of Dreyfus, wrote that if there were striking presumptions of error, the case should be reviewed; the only way to free the country of this nightmare was a complete airing of the facts. And Paul de Cassagnac, notorious as a defender of the General Staff, protested in moving terms in the *Autorité* against the use of secret evidence:

SOMEWHERE in this verdict there is a chasm—black, yawning, bottomless. Every conviction reached in the shadows of secrecy is judicial murder. It is vain to urge "secrets of State"—that is an act of cowardice. . . . The thought of the innocence of Dreyfus has always haunted me. It terrifies me.

.   .   .   .

Henry was now resolved to give battle all along the line. He had come to know the cowardice of his superiors, who were slipping deeper and deeper into the bog of their own original blunder, drawn steadily downward by weakness of character, professional solidarity, fear of certain newspapers which would never loose their hold and did not hesitate even to sully their names in order to strengthen that influence. In the light of this situation Henry now planned an offensive on a grand scale, which nearly won him a final victory. His plan envisaged a declaration by Esterhazy to the effect that a mysterious woman had placed in his hands a photograph of an important document she had found in Picquart's possession. This document Picquart had, as it were, purloined from a foreign embassy, and its contents seriously compromised highly placed personages in the diplomatic world.

Esterhazy, duly coached, wrote at once (October 31) a second letter to the President of the Republic, noting the existence of the document and concluding: "If I secure neither protection nor justice, and if my name is so much as pronounced, this photograph, which is at present in a safe place abroad, will immediately be published." The private life of Félix Faure was far from exemplary, and he feared the press more than anything else. Hence he was badly shaken by this threat, and summoned Billot and Boisdeffre. These three men knew the truth. They knew that Dreyfus was innocent, just as they knew that Picquart had never stolen a document which could have loosed a war, and that *a fortiori* no woman could have stolen it from him. Above all, they knew just what value they could attach to Esterhazy's word. Yet they were intimidated, and succumbed to the threats of this blackmailer.

Henry realized that his blow had struck home. With Esterhazy's aid he now contrived a third letter to the President of the Republic, who was insolently warned that the Government was being approached for the last time. Esterhazy's summons concluded:

IF I am protected, I will return the document to the Minister of War without a single person in this world having seen it; but I must be shielded quickly, for I can wait no longer and I will shrink from nothing to defend and revenge my honor, which has been so infamously sacrificed.

On November 6, Billot directed General Saussier to summon Esterhazy, and the latter was warned in the usual way: "The General will question you about the document. Refuse to talk, and say that you have it in a safe place. He won't press you in any event. All goes well." Saussier knew that no one wanted any complications, so he listened to Esterhazy's story, and then advised him simply to return the document without delay to the Minister of War. On the other hand, the Council of Ministers was lectured by Félix Faure, and, despite the caution urged by the Minister of Justice, Darlan, issued to the press an official communiqué stating that "Dreyfus had been legally and justly condemned."

Esterhazy and Henry had triumphed. But they desired to push their advantage too far. With good reason, Henry knew that Picquart's correspondence was being seized and read before being forwarded to him. He, therefore, dictated to Esterhazy a threatening letter for Picquart, which Esterhazy sent in his own name. The letter was followed by two telegrams, signed respectively *Speranza* and *Blanche*. The first ran: "Arrest the demigod. Everything is discovered, very serious business." The second read: "They have proof that the petit bleu was forged by Georges." Georges was Picquart's given name. These telegrams had been drawn up for the purpose of having them intercepted. They were then submitted to Gonse and Billot. At once the General Staff pretended to find in them new proof of Picquart's complicity with the defenders of the traitor, and directed the *Sûreté Générale*[6] to investigate his mysterious correspondents.

The two confederates, however, had misjudged Picquart. They had hoped to intimidate him. Instead, they induced him to come into the open and demand the truth. On November 12, 1897, just as Henry was promoted lieutenant colonel, Picquart sent to General Billot from Gabès a formal complaint. Meanwhile, Esterhazy, who had thus far never had in his hands the document with which he had threatened the President of the Republic, received it from Henry. And, upon the latter's suggestion, he made the *beau geste* of returning it to the Minister of War that very afternoon.

·   ·   ·   ·   ·   ·   ·   ·

Mathieu Dreyfus, however, had discovered a short time previously the author of the bordereau. He decided to denounce Esterhazy to the Minister of War, which he did in the following letter of November 15:

Monsieur le Ministre:

The unique basis of the accusation of 1894 against my unfortunate brother was an unsigned and undated letter indicating that confidential military documents had been delivered to a representative of a foreign power.

I have the honor to inform you that the author of that document was Count Walsin-Esterhazy, Major of Infantry, retired last spring by reason of infirmities of a temporary character. Major Esterhazy's handwriting is identical with that of the document in question. It will be very simple to secure specimens of this officer's writing.

I am, moreover, prepared to indicate where you can find such letters, of unquestionable authenticity and of a date prior to my brother's arrest.

I entertain no doubt, *Monsieur le Ministre,* that, now that you have definite knowledge of the author of the treason for which my brother was condemned, you will execute immediate justice.

MATHIEU DREYFUS.

After he had seen this letter in the newspapers, Esterhazy, on

6. The national body of plainclothes state police, subject then to the Minister of the Interior, concerned primarily with radicals, foreign refugees, attacks on public men, etc.; somewhat similar to Scotland Yard.

the suggestion of du Paty de Clam, wrote the following note at once to General Billot:

I HAVE read in this morning's newspapers the scandalous denunciation directed at myself. I hereby request you to institute an inquiry, and I stand ready to reply to all charges.

Esterhazy also asked the Minister of War for an acknowledgment of the document which he had returned to him, and Billot, influenced by Boisdeffre, actually agreed to write the wretched fellow the following letter:

MAJOR, I have the honor to acknowledge the receipt of yours of November 14, which enclosed the photograph of a document given you by an unknown woman and presumed to have come from the Ministry of War.

A second letter from the Minister advised him, in conformity with his expressed desire, to hold himself at the disposition of the Military Governor of Paris for purposes of the inquiry which had just been ordered. The inquiry was intrusted to General de Pellieux. As a disciplined soldier, de Pellieux felt that he could hold no opinion other than that of the Minister of War and the Chief of the General Staff. He did not for an instant think that it was his function, as an impartial investigator, to come to his own conclusions, to compare the texts of documents, to inquire into the possibility that a wrong had been committed. Throughout his investigation he viewed himself simply as the representative of the General Staff, whose duty it was to punish the scandalous attack on an officer—an officer whose private life was perhaps not without reproach, but whose military integrity was unquestioned. Furthermore, de Pellieux considered it his duty to pass severe judgment upon another officer who had dared to cast doubt upon the veracity of his superiors, and who, for reasons which he neither understood nor sought to understand, had created a disturbance in the service, and had done things not in keeping with the honor of a soldier. Even before de Pellieux began the study of the case, his mind was made up. In his eyes Esterhazy was the victim of an abominable plot, with Picquart the unwitting accomplice. His duty was to honor the one and punish the other.

Even the famous letters to Madame de Boulancy, which have already been mentioned,[7] and which Scheurer-Kestner submitted to the General in the course of the investigation, did not succeed in changing his point of view, which had already crystallized. When these letters were published in the *Figaro*, Esterhazy was at first frantic. Then he quickly denied their authenticity, and this became the official theory of those supporting his cause.

Meanwhile de Pellieux, despite all efforts, refused to resubmit the bordereau to handwriting experts, his excuse being that it had already been attributed to Dreyfus, that the case had been decided, and that it was not his function to reopen it. He concluded his investigation with a refusal to prosecute, which included severe animadversions on Picquart. Simultaneously, however, and acting under the inspiration of the General Staff, he advised Esterhazy to ask trial by a Court-Martial. De Pellieux even went so far as to draft, himself, the letter which Esterhazy sent to him:

NEITHER a refusal to prosecute, nor a judgment that there is not sufficient ground for prosecution, could give me the amends to which I am entitled. . . . I rely upon your high sense of justice to submit my case to the Court-Martial of Paris.

At the direction of the Minister of War, and in complete agreement with Boisdeffre, and even with Esterhazy, General Saussier refused to approve the official conclusions of de Pellieux, and, on December 4, 1897, he signed the order to prosecute. The preliminary examination was intrusted to an old Major on the retired list, Ravary by name, who exhibited all the pliancy which was expected of him. At the very beginning, moreover, Henry had reassured Esterhazy in these terms:

DON'T worry. Ravary is under our thumb, and will be coached. We will show him what is necessary, and no more. That's settled. Everything is going splendidly.

As a matter of fact, Gonse summoned Ravary, and in his own characteristic fashion familiarized him with the situation. Moreover, the Major reported the progress of his inquiry to the Gen-

7. *See* p. 60.

eral each day, a fact which permitted Henry and du Paty de
Clam to transmit a summary to Esterhazy and to tell him what
replies he should make. The preliminary inquiry was completed
December 30, and found for a discharge of the accused. But on
January 2, as had been agreed earlier, the Military Governor of
Paris rejected the findings of the rapporteur,[8] and sent Esterhazy before the First Court-Martial. He appeared January 10,
1898, and on the following day was acquitted by unanimous verdict.

This sham trial was, without any question, simply a disgusting
farce for which the generals themselves had written the scenario.
It strikingly confirmed the truth of Ravary's saying (of which,
however, he did not grasp the really profound meaning) : ''Military justice is not the same as the *other kind.*'' On the other
hand, this melancholy day marked the beginning of a still more
passionate struggle for the triumph of truth. Events now followed in rapid succession.

8. *See* Appendix II.

CHAPTER VIII

DEVIL'S ISLAND

THE Affair had now been magnified to an extent unsuspected by Dreyfus, unjustly shut away upon his solitary isle. The Court-Martial's decision of December 22, 1894, had condemned him to detention in a "fortified enclosure"; that is, to live beyond the borders of Continental France, in a place where surveillance would be possible, but where he might enjoy all the freedom compatible with this necessary supervision. His wife and children had the right to join him there. The place of detention specified by law was Ducos Island in New Caledonia.

According to the letter of the law, deportation never resulted in the actual imprisonment of the condemned. Its object was simply to restrict his liberty, and it imposed upon him no other limitation than that of not leaving the place to which he had been sent. But the Government now introduced special legislation, inspired by General Mercier, and accepted by Parliament on February 9, 1895. This law set aside, in addition to Ducos Island, the Salvation Islands, for prisoners being deported oversea for confinement in a "fortified enclosure."[1] And it was the Salvation Islands that were chosen for Dreyfus. Subsequently, when Dreyfus, in spite of the intervention of the Minister of War and in spite of the judgment of the Court-Martial, continued to proclaim his innocence, General Mercier decided to stifle his voice. By an unprecedented abuse of his powers, and without any justification for such a measure, Mercier changed the penalty of deportation to that of prison confinement.[2]

Dreyfus had been at the Ré Island Station for a month when he was placed on board the *Saint-Nazaire*, February 21, 1895, bound for the Salvation Islands. It was only seven degrees above zero. He was placed in a felon's cell in the forecastle, entered by a barred gate. His teeth chattered in the icy blast which swept

1. *Enceinte fortifiée.*   2. *Réclusion cellulaire.*

into his cell. He was tortured by hunger, and agonized in spirit. He felt that he had been utterly abandoned, and for long hours he wept.

After a horrible crossing, Dreyfus reached his destination at the Salvation Islands on March 12. The Islands are located some ten miles off the coast of French Guiana. In the order of their importance they are: Île Royale, seat of the penal administration; Saint Joseph's Island, to which infirm and insane convicts are sent; and finally Devil's Island, a barren rock with scattered clumps of cocoanut trees, some 1200 meters long, and 400 wide. The island had previously sheltered a leper colony, whose cabins had just been burned. The climate was so unhealthy that even an attempt to raise goats had failed. And it was here, on this wretched pin point of land, that, for more than fifteen hundred days and fifteen hundred nights, Dreyfus was destined to experience suffering unparalleled in the history of modern times.

No preparation had been made for Dreyfus. At first he was confined in a prison cell on Île Royale, with all the shutters barred. Finally, on April 13, he was taken to Devil's Island, where he was placed in a stone hut, thirteen feet square. The hut had been specially constructed for his use and was provided with an extension at one end—a tiny room, six-and-one-half by ten feet, in which a guard was constantly on duty. The guard had formal instructions never to speak to the prisoner and never to let him out of his sight.

During the early part of his residence on the island, Dreyfus was permitted to move about freely in an area some six hundred feet square—a bare and open space without a single tree to shade him from the tropic sun. No one could speak to him. He was without even the bare necessities. He was too proud to make a request which might be refused, and so he set about cleaning his hut himself. He prepared and cooked his own food. He washed and mended his own clothes. He even had to fashion dishes from discarded jam tins. He could not move an inch without finding himself in the shadow of a guard, armed with a revolver, and later with a rifle as well. Of all the tortures he was obliged to endure, this silent and eternal inquisition was the most terrible. In his unending solitude, which would already have been unbearable to most men, he had still to face this horror of eyes forever fastened on him—spying out his every movement, seeking to read his inmost thoughts.

.   .   .   .

In the early part of September, 1896, a rumor that Dreyfus had escaped was current in Paris. It was promptly denied— Dreyfus had done nothing whatever to justify a supposition of this kind. But André Lebon, the Colonial Minister, took his role as jailer in tragic vein, and telegraphed an order to confine Dreyfus to his cell and to put him in irons. Fearing that his orders might not be executed with sufficient rigor, Lebon summoned one Deniel, who had a reputation for brutality and who was at that time in France. The Minister gave Deniel a lecture and dispatched him to the Salvation Islands as new head of the penitentiary.

In accordance with the Minister's orders, Dreyfus was placed in double irons on the night of September 6, and this torture was continued for forty-four nights—until October 20. This "measure of safety"—to use administrative language—consisted of two irons, in the form of a reversed "U," fastened by their lower ends to the bed itself. A crossbar was fastened to these irons, and to this bar were fixed in turn two shackles. The feet of the prisoner were placed in these shackles, which were held securely to the bed by the bar in such a way that it was impossible for the body itself to move.

Riveted to his bed by chains stained with blood, tortured by vermin and torrid heat, racked by spiritual torment, Dreyfus felt that his suffering had passed the limits of human endurance and that he should die. Then, during a night of sleeplessness, he saw the light of what he called his "guiding star," revealing to him the path of duty. He experienced a sudden surge of strength. He resolved to struggle and to live. And yet even now his suffering was so great—his heart sickened, his mind crushed beneath the weight of his afflictions—that, on September 10, 1896, he ceased making entries in the melancholy diary which he had begun at the time of his arrival eighteen months before, and which he had not the strength to continue. In a final request he protested once more his innocence, and asked the President of the Republic to place his diary in the hands of his wife, if he should die.

. . . .

Meanwhile, a double palisade was constructed around Dreyfus' cabin. One of the fences stood eight feet high and was five feet from his windows, thus offering serious obstruction to both light and air. The other, a little farther away, was an impenetrable barrier constructed of thick planks of wapa trees, enclosing a space about one hundred and thirty feet long and fifty-five feet wide. Henceforth the prisoner had for exercise only a narrow walk without protection from the sun, and he was deprived of the view of the sea which had done so much to cheer him. More than this, the packages of books and periodicals which he had always awaited so impatiently were stopped. And the authorities were pleased to suspect that the profoundly affectionate and moving correspondence of Dreyfus and his wife was a mask for a secret code. Some of the letters were destroyed; others were delivered in a fragmentary form; others still were from time to time forwarded only in the form of copies, and so lost much of the charm and comfort which they brought.

Dreyfus' weakness at this time is revealed in his letters. He touched the depths of misery and sometimes called upon death to release him. He suffered from the bodily torments contrived by climate and by man. But he suffered far more from the thought of the crime which he was expiating for another, the thought of the stain upon his honor, of the unmerited affliction of his family, of the frightful injustice of which he was the victim. His embittered feelings gave vent to sudden fits of rage against the cruelty of his fate, and he was plunged in despair by the failure to plumb the mystery of the terrible wrong which had been done. Each mail was a fresh disappointment. As though in spite of himself, and with the regularity of a leitmotiv, the same words kept returning to his lips: "Always nothing. The culprit has yet to be found."

But these crises, terrible as they were, did not last. When his eyes turned to the cherished pictures of his wife and children, he quickly won control of himself. He wanted to live—to live that he might regain his honor, that he might expunge the terrible stain which sullied the family name. To this one end were molded his unbending will, his thoughts and hopes of every hour. Beyond that, he continued to exist, according to his own striking expression, "like a machine, unconscious of its own movement."

He lived. By a superhuman effort he succeeded in creating a spiritual armor of impenetrable steel. Henceforth, not the exhausting heat, nor endless insomnia, nor the bites of enormous mosquitoes which invaded his cabin and which he could not kill, nor fever, nor frequent attacks of cerebral congestion, nor dysentery, nor all the evils from which he had to suffer—nothing could undermine his grim fortitude. During the rare hours of relaxation he fought off the silence and loneliness by studying English, translating passages from Shakespeare, of whom he was a fervent admirer, and reconstructing from memory the elements of integral and differential calculus.

The cabin had now been deprived of adequate light and air, and the temperature inside never fell below 80 degrees. It had become so unhealthy and Dreyfus was in such a state of exhaustion, that the prison physician was obliged to intervene. Previously, in his report of April, 1897, he had noted the impairment of the prisoner's health. He added: "The regime of unbroken silence to which he is subjected has greatly affected his speech. When he speaks he has difficulty in articulating. Sentences no longer come readily, and he is obliged to repeat himself to convey his thought." After a second intervention by the physician, it was decided in August of the same year to construct a new cabin which would be situated on the "plateau," that is, on a higher level. The new cabin was somewhat higher and more spacious, but, like the first, it was surrounded by a thick palisade which excluded the view of the world beyond.

Neither this solid fence, however, nor the iron bars of the cell, nor the ever vigilant armed guard was sufficient to reassure Deniel, the Governor of the Salvation Islands. Unbalanced and vain, Deniel considered himself the repository of a "lofty national mission." He believed Dreyfus was obsessed with the idea

Dreyfus' hut and exercise yard on Devil's Island, sketched by one of his jailers. Note the excessive precautions taken to prevent his escape: the guard who followed him on his walks by day and watched by night from the little lean-to at the rear of the hut; the Hotchkiss gun and the guard on watch in the turret of the barracks.

Sketch of Devil's Island, showing the enclosure constructed for Dreyfus.

of escape, and of this, Deniel had a morbid fear. Feverishly he multiplied precautions. He increased the number of guards from five to ten, then to thirteen. In addition to the guards who relieved one another in the barred guardroom attached to the cabin, he placed guards on the roof and along the palisade. He encouraged his men to inform against one another, and no one was free from his suspicion. On the "plateau" he had an observation tower built, armed with a Hotchkiss gun, perennially loaded and pointed toward the sea. Boats were forbidden to come · nearer than three miles from the shore. The men on night duty in the guardroom were ordered never to be seated, but to march back and forth constantly. This they did, and the continual, monotonous, maddening noise of the wooden shoes which most of them wore added a new torment to those suffered by the prisoner.

The letters of Dreyfus and his family were viewed as disquieting by reason of their very emotional quality, and so they were submitted to the exclusive surveillance of the Governor who was afraid that, if the guards read them, they might be moved to abate the rigor of their regime. Frequently in the middle of the night, Deniel, for no other reason than that furnished by the anxiety of a disordered mind, would come in a small boat from Île Royale to make certain that his prisoner was still there. He decided finally that the protection of the windows—a system of bars reinforced by grating—was insufficient, and had two triangular panels added, making ventilation impossible and the air unfit to breathe.

After forty-three months of confinement, during which he had known nothing of the efforts being made in his behalf, Dreyfus finally learned on November 16, 1898, that the Criminal Division of the Court of Cassation had allowed his request for an appeal. Ten days later he was permitted to cross the threshold of the palisade. He was allowed to exercise in the narrow, sun-swept enclosure about the barracks of the guards. This spot offered few charms, but he was delighted to see once again his old friend, the sea, the voice of whose waves was a sympathetic echo of his own shaken spirit. Then, too, his heart was filled with high hope. He was certain that at any moment now he would receive the news of his deliverance. But, alas, he had not yet reached the

term of his suffering. Many weeks passed before the Court of
Cassation finished its investigation and set aside the judgment
of the Court-Martial of 1894. At half-past twelve on Monday,
June 5, 1899, Dreyfus was informed of the decision of the Court,
and on the ninth he boarded the Cruiser *Sfax,* and set out once
more for his own country.

There, in its larger lines, is the cruel tragedy of Devil's Island.
But those who would sound its depths should go to the moving
correspondence of Captain Dreyfus and his wife. With this sole
purpose in mind the letters which follow, chosen almost at ran-
dom, have been included.

> Dépôt de Saint-Martin-de-Ré,[3]
> January 21, 1895.

Ma bonne chérie:

Yesterday they gave me your sad letter, and then your telegram, to which I replied. How wretched we are! I think that no
one in the world has ever suffered as we two. You know there are
times when I am sorry that I promised you to live. After my conviction I had prepared everything for my death. I was ready to
appear before God, my conscience clear and at peace. You could
have vindicated my memory quite as well, and you would not
have suffered as much at the thought of my own torment. What is
really terrible about this situation is that I am completely in
sympathy with the measures which have been taken. Beginning
today, I am for everyone a convict, and one condemned for the
most heinous crime a soldier can commit. I am for everyone an
object of contempt. What can I say—that I am innocent! But
then why am I condemned, they quite logically ask?

What is essential, my dear, and what must be the object of
your every thought, is to discover the truth, by every means possible, by using our whole fortune. Money is nothing, honor is all.

If the Government would show a little pity for me . . . if it
would a little lessen my spiritual suffering, I should ask only one

3. Located about fifteen miles from La Rochelle, on the Island of Ré;
strongly fortified since the days of Vauban, and the concentration point for
convicts bound for French Guiana.

thing—that I should be cast nameless on a desert island which I might not leave, where I should see no one, until that day when, thanks to the investigations which must follow, the Government should discover the truth and restore my honor.

Take every care of your health, my dear, you need all your strength. Think of the children before you think of me. They need you, and they have only you now. You must not give yourself up to your grief. You have a task too lofty and too noble still to fulfill. . . .

ALFRED.

January 21, 1895.

Mon bon chéri:

Your good telegram of yesterday brought me great happiness. I was terribly worried without news of you, and so far no letter has come. Happily I didn't read the newspapers yesterday morning, and they tried to hide from me the sordid scene at La Rochelle. Otherwise I should have been mad with anxiety. What a terrible thing an angry mob is, poor Fred; what a frightful time you had! In any event you were not struck, I hope. I wept with anger, but there is nothing surprising in the attitude of the crowd; it is the result of reading these nasty sheets which live only by slander and filth, and which print no end of fables and lies, always readily accepted by the mob. But take courage, for among thinking men a great change has taken place, a change which everyone recognizes. I receive great numbers of letters from people who are indignant, people who swear your innocence and who tell me that we must have confidence and courage, that the truth will come to light. Only this morning I received, among others, a letter from an English lady with a bouquet of violets, emblem of innocence. She asked me to give it to you when I saw you again: "Bravest of the brave," she said, "that is the name your husband deserves. You can be proud of him. My sympathies were with the French Army in '70. Today I am proud of that sympathy, because I can tell everyone of the admirable conduct of a French officer in these circumstances. No officer, no matter of what nation, could have borne himself more bravely. The thought of Captain Dreyfus will remain an example to preserve me from all meanness in this life.'' That was so touching and so profoundly true that tears came to my eyes. Yes, *mon mari adoré,* I am proud of you. I have always had a profound love for you. Now I admire you, and wish only to be with you and never again to leave you.

Your children are too young to know how fine you are, but as soon as they reach the age of understanding they will deeply respect their father. They will restore to you in their affection and devotion the happiness which has been taken from you by this odious condemnation.

Adieu, mon bon chéri, je t'embrasse comme je t'aime mille et mille fois.

LUCIE.

Saint-Martin-de-Ré,
Thursday, January 31, 1895.

Ma chère Lucie:

. . . I ask myself in truth how I go on living. Night and day my thoughts are my only companions. There is nothing for me to do but to weep over our misfortunes.

Last night, as I thought back over my life, how I had struggled and worked to gain an honorable position . . . then, when I compared all that to my present situation, sobs caught in my throat and I thought my heart would break. I was so ashamed of my weakness and so afraid that the guards would hear me that I had to stifle my sobs in my covers. Really, this is too cruel!

Ah! how deeply I feel today that it is sometimes more difficult to live than to die! To die means a moment of suffering but then oblivion for all one's afflictions. . . . But I have no right to die, we have no right to die. We shall have that right only when the truth has been discovered, and my honor has been restored. Until then we must live.

How are our poor dear children? When I think of them, I burst into tears. And you? I hope that your health is good. You must take care of yourself, my dear. First the children, and then the mission which is yours—these impose duties on you, and you cannot fail.

Je t'embrasse comme je t'aime.

ALFRED.

Saint-Martin-de-Ré,
February 14, 1895.

Ma chère Lucie:

The few minutes that I had with you were sweet indeed, although it was impossible to tell you all that I had on my heart.

I pass my time in thinking of you, in filling my memory with your presence, in asking myself by what singular destiny I have been separated from you. Later, when they tell my story, it will seem an unlikely one indeed.

But what we must repeat to each other constantly is that we must seek vindication. My name must be distinguished once again by that honor which it should never have lost. I had rather see our children dead than to have their name dishonored. . . .

You have given me new courage. Your noble abnegation and your brave devotion have given me fresh strength to endure my terrible affliction.

I shall not tell you that I love you still more. You know how deep my love for you is. It is that which enables me to bear up under my suffering and under my spiritual torment—the love which you all have for me. . . .

ALFRED.

Saturday morning, February 15, 1895.

Mon pauvre Fred chéri:

How moving it was, and what a terrible shock, when we saw each other again. You, above all, my poor and dearly beloved husband, you must have been terribly shaken. For you had not been warned of my arrival and the surprise was too great. The conditions in which we were permitted to see each other were so painful. After a cruel separation of four months, it was terrible to be permitted to speak to each other only from a distance.[4] . . .

Ah! What anguish I felt as I parted from you, as I left Saint-Martin. For it had been such happiness to see and talk to you, in spite of the severe regulations to which we were subjected. . . .

LUCIE.

4. Dreyfus and his wife were only permitted to speak to each other from a distance and in the presence of the Governor of the Prison. They were forbidden to say anything whatever about the case. Mme. Dreyfus begged that she be permitted to embrace her husband, with his hands tied behind his back. This request was met with a brutal refusal. [Note of Pierre Dreyfus.]

Salvation Islands,
Tuesday, March 12, 1895.

Ma chère Lucie:

On Thursday, February 21, some hours after you left, I was taken to Rochefort and there embarked.

I shan't tell you of my voyage! I was transported as the vile wretch whom I represent would merit; that was only just. One can accord no pity to a traitor; he is the lowest of all scoundrels. So long as I represent this wretch, I can only approve these measures. My situation here is to be understood in the same light.

But your heart will tell you all that I have suffered, and that I suffer now. It is horrible. It is only my spirit which keeps me alive and which gives me hope that I shall soon see the triumphant day of vindication. It is that alone which gives me the strength to live. Without honor, a man is unworthy to live.

You who are truth itself, you swore to me on the day of my departure that you were sure of succeeding soon. I only kept alive during this terrible voyage, and I only live now, because of this promise of yours—and this you must remember.

I landed just a few minutes ago, and I secured permission to send you a cable. I am hastily writing these few words, which will go on the fifteenth by the English mail. It is a comfort to speak to you in this way—you whom I love so deeply. There are two mails a month for France—one by an English boat on the fifteenth, and one by a French boat on the third. There are likewise two mails a month coming to the Islands, one French and one English. Find out what the dates are and write me by both.

What I must say to you yet again is that, if you would have me live, bring about my vindication. Mere personal convictions, no matter what their character, help me not at all; they do not change my situation. What is essential is a judgment of rehabilitation.

When I agreed to live on after this tragic affair, I made for you the greatest sacrifice possible for a man of courage. I did it because of the conviction you have given me that truth inevitably comes to light. It is for you then, my dear, to do everything humanly possible in order to discover the truth.

Wife and mother, this is a task to move the hearts of wives and mothers, and induce them to yield the key to this terrible mystery. I must have my honor, if you wish me to live. That we must have for our dear children, too. Your sentiments are affecting your logic and that is never good. A judgment exists. Nothing will be altered in our tragic situation, until that judgment is reviewed. . . .

ALFRED.

When you have good news for me, send a cablegram. Each day I await it like the coming of the Messiah.

Salvation Islands,
July 15, 1895.

Ma chère Lucie:

I have written you so many and such long letters, during these months when I have been without news of you, that I have said and repeated many times all my thoughts and all my sufferings. Let me return no more to the latter. As to my thoughts, they are clear and invariable—and you know them well.

I appeal to my strength to stifle the beating of my heart, to bridle my impatience to learn that my innocence has finally been recognized everywhere and by every one. Although my energy is entirely passive, yours should be wholly active and animated by the ardent inspiration of my own.

If it were a question merely of torment, that would be nothing. But the honor of a name is at stake, the honor of our children. I will not have it— and of this you are well aware—that our children should ever be obliged to lower their heads. The light must be fully shed upon this tragic affair. Hence, nothing should be allowed to weary or to discourage you. Every door will open and every heart will beat for a mother who seeks only the truth, so that her children may have life.

It is almost from the grave that I say these words to you—for my life is not unlike death, with this added affliction, that I have a soul. . . .

ALFRED.

Sunday, July 21, 1895.

Mon Fred chéri:

Today it is raining, and I can't take the children for their walk. And so I have spent the entire afternoon reading the letters you have written since our frightful disaster. I have been terribly shaken. I have relived, hour by hour, those painful crises through which we passed. But all of that is over now; let us speak no more of it. I am calm now and full of confidence. I feel that happiness is coming. I should like to tell you what a touching thing Pierrot said to me. He came into my room just as I had burst into tears, and said to me: "Mama, you are very unhappy. Tell me why, and I will comfort you." I replied only with difficulty: "When you are older, you will understand." The poor little fellow stayed by my door for an age, returning often to repeat: "Mama, tell me, you are grieving because Papa is gone; are you less unhappy than you were a little while ago?" The music of his childish voice went to the bottom of my heart. Ah, if you could only hear the little dear! It would be such happiness for you. A ray of joy would warm your poor heart. Our children are very promising. They are strong, lively, fine looking, mischievous, and generous—willful, but persevering. They have all the elements which, properly guided, go to the making of fine character. We shall do our best and work to that end together, shall we not, my dear?

Bonsoir, mon mari adoré, je t'embrasse bien fort.

LUCIE.

September 5, 1895.

Mon bien cher mari:

What endless hours, what painful days we have experienced since this terrible disaster struck its stunning blow. Let us hope that we have finally surmounted the most arduous stage of our calvary, and that the future holds only happiness. . . . I am convinced that, with a will of iron, indomitable strength, and untiring perseverance, we can overcome every difficulty and plumb every mystery. I possess that will, and I shall possess it until the day of our triumph. It is your love that gives it to me and that keeps me from all weakness. I have ever before my eyes your beloved face and those of our children. I want to bring all three of you happiness and a tranquil future sheltered from suffering. But how far off all that is, *mon pauvre ami*, especially for you, solitary and alone, with no loved one near to comfort you,

Facsimile of a letter from Mme. Dreyfus to her husband, while he was imprisoned on Devil's Island. Note the official laisser passer of the Colonial Ministry, where all the Dreyfus correspondence was carefully scrutinized.

no one in whom you can confide and who by her affection could bring some solace to your heart. . . .

LUCIE.

September 25, 1895.

I have your good letter, my dear brother, and it is a great consolation and comfort to me to know that you are so strong and so courageous. I say to you, have faith, have trust. God will not permit an innocent man to pay for those who are guilty.

There is not a single day that I am not with you in heart and in thought. . . .

MATHIEU.

October 27, 1895.

My dear brother:

I can only keep repeating, always repeating: I have complete and unshaken confidence in the future. We shall discover the truth, and your honor will be restored. It is only a question of time. Continue then to be strong and brave, as you have been thus far. All our thoughts are with you. Our will is concentrated on one sole object: the discovery of those who are guilty. . . .

Your devoted brother,

MATHIEU.

Salvation Islands,
February 26, 1896.

Ma chère Lucie:

On the twelfth of this month, I received your dear letters of December, as well as those of the family. I need not describe to you the emotion they caused me; I wept, and that tells you all. . . . I received Mathieu's few words; tell him that I am with him always, heart and soul.

February 22 was the birthday of our dear little Jeanne . . . how much I have thought of her! I will say no more, for my heart would break, and I need all my strength.

Write me at length and tell me all about yourself and our dear children. I read and reread your letters each day, and it seems to me that thus I hear your dear voice, and this helps me to live. I will not write more, for I should be able only to tell you of the terrible length of the hours and the sadness of things—and to complain avails nothing. . . .

Salvation Islands,
April 5, 1896.

Ma chère Lucie:

I have just now received your dear letters of February, as well as all of those from the family. You in turn, my dear wife, have suffered the terrible anguish of waiting for news! . . . I have known this anguish, as I have known so many others; I have experienced so many disappointments. . . . Well, I say to you again, what does this matter! Your children live. We gave them life; we must restore to them their honor. We must push on to the end with our eyes fixed only on that object, with an indomitable will, and with that courage which comes from the feeling of absolute necessity.

I told you in one of my letters that each day brings with it the anguish of my affliction. . . . When evening comes, after an unceasing struggle with the agitation of my mind, the disorder of my reason, the revolts of my heart, I find myself in a state of terrible nervous and mental depression. I want to close my eyes, so that I will no longer think, no longer see, no longer suffer. I have to make a tremendous effort of will to drive away the ideas which depress me. Then the thought of you and of our dear children returns, and I say to myself again: however frightful your suffering may be, you must die in peace and in the knowledge that you leave to your children a proud and honored name.

If I recall this to you, it is simply to tell you once again what strength of will I consume in a single day, and all because the honor of our name and that of our children is at stake. That same will must animate you all. . . .

April 20, 1896.

Courage, *mon pauvre et cher Alfred,* our efforts will triumph, we shall succeed—be very sure of that. Although you suffer, we suffer also. But we must lift ourselves above all suffering and pain. These do not count, and should disappear in the face of the object to be achieved.

Courage, then, my dear brother. Strong in your innocence, continue to dominate your spiritual suffering, and wait patiently and with faith for the success of our efforts.

Je t'embrasse de tout mon coeur.

Ton frere qui t'aime bien.

MATHIEU.

Salvation Islands,
June 26, 1896.

Ma chère Lucie:

From your April letters I have sensed your sorrow at receiving only a few lines in the mail of the previous month. . . .

Your last letters, so affectionate and so touching in their poignant sadness, have deeply moved me. Once more you make a warm and moving appeal to my duties as a husband and father. You know, *ma bonne Lucie,* that it has been in the consciousness of these duties that I have drawn, and do still draw, the strength to endure all.

You tell me also that I must accept the certainty that a glaring light will be turned on this somber drama. Not only do I accept this certainty, but my faith and my confidence have always been complete. I know too well the sentiments of honor which animate all the members of our two families to have ever doubted. But to tell you that I wait patiently would be to speak falsely of my heart. When one endures torment such as ours, worse than death, strength and will must rise to the level of these tragic circumstances. As each hour which passes in these circumstances is for us a wound, each of these too long hours should be employed to end it all. I can only say to you then, and forever repeat, that your courage should grow each day.

What more can I say, dear Lucie? You must know that I live only in the thought of you and in that of our beloved children. We must then, dear Lucie, have no other thought, no other care, than that which is the inflexible and imperious command of our honor. I hope with all my heart, for both of us, for all of us, that we shall soon learn that this abominable torture is at an end. . . .

Your devoted,

ALFRED.

Beginning with the end of July, Mme. Dreyfus received her husband's letters only in the form of copies by a member of the penal service.

. . . .

Salvation Islands,
September, 1896.

I am writing you just as the July mail has come. The nervous reaction has been too great, too violent. I feel an irresistible need to speak with you after this long and distressing silence of a whole month. Yes, sometimes the pen drops from my hand and I ask myself what good it does to write! I have been dulled by so much suffering, my poor dear Lucie. . . .

I have endured so many things, that I am indifferent to life, and I speak to you as though from the grave, from the eternal silence which lifts one above all things. . . . I speak to you as a father, in the name of the duty which it is yours to fulfil toward our children. Go to the President of the Republic, the Ministers, to them who had me condemned. For, although angry passions sometimes mislead the most honest and upright men, their hearts remain generous, and they are ready to forget this same anger in the face of the terrible grief of a wife and mother who asks only one thing—the only thing we have to ask—the discovery of the truth, the honor of our dear children. . . .

Your devoted,
ALFRED.

October 10, 1896.

Papa chéri:

I want you to come back soon. You must ask God. I ask him every day.

Je t'embrasse beaucoup, beaucoup.

TA PETITE JEANNE.

October 10, 1896.

Chéri papa:

I cried this morning, because you do not come back, and that

makes me very sad. I want to say something which will please you : I am very good, and Mama told me that she was pleased.
Je t'embrasse beaucoup.

PIERROT.

December 15, 1896.

My dear Alfred :

I hoped that I should still receive some letters from you this month. I should have been so happy to have had a good long talk with you. But I received nothing, and so I went back to your October letters, and read and reread them. To my great happiness, I found there again that splendid strength which I so admire. It is this strength that sustains you in the terrible struggle you have accepted with such noble courage, a struggle which will lead us on to our supreme object, your vindication. The sentiments which you express, I share. We have each a duty to accomplish, however difficult it may be. Your duty is to strengthen yourself physically, with all the will that you possess; to dominate your nerves, so that you may not be disheartened. Thus you will be able to witness, with us all, the glorious triumph of truth. My duty, too, is simple and clear : to achieve our just right—the full and complete truth !

For two years we have been working toward this end, and we are certain that we shall achieve it. But how many obstacles we have encountered, how many difficulties we have overcome ! Each effort carries us one step farther forward, and today we are sure of success. . . .

LUCIE.

.   .   .   .

For two months the letters of Mme. Dreyfus to her husband reached the latter only in the form of copies written by a member of the penal administration.

.   .   .   .

February 1, 1897.

Mon bien cher Alfred :

Your letter of December 24, which I have just received, has deeply stirred me. You can imagine how I devoured that good letter. I read it and reread it, and I am not ashamed to tell you that I bathed it in my tears more than once. . . .

You see, my dear, that I am far from sharing your splendid character. You have a thousand times more reason to complain than I, and you endure your suffering with a strength and a will which could only belong to a character as strong as yours. You never complain. You are never guilty of acrimony or bitterness toward anyone. Yours is a greatness of spirit I deeply admire and to which I should like to be equal. But I am so far from reaching it! In this terrible struggle, it is I who should bring the words of calmness, whereas it is really you who show me the way. I should blush, with your example before me. I should blush to speak bitter words, and thus allow my too full heart to overflow.

I am even more sorry to yield to my emotions, because there is no reason to be discouraged. I am full of hope and I am completely convinced that the truth will be recognized, that justice will be done, and that, finally, in the universal recognition of your innocence, you will have that vindication which is your due. Never fear, *mon mari bien aimé,* the truth will come to light, and France will have reason for pride in the nobility of one of her children. Doubtless this will all take a long time, and your impatience is only too well justified. But what is time in terms of the end to be attained! . . .

Salvation Islands,
February 5, 1897.

Chère et bonne Lucie:

It is always with the same deep and poignant emotion that I receive your dear letters. Your December letters have just been given to me.

Why should I speak to you of my sufferings? You must know what they are—stored up unendingly, without a truce which might restore my strength and fortify my courage and my mind, so shaken and exhausted. I told you that my confidence extended equally to all my supporters, and that I had the certain conviction that my appeal had been heard. I know you all, and am convinced that you will not fail in your duty.

One thing more I wish to add. There must not be brought into this terrible affair any acrimony or bitterness toward individuals. I repeat what I said at the beginning: the *patrie* rises above all the passions of men. Subjected to the worst torment and to the most frightful insults, when the beast in man is roused to ferocity and his reason made to stagger beneath the rush of burning blood—under these provocations, I have thought of death, I have wished for it, often I have summoned it with all my strength. But my lips were ever tightly sealed, for I wished to die, not only an innocent man, but a good and loyal Frenchman who had never for an instant forgotten his duty to his country. . . .

Beginning in March the letters were again transmitted in the original.

May 14, 1897.
My dear Alfred:

I do not want to have this mail leave without sending you the assurance of my deep and unchanging affection.

Your letters comfort us and bring us the greatest happiness. When we see you so strong and courageous, we follow, and, if that were possible, we are given new strength in the struggle for your vindication. . . .

Ton frère tout dévoué,

MATHIEU.

Le Vésinet,
June 17, 1897.

Mon bien cher Alfred:

Some days after my arrival here, I received your brave letter of April 24. I am touched by the sentiments you express toward me, and by the brave and noble counsel you give me. How many times I have reread them. . . .

Ah! When will God grant me the great happiness of seeing you again, of holding you in my arms, of restoring, through infinite tenderness and unceasing care, the wastes of mind and body which the torture of your long and bitter sufferings has occasioned? As I look at the children, I often think of the joy you will experience when you see them. You left them as babies, and, after the years of absence, you will find them transformed. How shall I describe our little Jeanne so that you may know her as she is, a large baby of confident manner, engaging face, rosy complexion, large blue eyes, and curly, golden hair. If you saw her now, you would find only a vague resemblance to the baby you left.

Pierre is a big boy, so big that one would easily take him for eight, two years more than his age. Since I had his pretty blonde curls cut, he appears still more serious and masculine. He has a fine disposition; he is sweet, reasonable, and rather excessively sensitive. This characteristic I am seeking to modify, since it can be a serious handicap in a nature which should be virile before all else. He is very logical, observing and intelligent. . . .

July 15, 1897.

Papa chéri:

Perhaps next month I shall know how to write all by myself. Mama is teaching me. Then I will write you fine letters, and that will make me very happy. I shall be so glad when you return. I want so much to see you. Your trip has been too long. *Je t'embrasse bien, bien fort.*

TON PETIT PIERROT.

July 15, 1897.

Mon petit papa:

I send you many kisses. Mama has bought me a pretty vase to put some beautiful flowers in, when you return. We have great fun with Magui and Mimi.

Je t'embrasse avec mes petits bras.

TA PETITE JEANNE.

. . . .

Once again, from August 10, 1897, to August 7, 1898, the letters from Dreyfus to his wife reached her only as copies made by a member of the penal administration.

. . . .

August 30, 1897.

Mon bien cher mari:

. . . Clearly we are entering a more promising stage. We have suffered torment, passed through a period of anguish, of uncertainty, of illusions, of disillusionment, of high hopes which quickly vanished—but we have finally found the way. At the end we see victory, the triumph of right and of justice, the vindication of an upright and honest heart. My most recent letters have told you all that I can tell you. The present letter will only confirm the good news, will assure you that we shall triumph and will make you share our complete confidence in success. I am deeply distressed to be unable to explain further, but there are matters of such gravity and such importance that one does not dare to put them down on paper. May it suffice you to know that your honor will be restored to you, and that the future will hold the happiness which you have so much merited. . . .

LUCIE.

Salvation Islands,
January 6, 1898.

Dear Lucie:

I have not yet received your letters for October or November. The last news I had from you goes back to September. Hence I shall speak less than ever of myself, less than ever of our sufferings, which no word can serve to diminish. I wrote you a few days ago, but I was in such a state that I no longer remember what I said. But, although I am totally exhausted in mind and body, my spirit remains as intense as ever, and I want to say to you words which should sustain your courage. I have placed our fate, the fate of our children, the fate of those innocent ones who for more than three years have been struggling in the midst of uncertainties, in the hands of the President of the Republic and the Minister of War, asking that an end be made of our shocking affliction. I have placed the defense of our rights in the hands of the Minister of War, whose function it is to have amends made for this long-standing and terrible wrong. I am waiting impatiently. I should like to hope that I shall yet enjoy some happiness on this earth. But what I have not the right to doubt for a single instant is that justice will be done, that justice will be rendered you and the children, so that you may have your day of supreme happiness.

I repeat then with all my strength: Courage, always courage! . . .

Your devoted,

ALFRED.

January 7, 1898.

Mon chéri:

Courage, courage, I can see approaching the end of our suffering, the moment when we shall finally be reunited, happy,
cleansed of this frightful stain which has been cast upon our
name. Your martyrdom will end and nothing will remain of
these sad days of suffering but a painful memory, which will,
alas, never be effaced, but whose sharpness will be lessened by the
happiness we shall find in being together once more, surrounded
by our poor children. My poor husband, how unhappy you have
been. What can I do to make you forget your martyrdom? . . .
I have so often said to you that it was your example which has
been my strength in this period of struggle and distress, your example which sustained and prevented me from yielding to despair. In the face of your heroism and the greatness of spirit
with which you endured this torture, I had no right to falter.
You were so splendid, so noble, I had such admiration for your
resolution and your courage, that I wished to show myself worthy
of you. Proud to be your wife, I was determined to be equal to
my task. It was thus that I avoided all weakness, all yielding.
You sketched for me the way of my duty; the road was there, I
had only to follow it. . . .

YOUR LUCIE.

Salvation Islands,
January 25, 1898.

Ma chère et bonne Lucie:

I shan't write you a long letter, for I suffer too much in thinking of you and the children. . . .

I have asked for my rehabilitation and the review of my case in
letters to the President of the Republic, the Minister of War, and
General de Boisdeffre. . . . I am awaiting their reply with feverish impatience and with what strength remains to me. . . .

ALFRED.

Salvation Islands,
January 26, 1898.

My dear Lucie:

In the last letters I wrote I told you what I had done, to whom I had confided our fate and that of our children, what appeals I had made. I need not tell you with what anxiety I await a reply and how long the minutes are. . . .

Here is the situation as I think I understand it, and I fancy that I am not far from the truth. I believe that General de Boisdeffre has never refused us justice. We have been deeply wounded, and we ask him for the truth. It has no more been in his power than in ours to reveal the truth. That will be done in a future which none can foresee. Men have probably been embittered, blunders have perhaps been committed—I know not—and all this has envenomed a situation already so painful. We must go back and raise ourselves above all this suffering so that we may envisage our situation objectively. As for myself, the greatest victim . . . for more than three years; I, who am almost dying, have just given you counsels of wisdom and of calmness. . . .

March 17, 1898.

Mon bien cher Alfred:

I read and reread your good letters very often. In spite of their profound sadness and the impression of pain and anguish which they breathe, it seems that I hear you speaking to me. And that is so sweet that it encourages me and brings me much comfort.

You seem to think, my dear, that our efforts have not succeeded, and that for three years we have sought the truth in vain. Thus, in your letter of the ninth of January last, you said: "The truth which we have been awaiting for three years has not come to light; it will do so in a future of which we know nothing." Fortunately I can tell you that you are entirely mistaken. The truth has come to light, it continues to come to light, and, in the very near future, it will blaze forth in the eyes of all.

We have been slow, that is indeed true! Three years, for all of us who suffer, and above all for you, who endure a martyrdom without name: three horrible years, the equal of a century. The first two years were especially terrible; we found ourselves in the blackest night. But if you only knew how our burden has been lightened, what mountains we have uplifted, and how much shorter the road ahead is, than that which we have come!

When I think of the darkness in which we were plunged and of which you, *pauvre cher ami,* could know nothing, I feel profoundly relieved and deeply gratified by the tremendous progress we have made. . . . My feeling that we shall soon be happy is so deep that I want very much to bring this certainty to you.

I know so well that your innocence will be discovered and recognized, that I only wish I could share with you this confidence, this certainty. I implore you to have faith in me, to keep up your courage! I swear to you that your vindication is coming, that nothing can hinder the march of truth. The truth is too strong, too pure, too evident for any human will to prevent it from becoming manifest. . . .

LUCIE.

From March until August 10, 1898, the letters of Mme. Dreyfus to her husband reached him only as copies. Moreover, a long letter which she wrote him on March 24, in which she gave him a summary of events in a very modest form and told him that the Vice-President of the Senate, Scheurer-Kestner, had become convinced of his innocence, was retained by the Colonial Minister, and was only given to Dreyfus in October, 1900. By order from above, it was forbidden to bring the prisoner on Devil's Island the least comfort in the midst of his suffering.

May 18, 1898.

Mon mari bien aimé:

I come to you again, impelled by a great desire to speak with you and to bring you that comfort so close to my heart which I wish so intensely to share with you. I am certain that we are at the very end of our suffering, and that your vindication is imminent. The children are safe; their future gives me no more anxiety. The name that you bear, and which we all bear with love, will soon be honored everywhere. I have only one sorrow, and that consumes me and breaks my heart—it is to think that you, my poor dear, are prey to the most hateful suffering, without a friendly voice, without a kindly word. . . .

Salvation Islands,
May 26, 1898.

Chère et bonne Lucie:

At the beginning of the month I received copies of your letters. I can find no expression adequate to the sentiment of profound admiration which I feel in reading your letters. Nothing could increase my love, that you know; night and day my thoughts are with you and the children. Nor could anything increase my respect for the greatness of your spirit, your heart, for the nobility of your character.

Beyond that I can add nothing to the many letters which I write each month and send by each mail. Although human strength, tried night and day by every torture, has its limits, my will, like yours, is inflexible. So long as the heart has not ceased to beat, crushed by its wounds, I shall still cry "Courage" to you. As I told you, I have by each mail requested the review of my case in letters to the President of the Republic. I am still in the deepest night; I know not what has been the final result of all the requests for review which I have directed to the Chief of State. For several months I have awaited a reply each day. I wait always to learn that the day of justice has finally dawned for me. . . .

Your devoted,

ALFRED.

.   .   .   .

Beginning in August, the letters were again transmitted in their original form.

.   .   .   .

September 26, 1898.

My dear Alfred:

Today we are overjoyed. I am so profoundly happy that I must at once confide in you my joy, which is also yours, and that of all of us. This letter is not to announce the welcome news to you, for I feel certain that you will very shortly be advised of it by cable.

It is only that I wish to be near you in my extravagant happiness, as I have been near you in my moments of deepest sadness. Finally, after telling you that an appeal has been granted, I want to recount very briefly what has taken place.

On September 3, as a result of events of great importance of which you will learn later, I was in a position to send to the Minister of Justice a request for an appeal, a request which was only awaiting the favorable moment to be presented. After examination of the dossier, the Minister agreed to transmit it to the special committee. Finally this afternoon, after suffering much anguish, I learned that the Cabinet had submitted the dossier to the Court of Cassation. Our future, our life then, are in the hands of the supreme tribunal, which will, in accordance with the documents it has in its possession, determine whether the judgment of 1894 should be set aside. And so we have arrived at the last stage of our journey, at the final crisis, which should restore to us what we have unjustly been deprived of, our honor; which should restore you to all your dear family who are overjoyed at the thought of seeing you, of taking you in their arms, of showing how they love you. To describe our emotion would be impossible. As for myself, I live only in the thought of your profound happiness as you receive this news. I should like to have the power, the superhuman power, to see you in that moment of supreme gratification. Let us only hope, in God's name, that this shock is not so great as to be fatal, and that your poor wasted body will not suffer from such a sudden blow.

I have dared say nothing to the children. They have known nothing whatever. They have been ignorant of our suffering. They have no inkling of our joy. They will know of your return only when you are free and come to greet them. So long as they are small, I do not wish them to know the sadness of life. They will have the happiness of seeing you again. Only later, when they have reached the age of understanding, will they learn to appreciate what you suffered for them—the heroism, the greatness of soul of their splendid father.

I hope with all my heart that this is the last letter that I will send you to that wretched place. We have still some weeks of anguish to pass through, but they will be less painful now that we feel that we are near the end. Our sufferings will be only those of two beings who love each other tenderly, and who wait feverishly for the time when they will once more be together.

I am so happy that my hand trembles, but I do my best to be calm. I do not wish to add to your emotion, for I fear to give yet another shock to nerves already so badly shaken.

Je t'embrasse de toutes mes forces comme je t'aime.

LUCIE.

· · · · · · ·

The following letter was not transmitted, and the Colonial Ministry did not give it to Dreyfus until October, 1900. Moreover, it is known that an order of the Court of Cassation was required to force the Government to advise Dreyfus that his request for an appeal had been allowed.

October 29, 1898.

Mon bien cher Alfred:

Finally, after terrible anguish, disillusionment, and frantic hopes, I was informed of the decision of the Court of Cassation— a happy judgment indeed, initiating the procedure of review, first stage in your vindication. My request for an appeal has been allowed by the highest court, and an investigation ordered to prepare all aspects of the case which have not been thoroughly sounded.

This was our most cherished desire. We wanted a striking demonstration of the truth, and, although this method may take longer, we would rather endure this melancholy situation in order that we may finally reach a solution so clear and so evident that no one on this earth can protest further. We know that you share this view, and that, to regain your honor in all its purity, you stand ready to prolong your suffering yet awhile.

At last you will be told, at last you will learn this joyous good news. What would I not give to witness your happiness; to see the first smile on your beloved face; gently—very gently, to prepare you for all these emotions; to tend you with my loving care! *Mon Dieu,* what happiness, what mad joy for you and for us all. My heart beats as though it would break at the very thought. What will it be like when the reality is ours? It is too beautiful;

one can't imagine such happiness. And the children, what will they say when they see their dear papa! They know now that I am happier; they see me less sad. They never cease talking of you and making all kinds of plans for your return. How much we shall have to say to each other! What inexhaustible subjects! Above all, how much to forget, how many crimes and acts of baseness we shall prefer not to mention. We shall remember the splendid acts of self-sacrifice, we shall recall our noble friends, and we shall lack both words and years in which to show them our respect and love.

I am hoping with all my heart that this letter will never reach you, that, when the mail arrives, you will have left that dismal island and be on your way to our beloved France. God grant that this torture continue no longer, and that we find happiness at last.

Je t'embrasse comme je t'aime de toutes les forces de mon coeur.

LUCIE.

Salvation Islands,
November 5, 1898.

Chère et bonne Lucie:

I have just received your September letters in which you give me such good news.

In my letter of October 27, I told you I had already been informed that I would receive a definitive reply to my requests for an appeal. I said to you then that I was waiting with confidence, not doubting that this reply would finally bring my rehabilitation. Hence, when you receive this letter, I think that it should all be finished, and that your joy and happiness will be complete. But during these days of happiness and relaxation, which will follow so many days of pain and suffering, I want all that lives within me, my thoughts and my heart which have not deserted you once these four terrible years, to add, if possible, to your joy. This, while we wait to renew at last that happy and tranquil life, which you deserve now more than ever for your greatness of soul, your nobility of character—all the noble qualities that a woman could manifest in such tragic circumstances. They are qualities that nothing has been able to impair, that suffering has only served to exalt, and that have proved to me that there is no ideal on this earth to which the soul of a woman cannot rise, and which indeed it cannot surpass. . . .

Your devoted,

ALFRED.

November 22, 1898.

Mon bien cher Alfred:

I do not know whether you have received my letters of the past months, in which I told you, in a general way, of our efforts to make possible a request for an appeal of your case. I then told you of the initiation of the procedure and of how the request had been allowed. Although each new success makes me very happy, it is marred by the knowledge that you, poor unfortunate, are in ignorance of these facts and are doubtless on the road to despair. Finally, last week, I was overjoyed to learn that the Government was sending you a cablegram, informing you that the request had been allowed, and advising you that documents were being forwarded which would enable you to prepare your defense. . . .

L. DREYFUS.

Cablegram.

Cayonne,
November 25, 1898.

Mme. Dreyfus. I rejoice with you—health good, both physical and spiritual.

ALFRED.

Salvation Islands,
November 25, 1898.

My dear Lucie:

In the middle of the month, I was informed that the request for an appeal of the judgment in my case had been allowed by the Court of Cassation. I was asked to prepare means for my defense. At once I took the necessary measures. My requests were immediately sent to Paris, and you must have been informed of them some days ago.

Events ought to move rapidly now. In my thoughts I am with the children and with you all, by night and by day, as I have always been—sharing your joy as you witness the end of this shocking drama rapidly approaching. Words are powerless to describe emotions so deep. It will be only a few weeks before we shall be able at last to forget our long suffering in the affection we bear each other, and in that of the children and our families. . . .

December 1, 1898.

Mon bon chéri:

I have been made doubly happy this week—first, in receiving your good cable which filled us all with joy, and which brought us at last news of the present from the day previous and not dating back several months, and further with proof that you are in good health; second, in receiving yesterday your letter of October 27, in which I find you confident, calm, serene. You seem to await your vindication with courage and the certitude that your innocence will be completely and handsomely recognized. We share this confidence, and we have no doubt that the judicial wrong will be strikingly revealed, as the result of a conscientious and honest investigation. . . .

LUCIE.

January 1, 1899.

Mon bien cher Alfred:

I have just had the delightful surprise of letters from you. And so the New Year begins well for me and I take this as a happy augury. Your good and affectionate letters give me great joy. You can imagine how I devour them; I read and reread them so eagerly, and wish that this joy could last forever. Like you, I had hoped that our deliverance would come more quickly. But, when you desire a thing so ardently, you wish to make events move faster than is possible, and you measure time, not by your reason, but by your heart. Misfortunes, however, are not repaired as rapidly as they are created. We have endured years of cruel suffering, and we shall have the strength of spirit to wait a few weeks longer, if that is needed. The investigation, which has been undertaken by the judges of the Court of Cassation, is long and minute. It should make the truth so strikingly manifest that there will no longer remain a doubt in anyone's mind. What are a few days of sadness and of suffering compared with an end so noble, so important, so essential to our future happiness?

I asked permission to send you a cable and I hope that you received it. I want especially on this day to remind you again that all our thoughts are with you, that our wishes are one with yours, and that our hopes and our happiness are greater every day.

I hope with all my heart that this letter will not reach you. Doubtless in February you will be, if not in France, at least on the way to our dear country. . . .

LUCIE.

February 27, 1899.

Mon bien cher Alfred:

. . . You cannot imagine how long all these details of procedure take, how minutely everything is examined, and how many difficulties of every conceivable kind have turned up. Meanwhile the months pass, and I think with dread of your worry, of your distracted anxiety, as you live through these interminable days and nights. But it is true, is it not, that, when you are on the verge of attaining an object, each little stone which has to be lifted seems a world in itself, and just that much more difficult because you thought you were nearer the end? We have still a few short stages to traverse, and during that time we must arm ourselves with patience, and then we shall finally reach the end of our martyrdom. In a few days, at most in a few weeks, the decision will be given, and you, my poor dear husband, will return to us at last. Then we can surround you with boundless affection, and, in the midst of your family, you will find happiness in their love and devotion. You will be overjoyed to learn of the great number of deeply sincere and devoted friends who have interested themselves in your cause with en-

thusiasm and who, in response to their feeling against the wrong
from which you suffer, have sacrificed personal concerns to give
themselves up completely to the cause of the triumph of truth. . . .

LUCIE.

April 1, 1899.

Mon bien cher Alfred:

I hoped very much that I should have letters from you soon,
and so I have waited to write from day to day, with the feeling
that I should still be able to reply by this mail. Now I can wait
no longer, for fear my letter will be too late. We are anticipating
most impatiently the final decision of the Court of Cassation. We
think that the final hearing will begin in the course of this month.
. . . These few months of delay, however painful they may have
been, have made it possible for us to establish your innocence in
a more convincing fashion. Although we have suffered this longer
torment, the truth has been made more strikingly evident, and
time has proved a powerful ally. . . .

This time I will not say *"adieu,"* my dear, but *"à bientôt,"*
for I am sure that we have reached the last stage of our calvary. . . .

LUCIE.

Salvation Islands,
April 8, 1899.

Dear Lucie:

I can only repeat what I said in my last letter, written at the
end of March. It is indeed long. The accumulated suffering occasioned by this unending torment is terrible, and the mind is
stupefied as it looks back over it. But the end is everything, and
I await with confidence each day the news that our frightful
martyrdom is finally over.

As I said to you long ago: innocent as I am of this abominable
crime, that innocence should be made manifest to the eyes of all
Frenchmen. It is with an assured and confident spirit that we
must resign to the high authority of the Court the task of accom-
plishing its noble mission of justice.

And so I hope that this letter is the last that I shall have to write you, and that soon I shall have the great happiness of embracing you and our dear children, and all our dear relatives. . . .

ALFRED.

Salvation Islands,
May 23, 1899.

My dear Lucie:

Since the few lines I wrote you on May 6, I have been awaiting each day the news of the end of our horrible martyrdom, for I had hoped that the Court would finally strike a balance between its duty to render justice and its respect for human rights.

For the sake of the good name of our dear France in the eyes of the world, I deeply regret the renewal in our century of the grievous spectacle presented before 1789, when innocent men were sacrificed to legal procedure and the delays of justice—procedure and delays against which rose the protests of all the writers of the eighteenth century—and with them the protests of certain magistrates, like the *Avocat Général* Sirven, the upright Malesherbes, and before them, the most illustrious of all, Montesquieu, who wished that henceforth justice should be tempered with humanity. . . .

ALFRED.

Salvation Islands,
Thursday, June 1, 1899.

My dear Lucie:

A few lines, so that I may speak with you in these days when, more than ever, if that is possible, my thoughts and my heart are with you all.

The hearings have finally begun before the Court of Cassation, and the rapporteur[5] has recommended annulment and the remanding of the case. I think that, if the Court does not annul without remanding, it will certainly bring in an annulment and remand the case, suspending punishment meanwhile. I very much hope that the judgment of the Court will reach me in time for me to catch this mail boat and come myself at the same time as this letter. Annulment with or without remanding of the case —it matters little to us. My trust in the justice of my country

5. *See* Appendix II.

is the same, whether it be placed in that of the Court of Cassation or in that of the Court-Martial. . . .

Your devoted,

ALFRED.

Cablegram.

Cayenne,
June 6, 1899.

Mme. Dreyfus. Salvation Islands, June 5. Heart and soul with you, children, all. I leave Friday. Await with great joy happy moment of embracing you. Kisses to all. Alfred.

．　　　．　　　．　　　．　　　．　　　．　　　．　　　．

On June 9, Dreyfus left his dismal island. On June 30, with indescribable joy, he caught sight of the shores of France. Since the Court of Cassation had unanimously annulled the judgment of the Court-Martial of 1894, Dreyfus thought that the truth was accepted by the public, and that he would be greeted by his family, his friends, and a crowd happy to make amends for the wrong done five years earlier. He fancied that the investigation of the Court-Martial, before which he was to be sent, would be a simple formality, since the case had been studied with great thoroughness by the highest court in the land, and the latter had decisively shown that there was no valid charge against him. His reception on board the *Sfax* had already been the source of disappointment, but his disillusionment was deep when he perceived the precautions which were being taken in connection with his disembarking. He, who was so happy at his return, had once more to repress the beatings of a tortured heart and control his sorrow.

At nine o'clock in the evening, in a heavy sea, a small boat came to take him off the *Sfax*. But it was so difficult to hold the boat at the bottom of the ship's ladder, that he fell in jumping and seriously injured his leg. At a quarter past two in the morning Dreyfus was landed at a small fishing port. A carriage was waiting and took him, seated between two gendarmes, to a station where he was put on a train. After a few hours' journey, and without exchanging a word with his companions, he got off and was taken in a carriage toward a large town. There he entered a somber building. He learned later that he was in the Military

Dreyfus returns from Devil's Island on board the cruiser Sfax. *Note his extraordinary emaciation.*

Sketch of the Salvation Islands, with Île Royale on the left, Devil's Island in the center, and Saint Joseph's Island on the right.

Prison at Rennes. It was six o'clock in the morning. At nine o'clock, he was advised that his wife had received permission to see him.

.　　.　　.　　.　　.　　.　　.　　.

Thursday, June 22, 1899.

Mon bon chéri:

I want you to have a word from me upon your arrival, so that you may know that I am there near to you in the same town, my heart beating with joy and emotion at the thought that I am going to see and embrace you. I know that we shall be violently shaken. One wonders how human flesh can withstand such terrible shocks.

How can I tell you what I felt the day I received your wire, with news of your departure. I was so happy that I thought I was living in a dream. All was changed within me, and I began to live again after long years passed with a bleeding heart. And what a solace it must have been to you to leave that dismal island, and how good those first moments must have seemed when you felt almost free and were on the way to your own country.

How I should like to have taken this journey with you, a journey I have often followed in my thoughts! It was so sweet to think that each hour, each minute, brought you nearer to me, and that we should soon find ourselves in each other's arms after this terrible, endless separation. What happiness, *mon Dieu!* But one more step to surmount, that of the Court-Martial, and then we shall be free of this horrible nightmare. This will mean yet another terrible ordeal, *mon pauvre ami,* but I have confidence. I know you will endure it bravely and with the serenity which comes from a pure conscience.

I shall leave our dear children on Saturday, the twenty-fourth, in the care of Marie. I have permission to see you, and I shall hasten to the prison as soon as the Governor will let me. . . .

LUCIE.

Rennes,
Saturday, July 1, 1899.

Mon bien cher Alfred:

It is four years now that I have fought and prayed and ardently hoped for this blessed day. I had prepared myself for this shock. I wanted to be strong and without weakness, but it needed superhuman effort on the part of both of us to control ourselves and to hold our nerves in check, so that we might bravely endure this great ordeal.

How quickly that hour passed. It seemed to me a dream, a beautiful dream, filled with emotion and sweet torment. I wanted to tell you a thousand things, to speak to you of the children, of our families, of all those whom we both love, but I was afraid to overtax you by introducing such affecting subjects. *Pauvre ami,* you, who have not spoken for nearly five years; you, who have suffered every affliction—you are still brave and courageous. You are worthy of everyone's admiration. The many tributes which I receive for you from France and from all parts of the world will prove to you how you are loved and honored.

A few weeks now and we shall have our happiness. These will be days of work, for you have much to do to inform yourself of all that has happened, and to acquaint yourself with the characters of the men who have taken part in this terrible drama. Some of them are vile and base, and deserve only pity. Others are great souls, with a purity, an elevation of mind, and a devotion which make one forget much villainy.

6 a.m., Sunday.

I wrote you yesterday. My heart was too full, and needed to pour out its burden. And where should I find sweeter sympathy than from you, *mon pauvre ami?* The joy of having you near me, in the same town, made me sleep more calmly. My heart pains less, and I rejoice at having seen you. I wait for this afternoon with a feverish impatience. . . .

Your devoted,

LUCIE.

CHAPTER IX

THE FIGHT FOR THE TRUTH

WHEN he arrived at the Military Prison at Rennes on July 1, 1899, Captain Dreyfus was in almost complete ignorance of the epic struggle of which he had been the center and which had just resulted in the setting aside of his conviction. The brief reports sent to him at Devil's Island by his lawyers, Maître Demange and Maître Mornard, had only given him a summary of the legal bases of their case. Dreyfus was still convinced that the wrong had finally been recognized on the initiative of his superiors. As a loyal soldier, he believed that they had heard his desperate appeals, that General Mercier had ordered the investigation, for which he had asked in his letter of January 1, 1895, which read:

Monsieur le Ministre:

In accordance with your order, I received the visit of Major du Paty de Clam, to whom I declared that I was innocent, and that I had never committed even an indiscretion at any time. I have been found guilty. I ask no pardon. But in the name of that honor which, I trust, will one day be restored to me, it is my duty to urge you to be good enough to continue your researches.

After I leave, let them search ceaselessly. That is the only pardon that I ask.

ALFRED DREYFUS.

But even this request was not granted. Once Dreyfus was gone, General Mercier and the General Staff had only one desire— never again to hear this wretched affair mentioned. Although the Minister of War failed in his duty, a man now appeared on the scene to take up the defense of the exile, and lend support to his protestations of innocence. That man was his brother, Mathieu Dreyfus. He abandoned the management of his mills, came to live in Paris, and devoted himself without stint to his new and trying task. Mathieu Dreyfus was a person of distinguished appearance and charming manner. His voice was warm and resonant. He was possessed of a sound intelligence and a fund of common sense. He succeeded in winning the respect of his worst enemies and the affection of his supporters by his integrity, his great courage, his simplicity, his discretion, and his tact.

In the beginning, Mathieu Dreyfus found himself in utter darkness. He wanted to peruse the contents of the dossier of the trial, which was the property of his sister-in-law, but Maître Demange could not let him see it. The eminent lawyer had indeed been warned that, since the trial had been held *in camera,* any indiscretion on his part would bring him within the purview of the law on espionage, and might result in a sentence of five years' imprisonment. Thanks to Major Forzinetti, however, Mathieu finally learned the actual basis on which the case had rested. On January 10, Forzinetti gave him a roll of papers which Alfred Dreyfus had confided to him, and which contained the copy of Bexon d'Ormescheville's accusation.

Some time later, Mathieu was told that Dr. Gibert of Le Havre, *compatriote* and friend of the President of the Republic, refused to believe in the treason of his brother, for which he could find no plausible motive. Mathieu Dreyfus visited Dr. Gibert and begged him to ask for an audience with Félix Faure. Dr. Gibert was received by the President of the Republic on the morning of February 21, and imparted to Faure his conviction. But the President answered that Dreyfus had been justly condemned, not merely on the basis of the bordereau, but on that of a document presented to the judges of the Court-Martial, a document which could not be revealed either to the accused or his lawyer, since it affected the security of the State. He authorized Gibert to tell Mathieu of this document. Gibert remarked to Félix Faure that a flagrant violation of the rights of the defense had been committed, and urged that the departure of Dreyfus for Devil's Island be delayed until a further investigation could take place. But the President was adamant.

When this visit failed to yield any immediate result, Mathieu Dreyfus got in touch with a number of Alsatians, notably General Yung, Scheurer-Kestner, Jules Siegfried, and Lalance, and with certain journalists, among whom were Judet, Fernand Xau, de Rodays, and Yves Guyot. He was received by all of them politely, by some of them with sympathy, but he got no really effective help. In April Maître Demange was told by a lawyer that, according to the Minister of Justice, Trarieux, a document existed which included the words: "that scoundrel of a D——." Demange hastened to call on Trarieux, who confirmed the statement, and said that he had been told the story by Hanotaux, Minister of Foreign Affairs, who in turn had heard it from General Mercier. And Trarieux added that, according to the latter, this document had been discovered after the condemnation of Dreyfus.

But these different fragments of evidence in the possession of Mathieu Dreyfus, evidence whose source he was unable to reveal, left him just as helpless as he had been in the beginning. About this time it was suggested to him that he get in touch with a young and very talented writer, Bernard Lazare, for the purpose of having the latter direct a campaign in his brother's behalf. When Mathieu Dreyfus approached Lazare, he discovered that the latter already had doubts of Dreyfus' guilt. And on Mathieu's suggesting that he publish an account of all that he had been able to learn to date, Lazare agreed without hesitation. Henceforth, he devoted himself with magnificent courage and selflessness to what then seemed a hopeless cause. Lazare had completed his account in June, but Mathieu Dreyfus wished to delay its publication until that auspicious moment which he hoped, from one day to the next, would appear.

Alas, the auspicious occasion failed to materialize. The melancholy summer of 1895 passed, and the winter brought nothing new. Mathieu was champing at the bit. In his unpublished memoirs, he tells of his futile investigations, of the frequent proposals of swindlers and of shady agents of the police, perhaps sent by the General Staff in an effort to compromise him. It required all his good sense and discretion to avoid falling into the traps set for him. He was forever on guard and was terrified when he stopped to wonder who could carry on, if anything should happen to prevent him from directing the campaign for his brother's rehabilitation.

Finally, in despair, Mathieu decided that he must arouse public opinion. And so, in April, 1896, he approached an English agency which was ready, for a financial consideration, to launch the rumor of the escape of Alfred Dreyfus. Just as he had foreseen and hoped, the newspapers seized upon this false rumor with avidity. Indeed, for the first time certain of them even evinced, if not sympathy, at least an element of pity for the suffering of the condemned man on Devil's Island. In an article appearing in the *Figaro* of September 8, Gaston Calmette published the disclosures of a former member of the administration in Guiana, noting that "current interest has again turned to this wretched fellow, who it was believed had disappeared, been lost, forgotten forever." The writer described Dreyfus' sufferings and recalled his unremitting cries of innocence.

When Mathieu Dreyfus decided that the favorable moment had at last come, he authorized Bernard Lazare to issue his pamphlet, which was published in Brussels and sent in a sealed packet to all the deputies, all the senators, and a certain number of people outside Parliament.

On September 14, there appeared in the *Éclair* an article obviously inspired by the General Staff. It analyzed the reasons for the conviction of Dreyfus, and revealed to the public the existence of a document from the hand of the German Military Attaché, which included these very words: "decidedly this beast of a Dreyfus is becoming too demanding." This article caused a considerable stir and brought an end to the press campaign for a time. Then, on November 10, a thunderbolt struck: the *Matin* published the bordereau. In this connection, Colonel Dreyfus reports the following in a note annexed to his memoirs:

IN 1907 I ran into Philippe Bunau-Varilla, a classmate at the École Polytechnique. He told me that he was the author of the appeal of my case. I expressed my astonishment. He then told me how in 1896 his brother, editor of the *Matin,* while at *déjeuner* at his house, told him that Teysonnières, one of the handwriting experts in the Affair, had offered him for publication in the *Matin* (for a financial consideration) a photograph of the bordereau, the actual handwriting of which had not up to that time been made public. When Philippe Bunau-Varilla saw the handwriting, he was astounded not to find any resemblance to mine. He actually had in his possession two letters of mine concerning a study I had made at one time on the Congo. Hence he could easily make the comparison. The two brothers were convinced of my innocence, and Philippe Bunau-Varilla warmly urged publication of the photograph of the bordereau in the *Matin.*

It is certain that its publication enabled my brother, Mathieu, to discover Esterhazy, and Colonel Schwartzkoppen to recognize the author of the bordereau. But, although this publication marked a significant step toward appeal and served my cause in an important way, it must not be forgotten that the real author of the appeal was Colonel Picquart, who found the petit bleu.

Be that as it may, in the month of November, 1896, Mathieu Dreyfus knew nothing of Lieutenant-Colonel Picquart's discovery, and had not the slightest inkling of the origin of the bordereau. He went to the most distinguished French and foreign experts and secured numerous reports, which demonstrated that there was no resemblance between his brother's handwriting and that in this central document. Months passed, however, without bringing any appreciable results. He had no way of knowing that during this time events of great gravity were taking place within the General Staff, and that "truth was on the march." Although he knew nothing as yet, the cause of which he had made himself the indefatigable champion was moving forward at a dizzy pace.

Lieutenant-Colonel Picquart, who "was determined not to carry his secret to the grave," had confided it to his friend and schoolmate from Strasbourg, Maître Leblois, who had promised to share it with no one except, in case of emergency, a member of the Government. But Leblois could not tolerate the idea that an innocent man should expiate the crime of another. While he was hesitating as to how to go about informing the Ministers, he decided to ask the advice of a very close friend, Charles Risler, Mayor of the Seventh Arrondissement, of which he was himself Deputy Mayor. Risler was less astonished by these disclosures than Leblois had expected. He told the lawyer that his uncle, Scheurer-Kestner, Vice-President of the Senate, had entertained serious doubts for many months—doubts inspired by two of his friends, Senator Ranc and Deputy Joseph Reinach, both of whom were convinced of the innocence of Dreyfus. Nevertheless, Risler added, Scheurer-Kestner had yet to see evidence which would completely convince him. On July 13, 1897, Risler accompanied Leblois on a visit to Scheurer. Leblois dissipated his final doubts. From that day forward, the two men, working side by side, devoted themselves wholeheartedly to the task of rehabilitating Dreyfus.

Louis Leblois was the son of a Protestant minister, then pastor of the Church of the New Temple at Strasbourg. After the War of 1870, Pastor Leblois had retained French citizenship for his six sons. The latter were obliged to leave Alsace, but the pastor considered it his duty to remain and, as George Sand has said, "sustain and console those who were unable to leave, and who held him by their cry of distress." He continued to preach in French, was suspended, then returned to his pulpit without having surrendered. Louis Leblois showed himself worthy of his father's example. When he learned the truth about Dreyfus, he hurled himself into the battle with high courage and complete selflessness.

Scheurer-Kestner was born at Thann of old Alsatian stock. He had been Deputy for Alsace and then for the Seine in the National Assembly.[1] Later he was made Senator for life,[2] and then First Vice-President of the Senate. His life had been a model of industry and integrity, and he enjoyed the very great esteem of his colleagues and of all those who knew him. A man of deep sympathy and rigid honesty, he no longer hesitated, in the face of the certain proofs which Leblois brought him, to take an official stand and to devote his entire energy to the cause of the victory of justice. The struggle in which he now engaged was to ruin his health. A few days before his death, when he learned that the Court of Cassation had set aside the judgment of 1894, he wrote this magnificent letter to his daughter:

Biarritz,
June 6, 1899.

Dear Jeanne:

You ask me if I am happy?

How many men are there who, after they have sacrificed themselves to a just cause, witness the triumph of that cause?

1. The representative body elected in February, 1871, to determine if and on what terms, peace should be made with the German Empire. As one of the Alsatian Deputies, Scheurer-Kestner vigorously opposed the cession of Alsace. Following the cession, he could of course no longer represent Alsace. He was elected Deputy from the Department of the Seine in the bye-election of July, 1871; was made Senator for life in 1875; was elected First Vice-President of the Senate in 1896.

2. In the French Senate, as orginally constituted, provision was made for the appointment of seventy-five Senators for life; no more were appointed following the law of December 9, 1884.

I am blessed beyond the ordinary, and I am keenly aware of it. True, I have said to myself on occasion that I have paid dearly, at the price of my health. But I say this without regret. If I should be offered the good health I enjoyed before the Affair, in return for defeat, leaving poor Dreyfus on Devil's Island, I should refuse that offer.

I had rather suffer and have accomplished something worth while. I enjoy the respect of those about me to an unusual degree. And it is, above all, pleasant to think that I shall leave to my grandchildren an honorable name. That will prolong my life a generation, and, since I am very fond of life, I am content. . . .

A. SCHEURER-KESTNER.

Unfortunately, the restrictions imposed by Picquart paralyzed action by Scheurer-Kestner for some time. He did confide his ardent conviction to his fellow officers of the Senate. But he refused to appeal to the Minister of Justice until he should be free to present to him officially the new evidence susceptible of starting in motion the procedure of appeal. And yet compassion for the innocent man suffering on that distant isle made Scheurer-Kestner wish to fortify Dreyfus' patience and courage with the knowledge that a highly placed personage had finally been interested in his cause. Accordingly, he asked Joseph Reinach to make contact with the Dreyfus family so that they might inform the prisoner. This was done at once. But Mme. Dreyfus' letter was intercepted and failed to reach her husband.

Scheurer-Kestner left for a vacation of some weeks at Thann and did not see Leblois again until September 10. Pursuing always the same policy, they decided that the Vice-President of the Senate should take the matter up with the members of the Government in the following order: the President of the Republic, the Minister of War, the Premier, and the Minister of Justice. These interviews took place at the end of October and the beginning of November. Their sole effect was to loose a terrific press campaign against Scheurer-Kestner, who was deeply wounded when his name was dragged in the mire and made the object of vilest slander.

Meanwhile, Mathieu Dreyfus pursued his endless quest for the author of the bordereau. Thanks to its publication in the *Matin*, he now possessed a facsimile. He had a large number of posters printed for distribution in the streets. These posters included reproductions both of the bordereau and of a letter of his brother. He was hopeful that, with good fortune, someone would recognize the handwriting of the bordereau and put him on the right track. But he was to have a long and anxious wait before word reached him, on the morning of November 6, that a banker, M. de Castro, had read his poster a few days before, while waiting for the omnibus at the Madeleine. M. de Castro declared that the handwriting in the famous document strangely resembled that of one of his clients. He agreed to meet Mathieu Dreyfus that afternoon at his club on the Boulevard Montmartre.

In his memoirs Mathieu Dreyfus describes his emotion as he went for this interview. M. de Castro, whom he had never met, was awaiting him in a small parlor in his club. He had brought with him a sheaf of letters from Esterhazy. Like the banker, Mathieu was at once struck by the identity of the handwriting. He rushed off to see Maître Demange, and tell him that he believed he had finally learned the name which he had been struggling for three years to discover. Demange had once defended the Marquis de Morès, after the latter had killed Captain Mayer in a duel at which Esterhazy had been one of the witnesses. He called for the dossier, found in it letters of Esterhazy, and in turn verified the identity of the handwriting.

There still remained one experiment to perform. Mathieu Dreyfus was aware that Scheurer-Kestner knew the name of the author of the bordereau. But he also knew that Scheurer had hitherto refused to divulge either the name or the source of his information. Was that name the same as the one he had just discovered? Mathieu Dreyfus had not seen Scheurer since the appeal he had made to him in February, 1895, when he had met with polite evasion. He now secured an interview for November 12. His heart beat furiously and he trembled with emotion as he told the Senator that he knew the name of the traitor.

"Who?" asked Scheurer.

"Esterhazy."

"Yes."

That "yes" lifted a heavy burden from the shoulders of the two men. At last Mathieu Dreyfus was in possession of a key element, a fact of fundamental importance, in the campaign to rehabilitate his brother. And Scheurer was now released from his oath, since he had learned from a new source what he had promised not to divulge. Henceforth he could act with more vigor. Henceforth he could proclaim the truth from the housetops.

On November 15, 1897, Mathieu Dreyfus denounced Esterhazy in an open letter to the Minister of War.

.   .   .   .

Under the influence of Scheurer-Kestner, whose frankly announced conviction impressed many people, the first phalanx of Dreyfusards witnessed the gradual growth of its ranks. Forzinetti, Dr. Gibert, Ranc, Reinach, Bernard Lazare were soon joined, among many others, by Senator Trarieux, former Minister of Justice and the subsequent founder of the League of the Rights of Man, and the great author, Émile Zola. Zola had consistently eschewed public life, but the intensity of the drama in the Affair captured his interest and his sense of duty prompted him to intervene. In the course of a walk, and quite by chance, he met de Rodays, editor of the *Figaro*. Zola, confiding his profound interest in the Dreyfus Case, struck a sympathetic cord in de Rodays' heart and the latter offered him the columns of his newspaper. Zola published three articles in November and December, but was obliged to desist in the face of vehement protests by subscribers against the side he was espousing. He then wrote two eloquent appeals in the form of pamphlets: A *Lettre à la jeunesse* and a *Lettre à la France*. Finally, following the acquittal of Esterhazy, he prepared an open letter to M. Félix Faure, President of the Republic. But before giving it to a publishing house, and with the object of providing for it the widest possible circulation, Zola decided to try one more appeal to a newspaper —this time to the *Aurore*.

The *Aurore* had been founded by Ernest Vaughan, who had established the *Intransigeant* in 1881 with Henri Rochefort, but who had separated from the latter some months previously after a collaboration of sixteen years. From its beginnings, the *Aurore* had taken a clear stand for an appeal for Dreyfus. Its principal contributors were Clemenceau, Bernard Lazare, Urbain Gohier, Octave Mirbeau, Henri Leyret, Lucien Descaves, and Pierre Quillard. On the evening of January 12, Zola read to the editors present his letter to Félix Faure. The letter caused a great stir and evoked general enthusiasm. That immortal document appeared next day on the front page, under the title, "I accuse," a title which Clemenceau had chosen as being incisive. The conclusion of the letter follows:

. . . MOREOVER, I do not in the least despair of victory. I repeat with a feeling of vehement certainty: truth is on the march and nothing can stop it. It is only now that the Affair is beginning, because only now are men assuming clear positions: on one hand, the guilty, who do not wish justice to be done; on the other, the adherents of justice, who will give their lives so that justice may triumph. When you drive truth underground, it grows and gathers so great an explosive force that, when it finally does burst forth, it carries everything before it. Indeed, we shall see whether there has not already been prepared—for a future date—the most shocking of disasters.

But this letter has grown long, Mr. President, and it is time to conclude.

I accuse Lieutenant Colonel du Paty de Clam of having been the diabolical author of the judicial wrong—unconsciously, I am ready to believe—and of having then for three years defended his pernicious work by the most absurd and culpable machinations.

I accuse General Mercier of having rendered himself the accomplice, at least by want of firmness, of one of the greatest iniquities of the century.

I accuse General Billot of having had in his hands certain proofs of Dreyfus' innocence and of having hushed them up, of having rendered himself guilty of the crime of *lèse-humanité* and *lèse-justice* with a political object and in order to screen the compromised General Staff.

I accuse General de Boisdeffre and General Gonse of having made themselves accomplices of the same crime—the one, doubtless, through clerical prejudice, the other, perhaps, from the *esprit de corps* which makes the War Office a sacred, unassailable ark.

I accuse General de Pellieux and Major Ravary of having made an infamous inquiry—I mean by that an inquiry of monstrous partiality— of which their report is an imperishable monument of naïve audacity.

I accuse the three experts, *Sieurs* Belhomme, Varinard and Couard, of having made a false and fraudulent report, unless a medical examination should find them to be suffering from defective vision and diseased judgment.

I accuse the War Office of having carried on in the press, particularly in the *Éclair* and the *Écho de Paris,* an abominable campaign, in order to screen their mistake and mislead the public.

Lastly, I accuse the first Court-Martial of having violated the law by condemning an accused man on the basis of a secret document, and I accuse the second Court-Martial of having, in obedience to orders, screened that illegality by committing in its turn the judicial crime of knowingly acquitting a guilty man.[3]

In preferring these charges, I am aware that I bring myself under Articles 30 and 31 of the Press Law of July 29, 1881, which punishes defamation. And I do so voluntarily.

As to the men I accuse, I do not know them, I have never seen them, I have no resentment or animosity toward them. They are for me merely entities, spirits of social maleficence. And the act which I perform here is only a revolutionary means of hastening the revelation of truth and justice.

I have but one passion—that of light. This I crave for the sake of humanity, which has suffered so much, and which is entitled to happiness. My passionate protest is merely the cry of my soul. Let them venture then to bring me before the Court of Assize and let an inquiry be made in broad daylight!

I wait.

This noble letter, a veritable summary of the Affair, gave the public its first view of the case as a whole. It caused a stir both in France and abroad, but in Parliament it was greeted as a scandal. Méline, the Premier, did not personally favor the prosecution of Zola, but he was overwhelmed by his followers who forced him to yield. A trial was ordered, the only opposition to the motion being that of a few Socialists. In a speech at Lille in 1900, Jaurès was to relate how the Socialists themselves were divided on the issue. Some of them believed there was no reason to take a stand in favor of a wealthy officer and a bourgeois writer, while others took the contrary view—that the Socialist party ought to combat injustice no matter who the victim was. Said Jaurès:

Ah, I recall the splendid words of Guesde, when Zola's letter appeared. The moderates among our Socialist comrades were saying: "But Zola is not a Socialist; Zola is above all a bourgeois. Are we going to fasten the Socialist party in tow behind a bourgeois writer?" Guesde rose as though suffocated by the sound of such language, walked over and opened a window in the room where the group was deliberating, and said: "Zola's letter is the most important revolutionary act of the century."

3. Esterhazy.

And when the cannibals of the General Staff continued to fall upon the victim, Guesde said to me: "What are we ever going to do, what are the Socialists going to do, with a humanity so debased and so degraded? We shall arrive too late," he said, with eloquent bitterness, "the material of humanity will already be rotten when it comes our turn to build the house."

In any event, from that day forward Jaurès, without waiting for a mandate from his party, undertook in his own name the most noble, courageous, and eloquent campaign in favor of judicial review of the case. He did not feel that his responsibility was at an end until the final rehabilitation of Captain Dreyfus was achieved more than eight years later, in July, 1906.

In compliance with the vote of the Chamber, the Government had Zola and Perrenx, editor of the *Aurore,* brought before the Court of Assize. The trial began on February 7, 1898. On the defense bench for Zola were Maîtres Labori and Albert Clemenceau. Georges Clemenceau, although not a lawyer, had been authorized to defend Perrenx. The complaint of the Minister of War, Billot, referred only to three passages of the letter, "I accuse," all relating to attacks on the Courts-Martial. Hence the trial was deliberately restricted in scope. Moreover, Judge Delegorgue, summoned to preside over the Court, was notably lacking in authority and independence. He knew the Government dreaded that the truth would come to light, so he endeavored to suppress all testimony of a character likely to produce new evidence concerning the Affair. Throughout the trial he constantly interrupted with expressions which have become legendary: "The question will not be put," "Witness, do not reply." On the other hand, he allowed the jury to deliberate under the influence of the clanking of sabers and of hostile manifestations against the accused by a mob carefully chosen by the General Staff.

And yet the truth could not be quite suppressed. By their own excessive zeal the Army chiefs helped to bring the truth to light. Thus, in the course of the trial, General de Pellieux, who had already testified once, asked to be allowed to testify again (because he had become fearful of an acquittal). The General declared that, since he was obliged to do so, he would reveal a fact which he had thus far suppressed. He had seen at the Ministry of War a document of unquestionable authenticity which had arrived in November, 1896, at the time when a Deputy, Castelin, had indicated his intention of making an interpellation on the Dreyfus Affair. This document included in particular the following sentences: "There is going to be an interpellation on the Dreyfus Affair. Never say anything about the relations we have had with this Jew." General Gonse confirmed the testimony of General de Pellieux and on the following day General de Bois-deffre, Chief of the General Staff, declared to the jury:

I SHALL be brief. I confirm in every detail the testimony of General de Pellieux, both as to accuracy and authenticity. I have not a word more to say. I have not the right to do so. I repeat, gentlemen of the jury, I have not the right to do so. And now, gentlemen, permit me in concluding to say one thing to you: You are the jury, you are the nation. If the nation lacks confidence in the commanders of its Army, in those who bear the responsibility for the national defense, then those in command are ready to leave to others this heavy task—you have but to speak. I shall not say another word.

In the course of the same session, Lieutenant-Colonel Picquart, replying to a question of Maître Labori concerning a document whose authenticity he considered doubtful, declared:

THAT is the one of which General de Pellieux spoke. If he had not mentioned it yesterday, I should not have done so today. It is a forgery!

And so the untimely act of General de Pellieux, which forced Picquart to give him the lie, revealed to the defense the existence of that famous document later known as the "Henry forgery."

Although the General Staff brought the full weight of its influence to bear on the verdict of the jury, the partisans of truth and justice succeeded nevertheless in making their voices heard. Their testimony was broken by interruptions of the Presiding Judge, who professed to be preventing Zola's lawyers from asking them certain questions. Among the many who spoke proud and generous words were Leblois, Scheurer-Kestner, Trarieux, Ranc, Émile Duclaux (Director of the Pasteur Institute), Anatole France, Grimaux (Professor at the École Polytechnique) and Jaurès. As to the famous report of Bertillon—that monument of folly collapsed beneath the weight of the testimony given by the most distinguished authorities of the Institute, the Collège de France and the École des Chartes. Nothing remained of it—and yet what was the use? In this atmosphere of violence and hatred, justice was trampled underfoot and its partisans were in constant danger of death. All the talent of a Labori, of a Georges and an Albert Clemenceau could make no breach in this wall of prejudice and wilful ignorance. In spite of their passionate efforts to bring the truth to light, in spite of their eloquence and their courage, Zola and Perrenx were convicted and given the maximum penalty. Long afterwards (on December 12, 1906), Georges Clemenceau, then Premier, was defending in the Senate a bill providing for the transference of Zola's ashes to the Pantheon. Clemenceau passed this judgment on the vanquished in this trial:

. . . THERE have been men to resist the most powerful kings, refusing to bow to them. But there have been very few men to oppose the masses; to stand alone against the distracted mob, often guilty of the maddest frenzy; to face the ruthless rage of the people, arms crossed and unprotected; and to dare, when a "yes" was demanded, to raise their heads and say "no." That is what Zola did!

. . . I have been close to Zola in his hours of anguish. I have been with him during those wretched flights which followed the sessions of the Court of Assize, flights accompanied by showers of stones, hoots, cries of "death." I was there when he was condemned—there were twelve of us—and I swear that I never expected to see such a display of hatred. Had Zola been acquitted on that day, not one of us would have come out alive. That is what this man did. He dared face his own epoch. He dared face his own country. He dared face humanity itself, in the name of truth and of justice.

The General Staff was avenged. And still the Government of M. Méline was not completely satisfied. Having secured the condemnation of Zola, it also visited disciplinary penalties on those of the defense witnesses who were subject to its immediate authority. Maître Leblois was removed from his office as Deputy Mayor of the Seventh Arrondissement. The learned chemist, Grimaux, member of the Institute, had his course at the École Polytechnique suspended. Zola's name was struck off the roll of the Order of the Legion of Honor. Lieutenant-Colonel Picquart had been recalled from Tunis to testify at the trial of Esterhazy and following the latter's acquittal, had been sentenced to sixty days' imprisonment. He was now brought before a Court of Inquiry and discharged from the Army "for serious misconduct in the service." Finally, the admirable Scheurer-Kestner, to whose character the Upper House was some years later to pay magnificent tribute, was the victim of a scandalous defeat for the Vice-Presidency of the Senate.

CHAPTER X

THE APPEAL AND THE TRIAL AT RENNES

IN May, 1898, shortly after the violent upheaval of public opinion occasioned by the trials of Esterhazy and Zola, general elections were held. The elections altered but little the strength of the various parties, but led to a certain number of changes in personnel. Of those who were defeated, the Dreyfusards could rejoice at the failure of the Colonial Minister, André Lebon, but they profoundly regretted that of Joseph Reinach, who had paid the price for his noble and courageous attitude in the preceding Parliament.

Joseph Reinach, distinguished writer, political leader of great wisdom, disciple and friend of Gambetta, had had doubts of Dreyfus' guilt as far back as 1894. Then he was rapidly convinced of his innocence. In the beginning he had restricted his activity to a discreet campaign of propaganda. It was he who had first disturbed Scheurer-Kestner. Then, when he began to foresee the possibility of more direct action, he got in touch with the family of the condemned man. He did not, however, make the acquaintance of Mathieu Dreyfus until December, 1897, but this marked the beginning of a warm mutual affection which grew with the years.

Joseph Reinach contributed to the cause his pen and a minute and searching power of analysis, and he became the eloquent protagonist of a judicial review of the case. When the Chamber unanimously applauded the speeches of ministers who declared the condemnation of Captain Dreyfus both legal and just, Reinach stood alone at his desk, arms crossed, proclaiming his conviction, meeting with steady gaze the looks of hatred and the insults hurled at him by frenzied colleagues. Both his intuition and his humanity, fortified by an extraordinary courage, pointed the path of duty to him and strengthened his conviction that he would one day triumph in the face of all. At the abominable calumny of his enemies, to the effect that he had formed a "Jewish Syndicate" of which he was the head, and which possessed unlimited funds for the purchase of adherents, he shrugged his shoulders and continued in his own undeviating path. Few men have been so insulted, so unremittingly reviled. To the elevation of mind and the heroism of this great and distinguished man, adequate tribute has never been paid. It is only just that we should do so here.

.   .   .   .

The Méline Ministry was overturned on June 14, 1898, and was replaced by a Cabinet headed by Brisson. On a number of occasions during the life of the preceding Parliament, Deputy Castelin had raised questions relative to the Dreyfus Affair. He now asked the new Minister of War, Cavaignac, how he intended to put an end to the agitation for appeal. Cavaignac asked for three days' time in which to examine the question. On July 7 he replied to the interpellation. He was so completely convinced by the documents submitted to him by the General Staff, that he considered it unnecessary to examine the question further. He resolved to crush the supporters of Dreyfus once and for all by revealing the content of these documents from the tribune of the Chamber. And so he described once again the so-called confession of Dreyfus which had been invented after the event by Captain Lebrun-Renault. Then he read three letters from the correspondence of the German and Italian Military Attachés. It was discovered shortly thereafter that two of these letters had undergone important alterations and that the third, concerning which the Minister declared he had "weighed the material and moral authenticity," was a forgery.

By a unanimous vote, and with only some twenty abstentions, the Chamber enthusiastically authorized the official publication[1] of the speech. But Cavaignac, by saying nothing of the bordereau, sole basis of the trial of 1894, had unwittingly strengthened the case of the partisans of appeal and the Dreyfusards held their heads higher than ever. "They talk," exclaimed Clemenceau, "hence they are lost." Jaurès, in a masterly series of articles entitled, "The Proofs," revealed in decisive fashion the inanity of the Minister of War's statements. And Lieutenant-

1. *Affichage*, voted by Parliament, provides that a speech be publicly posted in every commune in France.

Colonel Picquart, since he had been dismissed from the Army, considered that henceforth he had the right to speak his mind freely. On July 9 he wrote to Brisson:

Monsieur le Président du Conseil:
  Until the present moment I have not been in a position to express myself freely on the subject of the secret documents, which, it is alleged, establish the guilt of Dreyfus.
  Since the Minister of War has, from the tribune of the Chamber of Deputies, quoted three of these documents, I deem it a duty to inform you that I am in a position to establish before any competent tribunal that the two documents bearing the date 1894 cannot be made to apply to Dreyfus, and that the document dated 1896 shows every evidence of being a forgery.
  It would seem obvious, therefore, that the good faith of the Minister of War has been imposed upon, and that the same is true of all those who have believed in the relevance of the first two documents and in the authenticity of the last.

Brisson transmitted Picquart's letter to Cavaignac, who, resolved to crush all resistance, decided to prosecute the author. But, instead of using the letter, he reverted to an old accusation framed by that despicable trio, Henry–Lauth–Gribelin, which alleged that Picquart had been guilty of indiscretions, capitalized by his lawyer, Maître Leblois. In accordance with the espionage law of April 18, 1886, Cavaignac brought a complaint against both men. On his order, Picquart was arrested and incarcerated in the Santé Prison on July 13.

. . . .

By a singular inconsistency, however—a reflection of his impulsive temperament—Cavaignac decided to have the documents in the secret dossier verified, at the same time that he ordered the prosecution of Picquart and Leblois. For this task, he detailed an officer attached to his own immediate staff, Captain Cuignet. One evening, as Cuignet was working by lamplight, he noticed that a letter which began with the words, ''My dear friend: I have read that a deputy is going to make an interpellation concerning Dreyfus, etc.,'' presented the peculiarity of having been reconstructed with two types of *quadrillé* paper whose lines were of slightly different color, a characteristic only noticeable, however,

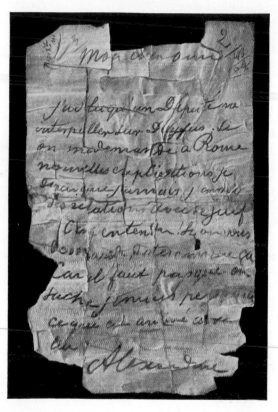

The famous "Alexandrine," one of Henry's forgeries, fabricated from fragments of two letters of Panizzardi.

when the document was held to the light. Naturally disturbed, Cuignet informed General Roget, the Minister's Chef du Cabinet, of his discovery. Roget verified the forgery and referred it to Cavaignac, who in turn examined the document and was obliged to admit the truth of what he had been told.

At two-thirty in the afternoon of August 30, in the presence of General de Boisdeffre, General Gonse, and General Roget, the Minister questioned Colonel Henry as to the origin of the incriminating document. There followed a dramatic inquisition. For a long time Henry struggled. He swore repeatedly that the document had been reconstructed from authentic fragments. Then, finally, he confessed that it was a forgery and that he was the author. He was arrested on the spot and taken to the Mont Valérien Prison. On the following morning, August 31, he committed suicide by cutting his throat with a razor.

No sooner had Henry confessed than General de Boisdeffre sat down in the Minister's office to draft a letter asking to be relieved of his position as Chief of the General Staff. As soon as General de Pellieux learned of the event, he asked to be retired:

Monsieur le Ministre:

I have been the dupe of men without honor. I can no longer hope to retain the confidence of my subordinates, without which command is impossible. And for my own part, I have lost confidence in those of my superiors who had given me forgeries with which to work. Hence, I have the honor to ask that you be good enough to retire me as having reached the age limit.

Finally, on September 3, while the text of his speech was still posted on the walls of all the communes of France, Cavaignac submitted his resignation as Minister of War.

.   .   .   .

Henry's confession opened the eyes of many people. One would think that the result should have been unanimous! But there were too many generals, too many politicians, too many journalists who were deeply intangled in the defense of a bad cause. They might still have done public penance and, like General de Pellieux, admitted that they had been mistaken. But many preferred to persist in their error. The Judets, the Charles Maurras were for a moment disabled. Then, with their customary bad

faith and social malevolence, they invented the inadmissible theory of the "patriotic forgery" and honored the forger. They
condemned themselves, once and for all, to the contempt of all
good people.

The Government itself, which was in the hands of weaklings,
dared not set in motion the procedure for appeal, although, on
September 3, Mme. Dreyfus had sent the Minister of Justice a request with this end in view. General Zurlinden had succeeded
Cavaignac and at first gave evidence of being favorable to a review of the case. He, too, now asked a few days in which to study
the dossier, and requested General Roget and Captain Cuignet to
enlighten him. These officers had already been put on guard by
the forgery they had discovered. One would reasonably expect
that their convictions would have been shaken, and that thence-
forth they would be more cautious. But they were blinded by one
idea—incomprehensible today—that the honor of the Army made
it essential that Dreyfus be guilty. And so they developed a new
theory which in a measure exculpated Henry for his act. They
conceived that Picquart had erased the name of the addressee of
the petit bleu and had replaced it with that of Esterhazy. Henry
had then been influenced by du Paty de Clam to answer this
forgery with another forgery. The second forgery would destroy
the possible effect of the first, by providing his superiors with a
flagrant proof of Dreyfus' guilt.

Zurlinden willingly accepted this new fable, and suggested to
the Cabinet that it issue an order to prosecute Picquart. Zurlinden added that he remained "completely convinced of the guilt
of Dreyfus." When the Minister of Justice asked to be shown the
secret dossier submitted by Mercier in 1894 to the judges of the
Court-Martial, Zurlinden replied that "there was no trace of the
submission of such a dossier." Finally, when the majority of the
Ministers declared themselves in favor of the transmission of
Mme. Dreyfus' request,[2] he resigned on September 17. He was
succeeded by General Chanoine, to whom he turned over the dossier against Picquart, which he had just collected. One of Chanoine's first acts was to name Zurlinden Military Governor of
Paris and to transmit to him the Picquart dossier, with the order

2. The transmission to the Court of Cassation of the request for a review
of the case by that Court. On the procedure, see Appendix II.

to institute an investigation. Zurlinden hastened to sign the order to prosecute and immediately had Picquart transferred to the Cherche-Midi Prison, where he was placed in close custody.

Thanks, however, to the tenacity of Brisson, who had now been won over to the cause of review, the Cabinet decided on September 26 to transmit to the Court of Cassation Mme. Dreyfus' request, which the Criminal Division[3] allowed on October 29. But the opposition was in no wise disarmed by this act. When the rumor had been circulated that the majority of the Criminal Division was favorable to the appeal, its members were showered with the most insulting abuse. The attacks became so violent that the Chief Justice, Mazeau—while stating that the impartiality of the judges was not in doubt—voiced his opinion that, under the circumstances, it would be preferable if the responsibility for the decision should not rest upon the Criminal Division alone. The Dupuy Government had meanwhile replaced the Brisson Cabinet. It seized upon this suggestion, which gave promise of somewhat pacifying opinion, and had Parliament pass the so-called Law of *Dessaisissement*, providing that, in requests for appeal, judgment should henceforth be pronounced by the full bench—the three Divisions sitting together.

The Court's investigation was long and minute. Rising above the passions of the moment, insensible to daily insults, the judges were determined to pass on the case with complete detachment. In a unanimous decision, on June 3, 1899, they set aside and annulled the judgment of December 22, 1894, of the first Court-Martial of the Military Government of Paris, which had condemned Alfred Dreyfus. At the same time, Picquart, who had been sent before the second Court-Martial of Paris, and who had submitted to the Court of Cassation a request in due form, was granted provisional liberty by the Court. On June 13 the Court of Accusation rendered a judgment that there was not sufficient ground for prosecuting either Picquart or Leblois.

. . . .

In the course of its investigation, the Court of Cassation had demonstrated the complete innocence of Captain Dreyfus, and had proved that no charge against him existed. The Court could

3. One of three branches of the Court of Cassation. *See* Appendix II.

then have set aside the judgment of the Court-Martial of 1894 without remand. Mme. Dreyfus, however, knowing that she was representing accurately her husband's sentiments, gave instructions to her eminent lawyer, Maître Mornard, to request that the case be remanded to a Court-Martial. As early as 1894, Dreyfus' defenders had pointed out that the acts for which he was being tried did not constitute a conspiracy aiming to provoke foreign powers to hostility against France (the political crime of high treason, envisaged by Article 76 of the Penal Code), but purely and simply the misdemeanor of espionage (misdemeanor at common law included in, and punished by, the statute of April 18, 1886). But Dreyfus, strong in his innocence, had categorically forbidden Maître Demange to raise the procedural point. He had directed him to defend nothing but his honor, and to give no attention to the penal consequences which might follow from an improper description of the offense.

Maître Mornard yielded in the face of the instructions he had received. In his plea before the Court of Cassation, which he finished June 1, 1899, he spoke as follows:

. . . In accordance with the orders of my client, gentlemen, I have been obliged to recommend that the case be remanded to a Court-Martial.

. . . I query whether it would not, in truth, have been more humane to move that the judgment be set aside without remand, as it was my right to do. But, in any event, I want to have it clearly understood that, if I have urged remanding the case to a Court-Martial, that was because I was obliged to yield to the very honorable sentiments expressed in Captain Dreyfus' letters. Dreyfus was dispossessed of his honor through the error of his brothers in arms. It is for those brothers in arms to return that honor to him. It is before them that he wishes to appear. . . .

As Maître Mornard had recommended, the Court of Cassation remanded the accused to a Court-Martial, and it was that of Rennes which was selected.

The first session of the Court, summoned for a term of five weeks, opened on August 8, with Colonel Jouaust as President. Although the latter appears to have been in the end one of the two judges who voted for acquittal, he conducted the trial in such

a way as to create a constant impression that he considered Dreyfus guilty. He lacked the authority to resist the generals, who
appeared to be masters of the Court-Martial. Nor did he dare
prevent those fraudulent manoeuvres which so vitiated the decision that four years later, at the time of the second review of the
case, the Minister of War declared in his report to the Premier
(October 19, 1903) :

THE war administration intervened in the trial at Rennes by introducing
the so-called "secret" dossier. . . . I have personally examined all the
documents existing in our archives, some of which went to make up the
secret dossier. In this way I became convinced myself that important
documents, favorable to the accused, had not been introduced, and that,
on the other hand, certain documents in the dossier had been the object, either of actual changes, or of misleading commentaries, which
perverted their meaning. . . .

If one wishes to understand the way in which a military tribunal passes judgment, one has only to go back to the final words
pronounced by Major Carrière, representative of the Government :

. . . You have listened to a great deal of testimony. I ask you to segre-
gate that testimony in two sheafs, in terms of its content—one asking
acquittal of the accused, the other his conviction.
It is your function to weigh those two sheafs, and to give to each the
just weight which you feel it ought to have. You will then award the
victory to that sheaf which weighs most in your scales of justice.
. . . In order to avoid all doubt in the minds of the judges, I should
particularly like to point out to them that the Court-Martial is not a
court similar to the Court of Assize. Here the judge has a double function. He acts, first, as juror, to pass on the question of guilt, and then,
as judge, to pass sentence.
. . . As a juror the law has given you very precise directions. . . .
The law does not hold the juror accountable for the way in which he
reaches his conclusions. . . . It directs him calmly, silently, and in all
sincerity, to interrogate his conscience, and to seek the impression made
upon his mind by the proofs brought in against the accused, and by the
arguments of his defenders. . . .

There was no way in which to state more clearly that the "just
weight" of the generals' testimony had annihilated the precise
arguments of the men who testified in behalf of Dreyfus, whatever may have been the rational or scientific value of these argu-

ments. And yet, in spite of all this influence, the military judges were still so disturbed in spirit that after they had voted five to two for conviction, they granted "extenuating circumstances" for a crime which admits none.

Thus, on September 9, 1899, the Court-Martial of Rennes bowed to the parole and the prestige of the generals. Once again a Court-Martial condemned Captain Dreyfus in a decision which scandalized honorable people in France and in the entire world.

CHAPTER XI

PUBLIC OPINION AND THE AFFAIR

IT would be perfectly safe to say that, until the summer of
1897, virtually the entire country was convinced of the guilt
of Captain Dreyfus. For the country knew nothing of General Mercier's illegal act in communicating to the judges documents unknown to the defense. Everyone reposed confidence in
the judgment of the Court-Martial of 1894, a decision accepted
as just and as final. This conviction was further strengthened by
intermittent campaigns in the press which overwhelmed the
wretched prisoner with abuse and fed the flames of anti-Semitic
hatred. Like a volcano which from time to time emits flame and
smoke, these attacks aroused men's passions, but soon subsided—
and the Affair was once again plunged in somber silence.

Of the first supporters of an appeal some had been convinced
of Dreyfus' innocence as far back as 1894, either because they
were stirred by his vehement protestations or because they could
not conceive of the commission of such a crime without motives.
Others, as soon as they learned the true posture of affairs, were
shocked by the violation of the law, and, without taking either
side on the merits of the case, demanded for Dreyfus—the words
are those of Émile Bergerat at least "the right to be innocent."

Although some men, however, thought that grievous errors had
been committed in good faith and in ignorance of the law, they
did not yet suspect—such was their ardent patriotism and their
deep respect for the Army—that certain highly placed officers
were capable of criminal acts. Even today, as one reviews this incredible story, one wonders how such folly could have taken possession of the General Staff and the Ministry of War. To be sure,
the recent experience of a neighboring country has shown us to
what crimes racial hatred can give rise. But France is a country
too proud of its generous tradition of liberalism to make possible
an explanation of this drama merely by anti-Semitism, so foreign
to French spirit. It is perfectly clear that the fact that Captain
Dreyfus was a Jew was connected with the terrible punishment

which was inflicted upon him. But that was only one influence which determined the desperate tenacity with which he was kept immured on that abandoned island, quite as though he had been struck from the rolls of the living.

The truth was that the Army chiefs were conscious of their blunder, but considered it contrary to the interests of the Army's prestige to admit that fact publicly. Any doubt of their infallibility seemed to them inadmissible. They were the incarnation of military honor and should never be subject to suspicion. Hence the basest turpitude seemed preferable to making amends for the injustice committed. This explains the criminal sophistry of a Mercier, the cowardice of a Billot, the complacent lies of a Boisdeffre or a Gonse, the hypocrisy of a Roget, the specious arguments of a Zurlinden or a Chanoine, the culpable docility of a Pellieux—not to mention the odious plots, more or less the results of influence from above, of an Henry, a du Paty de Clam, a Lauth, a Gribelin, or a Cuignet.

When, thanks to the noble voices of Scheurer-Kestner and of Zola, the truth finally became known, the public was divided into two opposing camps of unequal size. Among the opponents of appeal, who were the more numerous, three clearly defined views obtained. There were, first, those mentally obtuse people who in good faith remained convinced of Dreyfus' guilt. A second group, which had known the facts for a good while, was silent, through discretion or cowardice. There was, finally, a third group, and this was much the largest, which considered that it must at all costs uphold the honor of the Army, as personified in its chiefs. This group insisted, in the phrase of Goethe (not among his best) that "injustice is preferable to disorder," but it forgot the immortal words of another great German, Immanuel Kant: "When justice is gone, it is no longer important that men should live on this earth."

At this already distant period, no one yet foresaw that a war would inevitably involve the mobilization of all the country's man power. It was a widely accepted article of faith that only the active Army possessed value in wartime, and hence that it embodied the true glory of France. In the eyes of the great majority, to suspect an Army chief was to undermine the Army itself, to impair the very organ which was the incarnation of the

idea of the *patrie*. Nothing less than the Great War was required
to reveal the falseness of this point of view. It became rapidly
evident that, although the professional Army was essential to
provide the framework, and competent staffs were indispensable
to coördinate movements on the front as well as to organize and
direct the services behind the lines, the nation as a whole constituted our national Army. The cashiering of Army chiefs was
without influence on the troops who fought in defense of the invaded territories, in the hope that the victory of civilized nations
would end war once and for all. It was for these reasons they
fought, rather than for the trophies of war.

The defenders of Dreyfus were patriots as ardent as their opponents, even though their conception of patriotism differed. But
the Dreyfusards were obliged to combat this absurd theory of the
infallibility of the Army chiefs more sharply even than they had
to struggle for recognition of the judicial wrong itself. And yet
these picked troops, brave and tenacious, strong in the sanctity of
their cause, never once yielded ground. Under the influence of
Scheurer-Kestner, Zola, Jaurès, Trarieux, Anatole France, Louis
Havet, Octave Mirbeau, Paul Painlevé, and of many other eminent and unselfish men, this heroic cohort of the elite (of which
Mathieu Dreyfus and Joseph Reinach were the core) was soon
lost in the robust legions of the Cause. Henceforth, the latter had
on its side not only justice, but the strength of numbers—the
great mass of Frenchmen, intellectuals and workers. The moving
figure of the martyr became a symbol—even though he lived and
suffered still. The struggle was exalted above his personality. His
supporters aimed first of all, it is true, to rescue him from his torment. But they felt also that his example should serve the higher
cause of human solidarity, of tolerance, of justice.

.   .   .   .

In so far as it is possible to derive a conclusion from the Affair, to define its ethical meaning and its social significance, three
outstanding considerations command our attention. In the first
place, all classes were affected by a revival of political interest.
This was particularly true among intellectuals, who had hitherto
shown little interest in politics. Now suddenly the writer found
his study too confined. His laboratory no longer sufficed the sci-

entist. The lecture platform was too narrow for the philosopher and the historian. In great numbers they found their way to the public forum. This was true in both camps. There rushed to the aid of the General Staff, Jules Lemaître, François Coppée, Barrès, Syveton, Vaugeois and their friends, who split hairs over ambiguities, and for some time dominated public opinion. But their reign could not last. The defenders of the prisoner appealed to the people's intelligence and sense of justice, and in the end they were triumphant.

Among those who evinced a new interest in politics and who won great distinction in the struggle, none will forget the immortal example of the great Zola. Anatole France, that urbane and profound thinker, incomparable artificer of our language, sceptic whose irony failed to hide his deep sympathy for his fellow men—Anatole France deserted his ivory tower, never to return. To the very end, he interested himself in political questions, and his frequent pronouncements were reflections of a spirit at once generous and elevated. Francis de Pressensé, a man of broad culture, who had hitherto been absorbed by his studies, plunged wholeheartedly into the struggle, succeeded Trarieux as President of the League of the Rights of Man and died at the breach. Professor Grimaux, the distinguished chemist, preferred to lose his chair at the École Polytechnique and risk his life, rather than neglect the voice of his conscience.

Ferdinand Buisson, who taught education at the Sorbonne, after having organized the system of primary education at the side of Jules Ferry, went straight to the people, was elected to Parliament, and remained faithful to the high principles which inspired the Dreyfusards. The distinguished writer, Octave Mirbeau, hitherto a disciple of the theory of "art for art's sake," widened his horizon, took his place on the public platform, and became Zola's most faithful lieutenant. Professor Victor Basch, the eminent educator, although still very young at that time, frequented the workingman's districts, and devoted himself to the unselfish task of instructing the poor. Eventually he became President of the League of the Rights of Man, that admirable association which grew out of the Affair, over which he now presides with an authority which needs no emphasis. Paul Painlevé, illustrious mathematician who had been completely absorbed in his science, entered the combat to act as spokesman for the Cause before the Universités Populaires, another splendid organization whose origin was due to the Affair. He plunged into the political battle, occupied some of the highest offices in the gift of the Republic, and in its hour of trial, rendered his country services of inestimable value.

And there were others among the intellectuals, convinced Dreyfusards, who fulfilled their civic responsibilities with energy: Drs. Roux, Richet, Delbet, Reclus; Professors Lavisse, Gabriel Monod, Louis Havet, Gabriel Séailles, Georges Duruy, Appell, Aulard; the writers included Sully-Prudhomme, Edmond Rostand, Victorien Sardou, Marcel Prévost, Victor Margueritte, Marcel Proust, Georges Lecomte, Armand Charpentier, Paul Brulat; among the painters were Carrière, Roll, Claude Monet, *et al.;* and there were still others, of widely varying literary and scientific achievement, each of whom deserves warm homage.

The second fact which strikes anyone who studies with care this amazing period is the extraordinary patriotism openly manifested by many Frenchmen, regardless of political belief or religious persuasion. Men became aware that they lived in a steadily shrinking world, in which interdependence was each day a more obvious characteristic. And they were conscious of the danger to which these theorists of injustice exposed the country, which had by now become the subject of unceasing criticism beyond its frontiers, notably in the great British and American democracies. They became convinced that it was their duty to reconquer for France her universal prestige as a free, just, and humane nation—to wipe out the shameful stain which made her face no longer recognizable. This was, in truth, a moving spectacle. Primary-school teachers and savants, workers and bourgeois, militant Catholics and Freemasons, priests and Jews, nobles and shopkeepers, actors and writers, poor and rich—from every point on the horizon came citizens to enlist in this crusade. Their success was so striking that France's enemies, disturbed and envious, could not conceal their disappointment. Although Prince von Bülow, then German Minister of Foreign Affairs, had declared from the tribune of the Reichstag, on the previous January 24, "in the most formal and categorical manner," that Dreyfus had never had "either relations or connections of any nature whatever'' with German agents, he now expressed himself in these significant terms in a dispatch of September 27, 1898:

IT is not to be desired that France, as the result of a rapid and striking rehabilitation of Dreyfus, should secure once again the sympathy of liberals and Israelites. It would be preferable that the Affair continue to suppurate, that it discredit the French Army and cause a scandal in Europe.

But a wisp of straw could no more stay a torrent than could the malevolence of Herr von Bülow hinder true patriots from persevering in their vast effort to recall their country to her *mission civilisatrice*, to her universal influence. We well know how completely they succeeded.

Finally, a point of unquestionable importance: the Affair developed, alike among the people and among the elite, the sentiment of democracy and ideas of justice, of mutual understanding, of social progress, and of a real and fruitful social solidarity. It was the Affair which aroused the sense of revolt against injustice, a sentiment which leads so many Frenchmen of widely differing background to protest vehemently against the injustices of which men are victims, no matter to what nation they may belong. In short, the country emerged from the Affair purer, nobler, stronger, greater in prestige. One may conclude, without any exaggeration, that this valiant struggle against seemingly invincible forces was, contrary to the statements of certain disappointed men, a glorious action of which future generations may say with pride: it saved the honor of undying France.

THE MEMOIRS OF ALFRED DREYFUS

DREYFUS

(1899—1906)

CHAPTER I

IMMEDIATELY after my unjust condemnation of September 9, 1899, I saw my wife and did my best to console her. But we both suffered profound anguish. I had dreamt of the reparation of a terrible judicial wrong, and instead I had witnessed men give judgment contrary to truth and justice—men distracted by passion and by prejudice, perhaps influenced by treacherous manoeuvres carried out in secret. I was profoundly saddened that I could not see and embrace my children, after so long and cruel a separation. Ever since my return to France, I had been impatiently awaiting this moment of supreme happiness. Now it was still denied me. But, strong in the conviction of the justice of my cause, I pursued my claims with unyielding resolution. Despite my profound disappointment and complete physical exhaustion, I had no right to be discouraged. It was my duty to regain my honor—for my children and for myself.

In the few days immediately following the judgment at Rennes, I received thousands of telegrams and letters from France and from all parts of the world, expressing the indignant protests of good people against the injustice done. I also received a visit one evening in my cell from Dr. Delbet, Professor on the Paris Medical Faculty, who had been directed to make a report on the state of my health. There was so much intelligence and kindness in his face that I was strongly attracted to him from the very beginning. Despite the presence of the Deputy Governor of the Prison and the official character of the visit, which was made in the dim light of a lamp, I sensed from the first words we exchanged an elevated mind and warm human sympathies. Soon our conversation wandered from medicine and we lost ourselves in the realm of general ideas. The situation paralyzed all intercourse. Yet, without anything being said, we were drawn together by a mutual understanding which no words could express. As he left, Dr. Delbet shook my hand, and in that vibrant handclasp I was moved to the warmest feeling of attachment for him.

I was condemned September 9, 1899. That very evening I signed my appeal to the Appellate Court-Martial. But during the night of September 11–12, my brother Mathieu arrived at Rennes with a letter from General de Gallifet, Minister of War, to General Lucas, Commandant of the Army Corps at Rennes. General de Gallifet directed General Lucas that my brother, who came with an urgent message of the very greatest importance, should be admitted at once to my cell. My brother, moreover, was to see me without a witness—not even the Deputy Governor of the Prison. At six o'clock on the morning of September 12 my brother was in my cell. He told me that on September 11 the Government had decided, upon the proposal of General de Gallifet, to pardon me. But the Premier, Waldeck-Rousseau, and his colleagues found themselves thwarted in their plan by my appeal to the Appellate Court-Martial.

At first I greeted this proposal with resolute hostility, for I wanted nothing but justice. But my brother made me see, on one hand, the important effect which would result from a pardon immediately following a second unjust condemnation, and, on the other hand, the uselessness of my appeal on questions of law. As a matter of fact, even if my appeal should be allowed, the Court-Martial, before which I would be sent, would pass only on the questions of law. It would hear no witnesses and would not permit me to testify. My brother also made me see my duty toward my wife, my children, and my relatives. As a matter of fact, I was completely exhausted by five years of terrible mental and physical suffering. And I wanted to live so that I might accomplish my full duty, that I might continue the endeavor to appeal my case. After a prolonged discussion with my brother, I decided to withdraw my request for an appeal. On September 19 I was informed that the President of the Republic had signed my pardon.

On the next day the newspapers published the following statement:

THE Government of the Republic has given me my liberty. Liberty is nothing to me without honor. From this day forward I shall continue to seek amends for the shocking judicial wrong of which I am still the victim.

I am determined that all France shall know, by virtue of a definitive judgment, that I am innocent. My spirit can know no rest while there remains a single Frenchman who attributes to me the abominable crime committed by another.

TELEGRAMS-PIRBRIGHT.
STATION-BROOKWOOD. L. & S.W.R.

FURZE HILL,
PIRBRIGHT,
SURREY.

Septembre 22. 1899.

Angleterre

Cher Monsieur Le Capitaine Dreyfus -

Mon mari - L'Explorateur Africain Stanley -
Désire se joindre à moi - pour vous exprimer
toute nôtre sympathie - et toute nôtre admiration
pour nous - nôtre sympathie pour vos souffrances
si cruelles - nôter admiration pour vôtre Courage
héroïque - L'Angleterre entière partage nos sentiments.
vous n'avez que des amis ici - Un jour -
quand vous viendrez en Angleterre vous le
verrez bien. - J'espère que vous allez à présent
remettre vôtre Santé. et jouir de vôtre Chère
vie de famille - Vos souffrances n'ont pas été

Letter from Lady Stanley, wife of the African explorer.

At two o'clock on the following morning I left the prison where I had passed such melancholy days and where I had suffered so many cruel disappointments. A carriage was waiting and took me to a little station near Rennes. My health was sadly undermined, and needed immediate care. Nevertheless, I decided to remain in France and to visit my sister in the South, where I could rest in tranquillity and recover my strength for the coming struggle. At Nantes, where we took the train for Bordeaux, I was rejoiced to have an opportunity to greet my brother, Mathieu, and my nephew, Paul Valabrègue, who were waiting to see me on my way.

As the train rolled on, I experienced a keen pleasure in watching the fields and meadows go by. Everything interested and amused me. It seemed that I was being restored to life after a long and horrible nightmare. . . . We stopped for some hours at Bordeaux, and then went on toward Carpentras. About ten o'clock the next morning we arrived at the country place of my sister, Mme. Joseph Valabrègue at Villemarie. The emotion we all felt cannot be described. Now, finally, came a period of calm, of relaxation, in this long succession of afflictions which had been the lot of all of us.

My first thought after liberation was of M. Hanotaux-Kestner, whom I knew to be very ill. To my great sorrow, I learned en route of the great blow which had descended upon us all. Scheurer-Kestner was no more! I had impatiently awaited the moment when I should be able to pay him my respectful homage, to express my admiration for his character and his loyalty, and my gratitude for the generous enthusiasm with which he had undertaken the cause of an Alsatian, innocent of the detestable crime for which he had been condemned. Alas! my gratitude went only to a grave. I shall never forget how much I owe to Scheurer-Kestner.

. . . .

My wife rejoined me on the evening of my arrival at Carpentras. The passions aroused by the Affair were still so violent that she had felt obliged to come by way of Paris so that my departure from Rennes would not be known. This was really the first day of our reunion, for in our conversations in prison the situation had been too melancholy and too painful to exchange impressions and to give voice to those feelings which were in our hearts. Now, after five years of the most cruel and undeserved afflictions, we could once more freely enjoy each other's company.

On the following day my wife's family arrived with our children. I was deeply moved when I saw again these dear little ones for whom I had lived, and from whose memory I had drawn such strength. I had feared that there would be a moment of astonishment, of fright, when they beheld a father whose face they no longer knew. But they at once threw themselves into my arms and were most affectionate. Their mother had talked constantly to them of their absent father. These few precious moments made me forget many hours of sadness and sorrow. The days which followed brought hours of delightful family intimacy, as well as of the repose which we all needed so much.

Major Forzinetti visited me and I greeted with joy that loyal and gallant soldier, whom I had learned to know during my melancholy sojourn in the Cherche-Midi Prison in 1894. In Forzinetti were united the most elevated feelings of humanity and the strictest conception of his duty as a soldier. We recalled the poignant emotion which drew us together even at the moment of parting, on the morning of January 5, 1895, as I went to the worst torture that can be inflicted on a soldier: degradation. I knew with what courage and what vehemence this gallant man had proclaimed the truth on all sides, had cried aloud the frightful judicial wrong of 1894.

On September 23 we read, with tears in our eyes, Zola's splendid letter to my wife, in which the great author expressed, in characteristically poetic spirit and with infinite tenderness, the feelings we both had during those first days of reunion. I also read in the newspapers General de Gallifet's unfortunate order of the day to the Army, in which he declared that the incident was closed. To refer to this crisis, a distinguishing feature of one of the greatest struggles of the age, as an ''incident'' was to reveal little discernment. The incident was not closed, either from a judicial point of view, which would have been monstrous, or from the point of view of the nation, which was engaged in a political battle against the united forces of falsehood and injustice.

Letters and tokens of sympathy continued to arrive in great

numbers. Meanwhile, I saw in turn all the members of my family whose unwavering sympathy I had had during these five unhappy years. I also received visits from several friends. I knew with what courage and self-sacrifice all the friends of justice had defended the cause of truth. I have for them the deepest gratitude, and in coming to know some of them, I learned to love them all. My sole regret is that I do not know them all personally, and I am taking this occasion to address to them a heartfelt tribute.

In this atmosphere of affection my strength gradually returned. My spiritual strength was unimpaired, but I needed to renew my physical vigor and above all to restore my nervous system, which had been so badly shaken. I gradually recovered the habit of walking. The first time I went out with my wife I had been able painfully to cover six hundred meters.

.   .   .   .

At this time came the unfortunate Amnesty Bill, introduced by the Government, a bill which represented the bankruptcy of right and justice. Happily I was excluded from the amnesty. But in extinguishing all prosecutions and suits connected with the Affair, it closed many doors to appeal: the questions and answers of the witnesses in the pending cases would have brought to light much false testimony and much new evidence. I sent a letter of protest on December 2, 1899, to M. Clamageran, Chairman of the Amnesty Committee of the Senate.

.   .   .   .

During the early days of January, 1900, expressions of sympathy again began to reach me in great numbers. It was physically impossible for me to reply to all of these, but I was deeply touched by them. The year just past had made me aware of an infamy and ignominy whose existence I had hitherto not suspected. But to my great joy, it had also revealed a constantly growing number of scientists, men of letters, and workers, who were determined to safeguard the honor and dignity of France. They supported the cause of truth and justice with an ability equaled only by their courage. . . .

.   .   .   .

Early in March the Amnesty Committee of the Senate was directed by the Government to accelerate the preparation of the Amnesty Bill. At this point I wrote another letter to M. Clamageran, Chairman of the Committee:

Carpentras,
March 8, 1900.

In the presence of the bill which has just been laid before the Senate, it is my duty to renew the protest which I had the honor to direct to you last December, when the question of an amnesty was introduced.

The bill extinguishes prosecutions and suits, from which I had hoped revelations, perhaps confessions, would result. These would have enabled me to appeal to the Court of Cassation the unjust decision of which I have once again been the victim.

The bill thus deprives me of my most cherished hope, that of having my innocence legally proclaimed—innocence so evident and so manifest that the Government of the Republic made it a point of honor to prevent the execution of the judgment of September 9, 1899. Indeed it destroyed this judgment, upon the proposal of the Minister of War himself, on the very day following that on which it had been pronounced. I asked no pardon. The right of the innocent is justice, not clemency.

The liberty given me I prized above all, because I thought that it would facilitate my campaign for reparation of the shocking wrong of which I was the victim.

I will go so far, Mr. President, as to ask the eminent jurists of the Senate this question: if the amnesty is voted and the suits and prosecutions are extinguished, what legal means are left me to obtain an appeal?

The writers who have been proceeded against, and who are relying upon their trials to bring new facts to light, have protested in the name of that truth which is once more being suppressed.

I protest still more bitterly, in the name of justice, against a measure which leaves me disarmed in the face of iniquity.

No one wishes more ardently than I for peace, for the reconciliation of all good Frenchmen, for the end of the shocking virulence of which I was the first victim. The amnesty strikes me to the quick. It benefits only scoundrels who abused the good faith of the judges; who knowingly had an innocent man condemned through lies, perjury, and forgery; and who cast me into the abyss.

This amnesty will redound to the exclusive profit of General Mercier, the principal author of the crime of 1894, who, by a strange irony of fate, will be called upon, as a Senator, to vote in his own interest.

I beseech the Senate to leave intact my right to truth and justice.

On the following day I read in the newspapers that Zola, Reinach and Colonel Picquart had likewise renewed their protests against the amnesty, and had asked to be heard by the Senate Amnesty Committee. They were received on March 14. Reinach demanded the right to confute his defamers in the only court where that was permitted. He declared that he was convinced that the cases then being tried would provide me the means of securing final amends for the most deplorable of judicial wrongs. Colonel Picquart insisted upon the insufficiency of the charge against him. He was determined not to be involved in the same bill with General Mercier and his accomplices. He recalled again the judicial crimes committed in 1894 and the years following. Zola emphasized the necessity of recalling the national conscience from the shadows into which it had been plunged. It was his wish that France should find herself once more the France of liberty and justice, loved throughout the world. He asked that there be no interference with the work of the commissions of inquiry, and that they be permitted to summon all the witnesses and undertake to bring to light the whole of the amazing truth.

CHAPTER II

MY health was beginning to improve, but summer, a hot season in the South, was coming on. And so on the advice of physicians, I decided to go for a stay in Switzerland, on the shores of the Lake of Geneva, where the climate is both temperate and stimulating. There I would complete the convalescence so happily begun at Carpentras. We left on April 20, 1900, and took up our abode in the Villa Hauterive at Cologny, on the shore of the lake. From the steps of the villa one looked out upon the lake, more than a hundred and fifty feet below. Beyond, rose the Jura, their summits still covered with snow. Below and to the left, at the foot of the pass between the Jura and the Alps, lay the city of Geneva. The view was restful, and yet the eye had far horizons.

The changes in light were exquisite—at times the colors in the distance were softened by an intervening veil, again they were aflame with contrasts. In the evening the sun sank in brilliant light behind the Jura—a silver luster on the lake; beyond, in the shadows of the Jura, the verdant hills along the shore; and in the distance the deep violet of the Jura in silhouette against the vaulting heavens, afire in the splendors of the setting sun. What delicious repose this was for all of us, after so many years of sadness! What peace of spirit lies in the precious solace of nature! Our children, who had already been greatly benefited by their winter in the country at Carpentras, were delighted by the great expanses of lawn, where they could play to their heart's content. As we looked on, my wife and I would sometimes exchange a silent glance, and our thoughts, shadowed by the sadness of the past, were brightened by this present prospect.

After the trial at Rennes, a committee which called itself "Nationalist" (no one ever knew why, for patriotism does not, I think, consist of the spiritual humiliation of one's country) had published General Mercier's testimony in pamphlet form. This venomous and treacherous pamphlet was now once again circulated in great numbers, as though it was feared that there would be another awakening of the public conscience against falsehood, forgery, and injustice. On May 7 municipal elections were held in France. The Nationalists won a partial success in Paris, a result of the weakness of the Republicans who did not dare to set forth categorically their program and ideal of truth and justice. In the provinces, on the other hand, victory went to the Republicans. On the second ballot, May 14, the Nationalists won a final triumph in Paris after a hot campaign of slander and abuse.

On May 22, as Parliament reconvened, an interpellation took place concerning an article published in the *Éclair,* which stated that the Government was intending to revive the Affair. The Chamber of Deputies passed an order of the day,[1] directing the Government energetically to oppose any such move. How many similar orders of the day have we witnessed? And what have they done to hinder the march of events? During this same session of the Chamber, Waldeck-Rousseau, the Premier, was so far lacking in moral courage that he used the words: ''There is no longer a Dreyfus Affair.'' He had the right to say only that the Dreyfus Affair was, in his view, ended, in so far as it was a political question. But he should have added that it still remained, like all cases in this category, within the province of the courts. No Chamber has the right to bind the judiciary, to suppress the articles of the Code providing for appeal on the basis of ''new evidence.'' Waldeck-Rousseau permitted the adoption of an order of the day which was in fact ambiguous, and which, if it had possessed any judicial value whatever, would have meant the end of all justice.

Immediately following the session of the Chamber, the Government directed the Amnesty Committee to submit its bill to the Senate. Thereupon Émile Zola sent an admirable letter of protest to the Senators. The discussion of the Amnesty Bill began in the Senate on June 1.

1. The Chamber of Deputies regulates the transaction of its business by what is known as the ''order of the day,'' the agenda of the Chamber. In the Dreyfus period this agenda was fixed at the end of each session by the President, and was then submitted to a vote of the Chamber. The term ''order of the day'' is also, by extension, used of motions affecting the agenda: ''the order of the day, pure and simple,'' calling for a return to the agenda, without comment on the question under consideration; the ''qualified order of the day,'' calling for a return to the agenda but with a definite expression of opinion, indicating approval or disapproval of the government's policy on the question under consideration.

Under the pretext of a false pacification, the amnesty violated every principle of justice. In any case, I was rejoiced to hear at last from the tribunal of a French assembly words which branded with flaming iron the crime and the principal criminal. It is to three courageous men, moved by a sense of duty, that I owed this solace: MM. Trarieux, Delpech, and Clamageran. Delpech pilloried General Mercier and recalled the crimes which remained unpunished. Boldly he told the country the truth. In an admirable speech, reflecting intelligence and understanding, Trarieux laid bare with remarkable clarity all the defects of the proposed amnesty. And Clamageran protested not less eloquently in the name of justice. But, despite the efforts of these brave men, the amnesty was adopted by the Senate. It then returned to the Chamber, where the committee could not agree on the additions proposed by certain members. Parliament rose during the first part of July without daring to take a final vote.

CHAPTER III

IN August I received a visit from . . . Joseph Reinach. We examined the situation at length, and recognized that there was little likelihood that my investigations would result, in the near future, in the discovery of new evidence sufficiently serious to warrant submission of the case to the Court of Cassation. We came to the conclusion that we ought to make direct contact with those who had the proofs of Esterhazy's guilt. For this task I turned to my devoted and energetic brother, Mathieu, and asked him to visit me at Cologny. We agreed that he would induce one of our friends from Mulhouse, M. Sandoz, to write to Schwartzkoppen, whom he knew, and ask the latter for an interview for my brother. In the course of this interview Mathieu was to point out to Schwartzkoppen those moral obligations from which he could not escape, and ask him to give evidence before the French Ambassador in Berlin, at the same time furnishing in support of his statement the documents delivered by Esterhazy, and especially the documents enumerated in the bordereau of 1894. Two weeks later my brother informed me that Schwartzkoppen had refused the interview requested by M. Sandoz. In refusing, Schwartzkoppen pointed out that he could add nothing to what he had stated officially, namely, that he had never had any relations with me, direct or indirect. The former German Military Attaché at Paris placed his own interest above the duty which his conscience should have prescribed. This, moreover, was no matter of recent date.

September 9 was the melancholy anniversary of the judgment of Rennes. . . . On the next day I received from Trarieux, one of the founders and President of the League of the Rights of Man, this splendid letter:

Paris,
September 8, 1900.

WE are on the eve of September 9, and we do not wish to be guilty of permitting this baneful anniversary of the judgment of the Rennes Court-Martial to pass without bringing you once more the sympathy which your adversity deserves.

Doubtless your physical suffering is over. Thanks to a humane act of amends, you are free once more and with your family. But we realize the bitterness which must remain in your heart as you witness the persistent spiritual effects of a wrong which justice has not thus far repaired. So long as this torture causes you anguish, all those who undertook your defense and fought injustice will remain, with you, dissatisfied for the future.

We know not when it will be possible to reveal to the eyes of the most obstinate the terrible judicial wrong of which you were the victim. Time will accomplish nothing. Whatever happens, the authority of the *chose jugée* does not dominate man's reason as completely as certain interpreters of the law insist it should. It requires that your condemnation be carried out in all those respects which the subsequent pardon could not efface, but it does not in any sense deprive us of the freedom of personal judgment and the right to retain our conviction. . . .

It is no longer of you alone that we think, but of the legions of the weak and disinherited who need a helping hand even more than you do. To them we offer our protection and our aid. Henceforth, every victim of an abuse of power, of an illegal act, of an injustice, can find succor in the association which we have founded. And thus all those whom we aid will remain beholden to you for that support. Once more, good will have come from evil, and your long suffering will have served to bring comfort to others in distress. . . .

There also came to me a very moving letter from Mme. Marcellin Pellet, daughter of the lamented Scheurer-Kestner:

As I think back over the sorrowful days of the past year, I feel once more your anguish, which we shared. In memory of my noble father, and as he would himself have done, I send you the renewed expression of my ardent desire for your final victory. Your cause, which today is that of all honest men, is also that of Frenchmen who have implicit confidence in their country's greatness and its sense of justice.

I replied to M. Trarieux:

Cologny, near Geneva,
September 13, 1900.

WHILE we were in Caux last Monday we visited Montfleuri, and my wife reminded me that Mme. Trarieux had been there last year. We at once spoke of you with profound gratitude; and then, by a curious coincidence, your splendid letter came right afterwards. . . .

Your letter, inspired by such noble and generous sentiments, is also a touching tribute to the cause of justice. I thank you for it from the bottom of my heart. I was also deeply stirred to see how clearly you had sensed my feelings, and how well you had understood the sad burden which I bear. To be sure, I have been given my liberty once again. I have returned to my family, after so many years of painful separation. I have found many friends, still unknown to me at Rennes, who, faithful to the principles of a France which stands for right and justice, have undertaken with great courage the defense of an innocent man. On the other hand, I have lived through five years of terrible torture for the sake only of my honor. The moral effects of the injustice are still there; the spiritual torture is unabated; justice has not been done. My unchanging goal is the judicial review of my case. The League of which you are President has undertaken the great and noble task of bearing aid to all those who are victims of injustice. This splendid work of fraternity has my deepest and most heartfelt sympathy.

Upon receipt of my letter, M. Trarieux wrote me, asking permission to publish it (changing only the personal passage relating to Montfleuri). I willingly acceded.

The shameful lies to which newspapers resorted knew no limits. At this particular time I was the luncheon guest of friends at Anthy, near Thonon-les-Bains in Haute-Savoie, and I was well received everywhere we went. But the *Moniteur universel,* and subsequently the *Libre parole,* carried stories to the effect that I had been greeted by hostile outcries. On October 3, I read with great indignation an article in the *Petit parisien,* the newspaper of M. Jean Dupuy, then Minister of Agriculture. The article opposed revival of the Affair, and concluded in these words: "Returning to an expression which we used the very day of the Rennes Judgment, and to which we still give our most formal support, the decision of the Court-Martial constitutes the legal truth. The future will, if possible, assume responsibility for the historic truth." The *Figaro* reproduced this article; it suggested that it had a semiofficial origin, and approved it in every detail. What cowardice! The third and sixth paragraphs of the article were completely inadmissible, and on certain points entirely inaccurate:

DOUBTLESS it would be going too far to say that, when the former Captain withdrew his request for an appeal, he admitted his guilt, and recognized the justice of his condemnation. But it would also be contrary to the truth to maintain that this renunciation, whose aim was to obtain a pardon solicited by his family, did not constitute the acquiescence of Dreyfus in the definitive termination of the case.

And again:

FOLLOWING the judgment of the first Court-Martial, which had involved certain illegal acts, an appeal seemed to impartial minds to be inevitable. But at Rennes all the forms prescribed by law were observed. One must, therefore, defer to the decision of the judges, unless one wishes to set at naught all judgments, the decisions of all courts—in short, the very bases of the social order.

I decided to protest energetically against such outrageous misrepresentations. The paragraph concerning the pardon was a falsehood, since it was the Government which asked me to withdraw my request to the Appellate Court-Martial (a request from which I had, however, nothing to gain), so that my pardon could be signed by the President of the Republic. I had withdrawn my request and accepted the unsolicited pardon, only with the explicit and definite proviso that I would continue to seek amends for an atrocious judicial wrong. A note to this effect appeared in the newspapers on the very day of my liberation, and had been communicated to the Government before its publication. Hence the latter was not without knowledge of my intentions.

According to the article in the *Petit parisien*, the Government was alleged to believe that the question had been ended by the pardon; let the future establish the historic truth! Decent people do not recognize two truths, one legal, another historic. In their eyes there is only one truth—that which I hoped to establish, with or without political aid. This was no controversy over an historical point, but a question of the legal reputation of a living human being, determined to fight for the review of his case.

Just as I was writing the letter of protest to the *Petit parisien*, the Paris mail arrived with the following letter from Joseph Reinach:

October 2, 1900.

WHEN I read in the *Temps* the article from the *Petit parisien* (represented as semiofficial by the *Figaro*), I wrote a warm letter to Jean Dupuy. I pointed out that you might disregard statements respecting the withdrawal of your request for an appeal when they appeared in just any newspaper, but that obviously you could not permit them to appear with semiofficial approval—that you would be induced to declare that this withdrawal was asked by the Government, and that there are witnesses to testify to that fact. I asked that *Havas* publish a statement to the effect that the *Petit parisien* article was in no sense semiofficial.

I sent my letter to Dupuy, who replied at once, much annoyed, and gave me an appointment for this morning. Warm and animated conversation. I omit details. Conclusion: he will inform Waldeck-Rousseau and Millerand after this morning's cabinet.

On my own initiative, I wrote to Millerand, who telephoned me at noon to come and see him. I left Millerand, having learned that Waldeck-Rousseau had already talked to him and was much annoyed by the blunder of the *Petit parisien,* which had been accentuated by the *Figaro.* With his characteristic honesty, Millerand admitted that my memory was accurate and that you were in the right. But he considers that to reopen the Affair through this cheap exposé would be most unfortunate, especially at this juncture. It would mean a Nationalist insurrection against the Government for the most honorable of all its acts. I need not emphasize this point to you.

Let me add that not even our best friends would be willing to create an incident of such grave consequence, even as a legitimate reprisal.

On the other hand, I warmly uphold you as completely justified in opposing any attempt to sully your pardon through an allegation that you had renounced your rights.

It was agreed that Millerand should see Waldeck-Rousseau. A *Havas* note appears to be impossible. Instead, the *Petit parisien* will itself publish tomorrow a note to the effect that yesterday's article was in no sense semiofficial.

In my view, it is that note which must determine your action. If it is not clear, or if at the last moment Dupuy fails to insert it, you can make your protest as forceful as you like. If the note is in general satisfactory, then you could restrict yourself to a letter to the editor of the *Petit parisien,* with an energetic protest against the interpretation of the pardon.

I was completely in sympathy with the views of Reinach, who, with his usual devotion, had taken the initiative in these measures. I decided to withhold my protest and adopt a waiting attitude. In the afternoon I received a telegram from Reinach: "Am writing and sending newspaper." I learned from his letter of the following day that Millerand and Waldeck-Rousseau were in complete agreement concerning the insertion of the following note in the *Petit parisien:*

IT is important to note that the *Petit parisien* has spoken, as is always the case, with entire independence and on its own complete and exclusive responsibility.

Reinach and my friends considered that this semiofficial denial was sufficient, and were of the opinion that the incident should rest there. This view seemed to me wise, since the attitude of Waldeck-Rousseau and Millerand had been such that to insist would have been ungraceful.

CHAPTER IV

ABOUT this time I learned that the Prince of Monaco had made a short visit to Berlin and had been told the following story, for which, however, no proof was offered. He was told that General Boisdeffre himself had been responsible for the forgery of the so-called *bordereau annoté,* the false marginalia of the German Emperor, of which so much was made in the press at the time of the Rennes trial. The forgery had been carried out with the aid of an autograph letter sent to General Boisdeffre by the Emperor, following a conversation on the Gallic Wars. The General then had the bordereau delivered to the French General Staff by a Russian attaché. Furthermore, the Prince was told that Henry and Esterhazy had furnished information to the Russian General, Annenkoff, who coöperating with these two, had been concerned in other deals. Annenkoff had committed suicide precisely in order to escape the consequences of his participation in these different affairs.

Apropos the first part of this story, the legend of the bordereau annoté has never been cleared up. But what is curious about the latter part of the account—that concerning Esterhazy, Henry, and Annenkoff—is its similarity with a story once told by M. de Cyon to M. Léopold Favre of Geneva, and which the latter repeated to me. Or was it in fact M. de Cyon's story itself, which was now returning from the north? In any event, despite repeated requests, M. de Cyon has never been able to produce any proof of the accuracy of his allegations.

. . . .

The opening session of the Court of Cassation took place on October 15. Following the address of M. Ballot-Beaupré, chosen Chief Justice, M. Lafferrière, named Procureur Général, spoke as follows, addressing M. Ballot-Beaupré: "Your reputation as a magistrate, a reputation recognized by all, won for you the privilege of being rapporteur[1] in the most important case of the cen-

1. *See* Appendix II.

tury.'' The Avocat Général,[2] Dubois, then delivered a speech condemning the trial at Rennes:

LET me recall briefly the incidents in this trial, on which I need not comment: the courageous decision of the Minister of Justice; the investigation of the Criminal Division—act of indomitable faith in the truth; the Law of *Dessaisissement*[3] and the submission of the case to the full bench[4] . . .; the solemn proceedings; the vote which followed. Permit me to draw just one conclusion from these facts—and that conclusion has its significance at a time when the role of judges has been so unfortunately and so invidiously misrepresented: the highest Court expressed complete confidence in the absolute integrity of all its members. What a splendid lesson and example! The striking vindication of this confidence lay in the unusual, but completely justifiable, decision by unanimous vote to set aside the judgment.

M. Ballot-Beaupré, now Chief Justice of the Court of Cassation, was rapporteur for the appeal in the first instance. It is well known in what vigorous terms he proclaimed the illegality of the verdict of 1894 and attributed the bordereau to Esterhazy.

.   .   .   .

On the previous December 24 I had written to M. Decrais, the Colonial Minister, to ask for the return: (1) of letters from my wife which had never reached me on Devil's Island; (2) of letters of my wife which had been forwarded only in abridged and copied form; (3) of my personal notes. M. Decrais replied that his department still had on file the following documents, which were at my disposal: my diary, original and copy; thirty-six copybooks of my personal notes; and two signed letters from my wife. He added that my wife's other letters, ''intercepted by order, had been subsequently destroyed at the command of the Minister.'' I had the Colonial Administration send me the documents still in its possession. It must be noted that M. Decrais' letter proved that his predecessor as Colonial Minister, M. Lebon, had taken upon himself the responsibility, contrary to both law and justice, of having my wife's letters destroyed, letters which

2. The avocat général was assistant to the procureur général. There were six of them in the Court of Cassation.
3. *See* pp. 129, 279, note 1.
4. *Chambres réunies.*

had been intercepted and which ought to have been placed in my dossier.

.   .   .   .

On Sunday, October 28, Waldeck-Rousseau, speaking at Toulouse, outlined his program in anticipation of the convening of Parliament. I have taken from it the following passage:

WE were summoned to witness the last act of a moving drama which has profoundly stirred all of us, and which has divided the country. Despite all this, there have been some men who have gone so far as to assert that the "Affair" did not exist! We took steps to have the solution of the case confided to judges enjoying the most complete independence. Since we do not conceive that there can be reasons of state superior to the forms of justice, the decision of the judges has been respected.

Humanity has found satisfaction in a measure of mercy, approved by the magnanimity of our country, which was finally aroused.

Hence we felt no reluctance in supporting the order of the day of May 22 last, which directed the Government to resist every attempt to revive an agitation which henceforth has no justification. We have asked the Senate, as we shall ask the Chamber, to pass an essential law of effacement in order to assure a final pacification.

Waldeck-Rousseau was mistaken when he said that it was the *last act* which he had witnessed. He had witnessed only the *penultimate act*. He then maintained that the Government had taken steps to confide the solution to judges enjoying the most complete independence. What a complete error! What naïveté on the part of a statesman of such a vigilant mind! How the Government had been outwitted at Rennes! It had given to the authors of the crime of 1894 the greatest freedom to renew their treacherous manoeuvres. It had permitted its own representative, Major Carrière, instrument of the Minister of War, who stood at the head of the system of military justice, to place himself under the direction of, and receive his inspiration from, Maître Auffray, the attorney for the *Libre parole*.

In Waldeck-Rousseau's speech appeared also the ambiguous sentence in which he emitted a discreet—how very discreet— opinion on the fundamental issue in the Affair: "We do not conceive that there can be reasons of state superior to the forms of justice." Which means in plain language: whatever may be our opinion on the fundamental issue, nothing can prevent us from accepting the judgment, since the forms have been respected.

. . . .

During the month of November, 1900, some of my friends warned me that rumors as absurd as the following were circulating in Paris: that I was content with the pardon which, since I was remaining abroad, I obviously considered a final solution; that I feared for my life and dared not return to Paris; or again, and this was more serious, that my sojourn abroad had been imposed upon me on the day when I accepted the pardon (this last rumor was ridiculous on the face of it, since I had spent the preceding winter at Carpentras in the South of France). However preposterous these rumors might be, I had to cut them short. I had remained on the shores of the Lake of Geneva in the interests of my health, which had been seriously undermined, and that of my children. I was prepared to return to Paris as soon as my presence there was necessary. It was useless at this time since I had no "new evidence" which would permit me to submit my case to the Court of Cassation. But there was only one way to muzzle this rash gossip of certain embittered defenders of my cause—that was to return. I left for Paris on November 24, in order clearly to indicate that I enjoyed complete and entire liberty of movement and that I feared nothing and no one. I arrived on the morning of November 25.

How many tragic events had taken place since I left my home on the morning of October 15, 1894—never to see it again! What a terrible tragedy I had experienced! I lived again this horrible nightmare. But I had no desire to be swept along by the melancholy and depressing thoughts of the past. I quickly gained control of myself and fixed my thoughts on the future and on the goal I was determined to achieve.

During the first days following my return I greeted again the friends whom I had already seen at Carpentras, and above all I had the profound pleasure of meeting Émile Zola. I was delighted by his simplicity and moved by his sonorous voice, his warm sympathy, his heart overflowing with kindness.

. . . .

During my stay on the Lake of Geneva, there had been re-

*Mme. Dreyfus, with Pierre and Jeanne, the photograph
which Dreyfus had with him on Devil's Island.*

peated to me on several occasions a conversation which was said
to have taken place at the French manoeuvres of 1896 between
Colonel Chauvet of the Swiss Army and Colonel von Schwartzkoppen. I was also told that Colonel Chauvet had made a statement in writing to the effect that Colonel von Schwartzkoppen
had affirmed my innocence. The conversation had this special interest—that it had taken place at a time prior to the beginning
of the campaign for appeal. I sought confirmation of this story,
and during my stay at Cologny a mutual friend arranged an interview with Colonel Chauvet.

The latter confirmed the statements of Colonel von Schwartzkoppen. Chauvet, along with the foreign military representatives, was on his way to the manoeuvres of 1896 in the environs
of Angoulême. In the coach in which the group was traveling, he
found himself seated next to Colonel von Schwartzkoppen and
Colonel Panizzardi. All were reading the newspapers. Suddenly
Colonel von Schwartzkoppen exclaimed: "Here they are talking
again about that Affair. It's very annoying." He turned to
Colonel Chauvet and said: "I can swear on my honor that Dreyfus is innocent, and that he is paying for another. You see that
man (pointing out du Paty, who had been detailed to accompany the foreign attachés to the manoeuvres), well, I shouldn't
like to be in his skin, for he had an innocent man condemned."
Colonel Chauvet also told me that he had repeated Colonel von
Schwartzkoppen's conversation in a letter written before the
Rennes trial to M. Andrade, Professor in the Faculty of Sciences
of Montpellier. After the Rennes trial M. Andrade was supposed
to have sent this letter to M. Monis, Minister of Justice, thinking
that it would constitute new evidence.

Colonel Chauvet also told me that he stood ready to repeat
this conversation in a deposition before the French Ambassador
at Berne, if I should deem that useful. I first wrote to M. Andrade to obtain the text of the letter which Colonel Chauvet had
sent him, and to learn whether he had actually transmitted the
original to the Minister of Justice. M. Andrade replied on October 2, sent me the text of the letter, and declared that he had
in fact transmitted the letter to M. Monis, Minister of Justice, in
September, 1899, after the Rennes trial. The text of the letter
follows:

Thun,
July 6, 1899.

Monsieur le Professeur:

I have your letter of the fifth instant, and I hasten to reply. It is true that I had the honor to be present in 1896 at the army manoeuvres near Angoulême. Without any provocation on my part, Colonel von Schwartzkoppen one day entered upon a conversation with me about Dreyfus. Among other things, he said that a terrible judicial wrong had been committed in 1894, that Dreyfus was innocent, and, pointing out Colonel du Paty de Clam, "that he would not be in his skin, for it was he who had directed the investigation." Colonel von Schwartzkoppen had no reason *to swear to me on his honor* that he had had no relations with Dreyfus, for I had not asked him this question. Let me repeat, I had not invited this conversation in any way—this affair did not concern me. I did not prolong the conversation. Naturally it struck me with great force at the time, and on my return to Switzerland I recounted it to several of my colleagues. . . .

I sent the text of this letter to Maître Mornard, to determine what advantage we might draw from it and whether it would be useful to have Colonel Chauvet repeat his statement in the presence of M. Bihourd, French Ambassador at Berne. Maître Mornard was of the opinion that it would be helpful to have this conversation secured in a definitive form by the Ambassador. I immediately wrote this to Colonel Chauvet, who replied that he was prepared to give official confirmation to his conversation with Schwartzkoppen, but that he wished to be asked to do so. I replied to Colonel Chauvet that, since no prosecution was actually in progress, it was not the affair of the Ambassador to call for a deposition—he could only receive it. It was the function of him who had a statement to make to do so without compulsion. Moreover, I said that I considered it the duty of every man who was the possessor of an element of truth to offer it as testimony. But Colonel Chauvet never brought himself to take the initiative and testify before the French Ambassador at Berne.

.   .   .   .

At this time I had the pleasure of meeting M. Trarieux. I had only caught a glimpse of him during the trial at Rennes when his magnificent testimony had deeply stirred me. M. Trarieux was one of those characters in whom humanity is most profoundly honored.

I did not, however, forget what had become the goal of my life: to obtain the judicial review of my case. I profited by my return to write the following letter to the Prince of Monaco, urging him to act:

Paris,
December 7, 1900.

ON the occasion of my return to Paris, permit me to send you once again the expression of my appreciation and of my feeling of profound gratitude for the interest which you have taken in the cause of justice and truth.

Yours is a spirit too elevated not to make you sensible of how much sadness and pain there is still in my life.

To be sure, I have been given my liberty. I am with my family once again after so many years of terrible separation. I have found many friends united beneath the banner of truth and justice.

But I lived through five years of horrible torture only for my honor. I endured it all only that I might cleanse my name—the name which my children bear—of the shameful stain which has been placed upon it.

But the moral stigma of that injustice still remains, a situation as hateful for my children as for myself. I am insulted with impunity and my name is dragged in the mire, because legally I am a convict. I am the moral prisoner of this terrible situation; my hands are tied by it. It is improbable that the prosecutions and suits already begun will come to court, that testimony can then be taken by commissions of inquiry, and that new evidence will thus come to light which would enable me to request an appeal of my case. Hence the present situation may continue indefinitely.

Will not General von Schwartzkoppen now finally do his duty? Is it not time that he should tell the truth, the whole truth? Will not his conscience influence him to go to the French Embassy in Berlin, and there state the truth under oath?

For him who knows the truth, it is a duty not only before history, which will judge us all, but a duty to humanity, even more a duty to his conscience, to disclose that truth. It is for General von Schwartzkoppen to put his conscience at rest by making a deposition in the presence of the French Ambassador in Berlin, with supporting proofs of the crime committed by another, and among them the documents named in the bordereau. These will then enable me to resubmit my case on appeal to the Court of Cassation.

I hope that he who has the truth will finally accomplish the sacred duty which is incumbent upon him.

But this course of action was fruitless. General von Schwartz-koppen remained deaf to all entreaty!

CHAPTER V

THE discussion of the Amnesty Bill reached the Chamber on December 6. Two Deputies, MM. Guyesse and Vazeille, had the courage to define the question clearly and to state the truth. The Chamber listened to them in silence, and the remainder of the discussion was postponed. Lieutenant-Colonel Picquart then sent a superb letter to the Deputies protesting against the amnesty which tended to involve him who had fought for the cause of truth and justice with the authors (but too well known) of the crimes of perjury, forgery, and conspiracy.

When discussion of the bill was renewed in the Chamber M. Jules Louis Breton, with admirable courage, proclaimed the truth from the tribune. The end of the discussion came only some days later. The unjust law was passed by the immense majority of Republicans who did not wish to defeat the Ministry which was being attacked by all the forces of reaction. The law closed to me many avenues leading to the appeal of my case. I had now to exercise patience for long years, occupied by arduous and unceasing investigation, before I was able finally to succeed. I wrote to Deputies Jules Louis Breton, Vazeille and Guyesse to thank them for their courageous speeches which had pilloried with such remarkable effectiveness the authors of crimes against justice and truth. In the letter to M. Vazeille I added the following:

THERE is, however, one sentence in your speech which I did not quite understand. You said that I no longer saw in the Affair anything beyond my personal interest. Till my last breath I shall seek the judicial review of my case. And in seeking this end, which you describe as a personal one, it appears to me that I am fulfilling at the same time an ideal of justice and truth, which is that of all good Frenchmen, of all those unselfish and noble men who threw themselves into the battle to defend this ideal.

In answer to my letter to M. Jules Louis Breton, Deputy of the Cher, I received a very moving reply in which he said:

IN the course of the discussion of this Amnesty Bill, so unwisely introduced by the Government, I wanted to recall the infamies and the crimes which had been committed to keep an innocent man in prison. I was able to assert your innocence from the tribune, which had not yet been frankly done.

.   .   .   .

The *Intransigeant* of December 25, 1900, published an article in which the famous bordereau annoté was discussed. I was hopeful that Rochefort was finally going to bring to light this forgery, the most colossal to appear in the entire Affair, which had, moreover, seen so many. But my hope was disappointed. This article, which predicted new revelations, was followed by no others. Accordingly, I decided to write M. Waldeck-Rousseau, the Premier, the following letter:

I AM accused by certain newspapers of having sent to the Emperor of Germany in 1894 an infamous letter alleged to have received the marginalia of that Sovereign and then to have been purloined from an embassy. It is said to constitute a formal proof of the crime for which I have twice been unjustly condemned.

The bordereau which was produced in the trials of 1894, 1898, and 1899, is said to be only a copy.

This new falsehood, by reason of its origin, can only be received with contempt.

The journalist who is disseminating this story and who returns to it repeatedly, despite official denials, did not invent it. He is, according to his own story, only the echo of confidences brought him, along with brazen forgeries, by an agent of General de Boisdeffre.

Photographs of the forged letters attributed to the Emperor of Germany and of the bordereau annoté have been shown on several occasions. This false story has been recounted many times. Tomorrow for many deluded minds, that clumsy legend will become the truth.

I am completely innocent. Till my last breath I shall seek judicial recognition of that innocence through a review of my case.

I am no more the author of the bordereau annoté of the German Emperor (which is only a forgery), than I am of the original bordereau, which is authentic, and whose author is Esterhazy.

Except for Henry, all the principal authors of my unjust condemnation are still alive. I have not been deprived of my rights; I retain the right of every man to defend his honor and to have the truth proclaimed.

I have then the right, Mr. President, to ask you for an investigation, and I have the honor to request it.

There appeared in the *Fronde* for December 20, 1900, a still more explicit article on the bordereau annoté by Mme. Séverine. Its secret communication to the judges at Rennes was there affirmed. I made a personal investigation of this subject, but I secured only evidence much too vague for any convincing conclusion. Had the inquiry which I sought from Waldeck-Rousseau been granted, I was hopeful that the investigation of the use made of this forgery would lead to discovery of its role in the Rennes trial.

. . . .

On January 20 I was told the following story. A certain Streisser, attached to the Intelligence Bureau, sought out M. Montaigne, director of the Agence Nationale, to ask him a personal favor. At the same time, it seems, he unbosomed himself on his own behalf and on that of a relative, Major Bajac, who was then in active service, and who had formerly been attached to the same bureau. He returned some days later with Major Bajac himself. Both claimed that Esterhazy had been well known by Henry (of which there was no doubt), and by Sandherr; that he had been used by them in the service of counterespionage; and that, moreover, Henry had been guilty of treason in complicity with Esterhazy. The latter was said to have been paid by both sides. Esterhazy's account in the Intelligence Bureau, according to Streisser, was carried under the name of Moulins. If Esterhazy had been employed by Sandherr, Chief of the Intelligence Bureau, it would have been very surprising that neither Lieutenant-Colonel Cordier, Deputy Chief of the Bureau, nor Colonel Picquart, when he took over direction of the service, should have been told of this fact. Hence this story appeared to me highly questionable.

On the following day I received a visit from the Prince of Monaco, who wished to meet my wife and children. He was, as usual, most affable.

At a dinner I attended during the first part of February, it was my great pleasure to meet MM. Jaurès, Lanson, Dupuis, and Painlevé. Jaurès in particular made an unforgettable impression upon me. Clear eyes which lighted as he spoke; a kindly and good-natured smile; vivid and penetrating conversation, pointed with wonderful imagery and developed with serried logic; thick-set frame; impressive head—this was the impression I carried away of the man who exercised such sway over the masses. How many times I have seen him since then, and what delightful hours he has given me. His simplicity was so great! When he took his place at our table, he charmed us all with his extraordinary learning and his vivid and colorful conversation.

Jaurès spoke to me at length about the forgery known as the bordereau annoté. In his opinion, its fabrication preceded that of the "Henry forgery." It must have been devised as soon as Colonel Picquart had discovered Esterhazy, for the purpose of offsetting this discovery. In fact, it was then becoming impossible to deny the identity of the handwriting of the bordereau with that of Esterhazy. Jaurès reminded me of what Henry had said at the Zola trial: that, at the time of the trial of 1894, Sandherr had told him that he had a secret dossier more important than the one prepared by Henry. Sandherr was even alleged to have shown Henry a letter from this dossier, making him swear never to speak of it. Jaurès inferred that Henry's statement at the Zola trial was bait which would make it possible to bring forth, if necessary, the bordereau annoté.

M. Girodeau, under the pseudonym of "Vanex," was the author of the remarkable pamphlet which appeared in 1898 with the title, "Guilty or Not?" I asked for an interview to express my gratitude. I also wished to ask him—for he had been secretary to the Empress Eugénie—whether he could get any basic information bearing on the bordereau annoté from Émile Ollivier, who was said to have seen this forgery. When I saw M. Girodeau, a very gracious and charming gentleman of advanced years, he told me that Émile Ollivier's was a hazy mind, and that he would get nothing from him. Moreover, I learned later that Ollivier knew this document only by hearsay.

CHAPTER VI

WE left Paris on March 8, 1901, to return for the spring and summer to Cologny, on the shores of the Lake of Geneva. It was painful to leave my family and friends, but I was happy to find once again a little of that tranquillity which I so much needed. Since I had as yet no decisive or even important new evidence to justify an appeal, effective action in this direction was impossible. The numerous visits, incessant presentations, long conversations, the sight of disharmony among certain of my friends—all this had exhausted me. Finally, the winter, a very wet one in Paris, had caused a return of the fever of which I had had several attacks. The stay at Cologny was calm and restful. The mountains bordering on the lake were still covered with snow and the white shroud over their summits lent the scene, so cheerful in summer, an aspect of grandeur.

Upon the urgent solicitation of my friends, I decided to have Fasquelle publish my memoirs of the years 1894 to 1899 under the title, *Five Years of My Life*. As soon as I had returned to Cologny I set about correcting the proofs of my book. I sent them back to Paris by parcel post, an error, since such parcels pass through the customs and are examined. His curiosity was too much for the customs agent in charge of books: he read everything I sent to Fasquelle, and wrote me these affecting lines:

YESTERDAY as I was examining publishers' shipments, I read the sincere and moving story of your calvary. I am taking the liberty of sending you the sincere expression of my deep sympathy, of my firm belief in your innocence, and of my hope for your very early vindication, which cannot be far off now. In reading your story, I made the firm resolution never to do any wrong in my life. Please accept the expression of my deep sympathy and profound respect.

The publication of my book caused me a certain amount of annoyance. Various blunders were made by foreign publishers. They indulged in unseemly advertising when the book was announced, whereas I had expressed an earnest wish that such publicity be brief and dignified since the aim I was pursuing was essentially a moral one. The book appeared on May 1, 1901, and was well received. Fasquelle's advertising at the time of publication was fitting in every way, and in conformity with the ideas which I had expressed to them. On this occasion M. Gobert, expert of the Bank of France, sent me this very interesting letter:

Paris,
May 15, 1901.

Cher Monsieur:

I have received your splendid book with its inscription. I read it with eagerness, and with the sympathetic interest which you deserve for so many reasons.

You state—and this is not a rectification—that in 1894 only one man, Maître Demange, believed in your innocence. There were at least two: the expert Gobert and your lawyer.

On October 13—before your arrest and hence before Demange—that expert said to General Gonse: "General, if you have no other reasons for arresting the suspected officer, do not rely upon the anonymous letter. That officer is not the author. Search and I will aid you." I was right.

The same expert declared to the Minister of Justice on October 15: "Mr. Minister, at the present moment, ten-thirty o'clock, they are arresting the suspected officer (I already knew your name). I am very much afraid that they are making a mistake." And that was true.

On October 28, I said to my colleague, Pelletier, who confided in me the negative conclusions of his expert's report concerning you: "I congratulate you all the more heartily, since I don't know exactly what is behind this case; but I sense something dishonorable." That was also correct.

You see, *pauvre Monsieur,* that I, too, believed in your innocence in 1894.

I am told that you have been staying for some months in Paris. I should very much like to have the pleasure of meeting you.

Please be good enough to present my respectful greetings to Madame Dreyfus, and believe me, my dear Sir, to be,

Yours most sincerely,

R. Gobert.

. . . .

During the early part of June I had the honor of meeting, at the home of a mutual friend, Lord Rosebery, former Prime Minister of Great Britain. Lord Rosebery told me that, from the time of my degradation, he had had the feeling that I was innocent—a feeling which was changed to certainty by subsequent events. I sent him a copy of my book, *Five Years of My Life,* and he called to thank me. He told me that the Lord Chief Justice of England had been present at the trial at Rennes and that one day, as he was being driven to the courtroom, he said to his coachman, speaking of me: "But this man is innocent." The driver replied: "Well then, are the generals guilty?" The Lord Chief Justice then understood that the case no longer involved a question of justice, but a question as to who would emerge victorious from the struggle—the innocent victim or his superiors and accusers.

.   .   .   .

During this same month of June, I discussed the situation at length with my friends. The deposition which Esterhazy had made in February, 1900, before the French Consul in London, had just been published simultaneously, in two slightly different versions, by the *Siècle* and the *Indépendance belge.*[1] Although Esterhazy had been shown to be completely unreliable, I read the two versions and studied them with care. Except for the story of collusion, which had only a retrospective interest, there seemed to me to be only one aspect of real importance—Esterhazy's statement that he had written the bordereau. That statement, however, did not constitute an entirely fresh piece of evidence, since its author had already made it previously in letters to the *Matin,* confiscated on court order prior to the Rennes trial. He had repeated the story in letters to the President of the Court-Martial at Rennes. Moreover, this confession was juxtaposed with stories which were entirely false.

During the preceding month, and just at the time when the newspapers were publishing Esterhazy's deposition I had received a letter from Reinach in which he said that he saw "new evidence" in the former's confession, since that confession had

1. Esterhazy fled from France on September 1, 1898, following the disclosure of Henry's forgeries and the latter's suicide. He lived under assumed names, and was finally found dead on May 21, 1923, in a lodging house in Harpenden, a town of 5,000 inhabitants not far from St. Albans, Hertfordshire, England. At the time he was known as the Count de Voilement, and as a result of this incognito his death was discovered by the London press only on August 10 (*see New York Times,* August 17, 26, 1923).

now been officially received. I requested him to act as my representative and ask Maître Mornard for a legal opinion on the matter. On May 16, M. Havet wrote me expressing the same view; according to him, the Esterhazy deposition was of capital importance. He went on: "Beyond the theoretical and retrospective interest of the part concerning conspiracy—the sole aspect to strike me on first reading—there are two points of major importance: (1) the formal declaration that Esterhazy is the actual author of the bordereau; (2) the exact explanation of the way in which the bordereau fell into the hands of the Intelligence Bureau." He concluded by saying that it was my duty, with or *without* hope of immediate success, to demand an appeal, and that this opinion was shared by Colonel Picquart and Psichari.

As to M. Havet's first point, there was in fact the formal declaration of Esterhazy that he was the author of the bordereau. But I have already stated my opinion of that declaration, both from a legal and an ethical point of view. As to the second point, the way in which the bordereau had come to the Ministry, a mere declaration by Esterhazy would not suffice; a preliminary investigation would be essential to verify the accuracy of his statement. As for my own duty, I deemed that it did not consist in inviting a defeat, but in achieving the object I was pursuing—the legal review of my case. A defeat before the Court, by reason of legal niceties which the public would not have understood, would have been extensively exploited by our adversaries, and would have meant a retreat. I could not, therefore, view my duty as M. Havet understood it. I replied to him that I had asked the opinion of Maître Mornard and that I was awaiting his response.

On May 18, I received another letter from M. Havet which stated that, in his opinion and that of Colonel Picquart, we must go ahead at all costs, no matter what the consequences. I replied that since he was to visit me at Cologny some days later, I would tell him then what my objections were. Finally, on June 11, Maître Mornard's opinion reached me. It was flatly unfavorable to a request for an appeal, based on Esterhazy's official deposition in London. To this opinion, Maître Mornard added a letter he had received from Colonel Picquart, which included the following: "The prospect of a failure would not hinder me, far from it. . . . If there were only one chance in a thousand of success, I should still say that our duty was to march forward." I held the contrary view. One does not engage a battle which may have such serious consequences—as much from the point of view of the country's interest as from my own—in the face of almost certain defeat.

My decision had now been reached. I wrote my friends that, after having consulted Maître Mornard, I felt that we must resolve to wait still longer, however discouraging that might be. If we were to have serious chance of success, we must pursue with more energy than ever our search for evidence from a less suspect source, or else obtain verification of certain elements in the Esterhazy evidence. It should be noted, moreover, that when I later presented to the Court my request for an appeal (which was finally successful), I cited Esterhazy's deposition before the French Consul in London as one of the elements of fresh evidence on which I was relying. The Court refused to accept it as "new evidence." Hence I had been well advised not to base a request for an appeal on this single fact, not to undertake, to speak frankly, a bootless offensive.

Toward the end of October, 1901, we took our final departure for Paris, regretfully leaving behind us the delightful shores of the Lake of Geneva. The people there had been most cordial and had done much to make our stay agreeable. Before our departure I received from Marc Debrit, editor of the *Journal de Genève*, the following letter, which greatly touched me for it expressed sentiments whose sincerity we had been in a position to appreciate:

Cher Monsieur:

I learn that you are leaving us, not, I hope, for good. For you are aware that you have Geneva's affection—and I should like you to preserve a kindly memory of that fact. You will nowhere find a milieu more deeply cordial. And I trust that you will one day return, no longer as you came, a martyr of destiny, but after you have obtained that complete vindication which is your due.

CHAPTER VII

WE reached Paris on October 26, 1901. . . . During the month of November, I brought together all the facts which I then had concerning the forgery known as the bordereau annoté, and the occult role it was supposed to have played. I arrived at the following conclusions. In the face of the insufficiency of the accusation, the Rennes judgment remained incomprehensible. The surroundings, the pressure exerted by the generals, the lies of the Merciers, the Deloyes, the Rogets, and others, accepted by the members of the Court-Martial as words of truth, were not adequate, it seemed to me, completely to explain my unjust condemnation. On the contrary, everything was explained by the hypothesis that either the contents of the bordereau annoté were secretly communicated to one or several of the judges at Rennes, or, what seemed to me more probable, its existence was affirmed. Moreover, the bordereau annoté and the so-called letter of the German Emperor, which had been discussed in the press, were probably one and the same document. No one had ever seen this letter of the German Emperor, but it is conceivable that those who fabricated the bordereau annoté sometimes referred to it as the German Emperor's letter, since the alleged marginalia were signed ''Wilhelm''—unless there were actually two forgeries.

The official proof of the existence of this document was the testimony of Paléologue before the Court of Cassation in 1899, when he declared that Lieutenant-Colonel Henry had, on the second or third of November, 1897, alluded to a letter of the German Emperor. Furthermore, it had often been spoken of in the newspapers at this time, and in certain *salons*. The existence of the bordereau annoté was again referred to by the newspapers during the Rennes trial. The *Gaulois* of August 14, 1899, published an article entitled, ''Open Letter to General Mercier.'' This letter, in which was related the history of the alleged bordereau, the one which had had to be returned but of which photographs had been kept, concluded: ''You possess one of the copies of this photograph and you took it with you to Rennes. These facts explain the substitution of Esterhazy. He could truthfully say that the bordereau had been written by him, and you could declare with equal truth that it was the work of Dreyfus.'' The *Gaulois* article was copied by the *Libre parole* and the *Intransigeant* of August 15, 1899.

After the Rennes trial, there appeared in the *Croix* of September 21, 1899, an article entitled, ''Why was Dreyfus pardoned?'' It follows:

THE Dreyfusards themselves are surprised at the speed with which the President of the Republic has pardoned Dreyfus, for some of them were relying on a new trial which would result in acquittal. They were obliged to give up that hope, on the threat that a photograph of the original of the bordereau would be produced, a document which a statesman, in a situation to be well informed, assures us contains the following annotation in the hand of Emperor William: "Send me as soon as possible the documents indicated, have this scoundrel of a Dreyfus hurry. Wilhelm." General Mercier has photographs of the said bordereau, and seven other persons have copies.

On September 20, 1900, there appeared in the *Fronde* an article by Séverine, with the title: ''The Scapulary of General Mercier.'' She related that a gentleman of good birth and of widely recognized respectability had vainly attempted to convince her of my alleged guilt by telling her the story of the bordereau annoté On December 25, 1900, the *Intransigeant* published an article by Rochefort, concerning the same document, which confirmed Séverine's story in so far as the document's existence was concerned. It is true that Rochefort was not explicit as to the condemnation at Rennes, but he declared that this document was the reason for my conviction. He concluded his article: ''At this time (before Rennes), it was perhaps patriotic to be silent. It is now patriotic to speak.'' At once I wrote to M. Waldeck-Rousseau, the Premier, the letter which I have quoted above,[1] requesting an investigation. I was also hopeful that, when this letter was published, Rochefort would speak and say all that he knew. But the investigation was not granted and Rochefort at once lapsed into silence.

Later I was told by Reinach of the conversation which Lieu-

1. *See* p. 166.

tenant-Colonel Jourdy, now General Jourdy, had had with M. Wyroubof, Professor in the Collège de France. Lieutenant-Colonel Jourdy, who was an alternate judge at the Rennes trial, said that "during the whole trial the judges frequently spoke of the bordereau annoté, whose existence had been revealed to them during the trial by the *Intransigeant* or the *Libre parole,* and that *several* of them considered the bordereau on thin paper to be a 'tracing.' " It is obvious that, in order to believe the bordereau on thin paper to be a tracing, it was necessary to suppose that the bordereau on heavy paper (that is, the bordereau annoté) was authentic.

Maître Demange told me this story. A short time after the Rennes trial he encountered on the train Captain Moreau, adjutant to General Chamoin, representative of the Ministry of War at the trial. Maître Demange evinced astonishment at the "extenuating circumstances." Captain Moreau replied: "They are, however, easily understood. In the juryroom, when Colonel Jouaust, President of the Court-Martial, saw that conviction was certain, he intervened sharply and forcefully. His statements won back two or three judges. They looked for a solution, and the result was 'extenuating circumstances.' " To what did the explanations of Colonel Jouaust refer? May we not think that they referred to the legend of the bordereau annoté? In summary, I now understood that here was a question for which it was of the first importance to seek an answer.

. . . .

In the *Grande revue,* of which he was editor, Maître Labori published an article in which he expressed regret that I had accepted the pardon, and that I had consistently refused to countenance an agitation which I considered sterile. Some days later, in the *Petite république,* Jaurès wrote a remarkable criticism of this article, analyzing in noble and forceful words the situation in which I had been placed:

AND then, what purpose would have been served had he refused the pardon and walled himself up in his prison? It is an illusion to believe that by that fact the battle would have been maintained and inspired. The appearance of fresh evidence, juridically necessary to renew the campaign for appeal with any hope of success, would not have been hastened by one minute; the public mind would have been wearied by idle gossip; and the national conscience would have been annoyed, rather than shocked, by a punishment for which Alfred Dreyfus himself would have been responsible, and from which the material element had been removed. Finally, after the Rennes verdict, in which the vote of two judges for acquittal and the extenuating circumstances had emphasized the anxiety of the Court, the pardon, tacitly accepted by the whole nation, already had the character of partial amends. It was the sole means by which the French conscience could free itself in a measure and correct, in so far as it depended on her, the infamy of the legal judgment.

It will not appear in history as a renunciation of justice but, on the contrary, as humanity's pledge of complete justice. . . .

And further on:

BUT, although that vehement and poignant aspect of the drama appears to be at an end, it is not forgotten. And on the day when the complete truth is legally proclaimed, on the day when the justice of the courts is forced to shatter the monstrous judgment of Paris, the battle which we have undertaken will reveal its full significance. . . . Truth has not said its last word against the forgers and the traitors. The sovereign word, which it will one day pronounce with the serenity of the law, will not only restore legal honor to an innocent and outraged man, but will add to the weight of discredit under which these powers of untruth are slowly descending.

On January 2, 1902, I received a splendid letter from M. Trarieux, in which he expressed his wish for my final vindication and spiritual rest. Alas, instead of being able to concern myself solely with this final vindication, which I pursued with all my strength, I was only too often obliged to intervene to pacify conflicts which arose among the friends of my cause, and to reply to more or less ungracious criticism. Although the infamous attacks of the opponents of truth left me indifferent (so great was my contempt for them), the excitability and the undisguised bitterness of certain of our friends were not without their painful side.

In an article which appeared in the *Bloc* of February 2, Clemenceau declared that, owing to the fact that I had accepted the pardon, "Waldeck-Rousseau could arrest the course of justice, with the aid of the condemned man himself.'' I called on Clemenceau the next day. He told me that he had wished to make no criticism of me, but that it was his conviction that accepting the pardon had meant the death of the Affair, from the point of view of the public. . . . Accepting the pardon, however, hindered nothing; quite the contrary, it allowed me to achieve the final triumph. In any event, I replied to him that I had a very different conception of the matter but that every man had a right to his own opinion. What was inadmissible was to conclude, as he did, that because the pardon had produced unfortunate results, I had helped to bring about those results. He declared that this had not been his thought. But that was what everyone read in his words. On the next day I learned that Mathieu, as soon as he heard of the article in the *Bloc*, had sent Clemenceau this letter:

THE following passage in your article in yesterday's *Bloc*—"It is then that Waldeck-Rousseau and Millerand appear . . . they can arrest the course of justice with the aid of the condemned man himself"—pained me deeply, and I am too fond of you not to tell you so frankly.

Recall what happened at the Ministry of Commerce, forty-eight hours after the condemnation—your emotion when I said to you: "I will not separate myself from you; if you persist in wanting the pardon refused, I agree." And then, after a long silence, your words: "If I were your brother, I should accept." And then the mission I was given, and the pressure I had to exert on my brother to wrest from him the withdrawal of his request for an appeal. After I have recalled these facts, do not your words seem to you unreasonable?"

Clemenceau replied to Mathieu in the following letter:

I AM deeply sorry to have caused you pain, but I can only say to you what I said to your brother this morning when he came to present his own grievance.

I attack no one, for I know what excuses can be offered. I simply stated an undeniable fact without which our defeat would be changed to triumph, not for you, but for France and the ideal involved.

You must know, my dear friend, that I am much more inclined to defend you than to attack you. But how could you refuse me the right to place a fact in its historical context, when a review of political events imposes that obligation upon me? Moreover, your brother understands that perfectly, and he thanked me on parting.

I wrote to Mathieu:

CLEMENCEAU's letter confirms in general what he said to me. As a matter of fact, I recognized his right to interpret a fact from a historical point of view. But I added that his words were ambiguous, since it appeared that he meant that I had had a hand in the results which, according to him, had flowed from the pardon. Whereas in reality I could not know, much less foresee, these alleged results. . . . As we parted I did in fact thank him, but I thanked him for the cordial sentiments which he expressed concerning both you and myself, and not for the words he had written and of which we had justly complained. . . .

The parliamentary elections which were to take place April 27 occupied public attention at this time. The Nationalists were still active, thanks to the weakness of Waldeck-Rousseau's Government. If Mercier and his accomplices had received the punishment their crime warranted, the situation would have been very different. Two days before the elections, the Nationalists made use of an ambiguous letter written by General de Gallifet during the Rennes trial. This letter threw light upon some obscure points in the drama. It revealed that the members of the Government had had the intention of bringing the unjust and illegal judgment of Rennes before the Court of Cassation on a plea of abuse of power, but that General de Gallifet had caused them to retreat when he drew in lurid colors the imaginary specter of the Army in revolt. . . .

I also saw Maître Demange who had had a long conversation with Waldeck-Rousseau. The latter, said Maître Demange, was as sympathetic as ever toward my cause. He also told me that, in the period between the proceedings before the Court of Cassation, in 1899, and the Rennes trial, the Government was said to have had our Ambassador at Berlin ask semiofficially whether, if the documents enumerated in the bordereau were asked for officially, they would be surrendered. It appears that the reply was negative, and would be even in the case of an official request. I was of the opinion, however, after what had been told me previously, that the response was only negative because the request was only

semiofficial. Furthermore, Waldeck-Rousseau told Maître Demange that, following the request for an inquiry which I directed
to him at the end of 1900 and which involved the bordereau annoté, he had done everything that he could to throw light on the
role played by this forgery, but that he did not succeed largely as
a result of the ill-will of the soldiers. . . .

CHAPTER VIII

I SEIZED upon the occasion offered by a splendid article in the *Radical* by Ranc to send him the following public letter, for the purpose of dissipating the shameless stories which were regularly appearing:

July 28, 1902.

My dear M. Ranc:

. . . Since everyone knows today that I am not the author of the bordereau, some people are spreading the rumor that I had in fact never had anything to do with Germany, but that I had had traffic with Russia. This does not appear in print, but it is spread as a rumor. According to some people, I sold to Russia our real mobilization figures which revealed the falsity of the figures produced by General de Boisdeffre at the time of the conclusion of the alliance.[1] According to others, I was directed by General de Boisdeffre to give to Russia our mobilization figures (which the General himself had placed in my hands), so that the figures obtained by spies would confirm the official statistics.

You shrug your shoulders, *cher Monsieur et ami,* in the face of such nonsense!

Some weeks ago General de Gallifet said to our friend, Joseph Reinach, who authorized me to make whatever use I liked of the statement: "The bordereau was by Esterhazy, who had two accomplices. As to Dreyfus, he never had anything to do with Germany. But someone, whom I cannot name, told me at Marienbad that Dreyfus had been in the service of Russia." Joseph Reinach protested, but General de Gallifet held his ground.

Need I tell you that this whole story is an abominable lie, and that I have never had anything to do with Russia, any more than with Germany. You will do me a great service, my dear M. Ranc, in publishing this letter. It is my only means of crushing this stupid and odious legend. It must be brought out into the full light of day, if it is to be destroyed. People will perhaps believe the Russian Government when it declares that it has never had any traffic with me. I defy General de Boisdeffre to say that I had any relations with Russia.

M. Hugues le Roux declares that M. Félix Faure said to him: "The review of the Dreyfus case is essential, because it is legal." M. Félix Faure is supposed to have known better than anyone else all the circum-

1. The Franco-Russian Alliance, concluded 1891–94.

stances relating to the Franco-Russian Alliance. He also knew that I was absolutely and completely innocent.

The day will come when impressive new evidence will permit me to solicit a legal review, to seek again my legal honor. But meanwhile, help me to put an end to this silly legend which circulates in the dark.

General de Gallifet replied in the *Journal des débats,* in an absurd letter to which I replied in turn on August 4, protesting the inaccuracy of his memory.

.   .   .   .

One of the judges in the Rennes trial, Major Merle, had retired and was living at Montpellier. I had already made several attempts, through Major Merle and through other judges who were at Rennes, to discover the influences which made themselves felt there. One of my friends, Dr. Dumas, whose family lived in the South and who had a brother-in-law at Montpellier, was good enough to undertake a fresh attempt. Moreover, I had decided that if we should fail again I would ask the Minister of War for an inquiry. But I learned that Major Merle would be absent from Montpellier until October 10, hence that Dr. Dumas could not see him at this time. . . .

I called on M. Trarieux . . ., who told me that he had seen General Percin, General André's Chef du Cabinet. He asked General Percin whether he thought that General André would grant the inquiry I would perhaps solicit. General Percin replied: "I cannot answer for General André. He is as convinced as you and I of the innocence of Captain Dreyfus. But if he should receive a request for an inquiry, it seems clear to me that he would do nothing without the advice of the Cabinet." I told M. Trarieux my reasons for waiting until October. I wanted to do nothing before I learned the results which I hoped Dr. Dumas' step would produce.

.   .   .   .

At six o'clock on the afternoon of September 29, I was deeply dismayed to learn that Zola had died in the course of the day, asphyxiated by gas from an improperly functioning chimney, and that Mme. Zola was in grave danger. Overwhelmed by this terrible tragedy, I hastened to the Rue de Bruxelles, but I was unable to gain entry to his house for they were at that very moment taking Mme. Zola to a hospital in Neuilly. I returned to Zola's home on the next day. With an indescribable sense of grief I saw him stretched upon his bed, his face as calm and tranquil as though he were asleep. I was deeply shaken to see this dear and noble friend, who, in his full vigor and in the midst of his labors, had been struck down by a senseless accident. His creative power and his genius as a novelist are well known, but enough has never been said of his generosity and unselfishness. I went each morning to meditate over the mortal remains of Zola. How I loved this man, so upright and so kind! His innate goodness reflected a noble conscience.

On October 2 I saw Mme. Zola, whose life had been saved. Our greeting was sad indeed. Together we mourned our loss. Mme. Zola then made a very grievous request of me. I considered it a duty to be present at the funeral of her husband, but she was fearful lest my presence should give rise to hostile demonstrations. "If anything should happen to you," she said, "or if unpleasant incidents should occur, I should never forgive myself."

I assured Mme. Zola of my respect and devotion, but I replied that I feared nothing, that I despised the insults which might be proffered by a few worthless fellows, and that it would be very painful to me to fail in a cardinal duty. And I expressed to her my firm resolution to be present at the funeral. But she was insistent and begged me again to accede to her request. Faced by so urgent a wish, I yielded, asking in return only the honor of watching over Zola during the final night.

Two days later when I arrived at Mme. Zola's house, I found her deeply moved by a telegram she had just received from Anatole France which read about as follows: "Under these circumstances, it is impossible for me to speak at Zola's grave." She explained to me that she had asked France to extol Zola as a literary figure and novelist, that France had replied that he must also refer to the author of the letter, "J'accuse," and that he could only do that in a forceful manner—otherwise his words would have no meaning. Mme. Zola had then sent him this telegram: "Relying upon your tact, I leave you your liberty and am counting on you." But Anatole France had interpreted the words, "relying upon your tact," as a restriction and had so replied in the telegram which had just arrived. Mme. Zola asked my advice. I told her that she had simply to reply to France that she gave him complete liberty, without any limitations whatever. This she did.

The evening of the same day a relative of Mme. Zola called on me to say that I need not keep my promise to absent myself from her husband's funeral. On the final night, that of October 4 and 5, I watched over the body of the great novelist, along with Mme. Zola, Mme. Laborde, Octave Mirbeau, and Alfred Bruneau. We passed a great part of the night in talking of Zola, of his too-little-known kindness and unselfishness. This indefatigable worker, this fighter, was at heart a shy person.

The burial took place on October 5. I accompanied this great and noble friend, whose loss was irreparable, to his final resting place. There were three eulogies. That of Anatole France, in the name of his friends, was admirable. These passages deeply stirred me:

I MUST, however, also refer to the struggle of Zola for truth and justice. Can I keep silent concerning those who were bent upon the ruin of an innocent man, and who, since they felt themselves lost if he were saved, overwhelmed him in the desperate audacity of fear? How can I exclude them from your view, when I ought to show you Zola, standing erect, weak and disarmed, before them. Can I keep silent about their lies? That would be to keep silent about his heroic integrity. Can I remain silent about their crimes? That would mean to be silent about his virtue. Am I to say nothing of the outrages and insults with which he was persecuted? That would be to say nothing of his rewards and his honors. Am I to be silent about their shame? That would mean to be silent about his fame. No, I shall speak. . . .

Let us envy him: he brought honor to his country and the world by the extent of his labors and by a noble act. Let us envy him: his genius and his heart made for him the greatest of all destinies. In him lived for a moment the conscience of humanity.

. . . .

I was again sadly bereaved in this month of October, 1902. On Wednesday, the fifteenth, we dined at the home of my father-in-law, M. Hadamard, who was in good health and very happy in the circle of his children. After dinner he suffered an indisposition, which passed. Then the pain returned and became more in-

plus sublime des spectacles, l'a-
veu d'une erreur. Ce jour là,
l'armée ne sera pas seulement
la force, elle sera la justice.

Mon cœur déborde, et je
ne puis que vous envoyer toute
ma fraternité pour ce que vous
avez souffert, pour ce qu'a souffert votre vaillante femme. La
mienne se joint à moi et
c'est ce que nous avons en nous
de meilleur, le plus noble et de plus
tendre, que je voudrais mettre dans
cette, pour que vous sentiez que tous les
braves gens sont avec vous

Je vous embrasse affectueusement. Émile Zola

Greetings from Émile Zola to Dreyfus upon his return to France.

tense. At three o'clock in the morning my beloved father-in-law passed away, the victim of angina pectoris. We suffered keenly and deeply from our loss. One needed to have known this splendid man to appreciate his integrity and his fine moral sense. As was admirably said over his grave: "Even during the storm of the Affair, no slander touched this unsullied life."

In October Dr. Dumas went, as arranged, to Montpellier, where he was presented by his brother-in-law to Major Merle. I received letters from him daily, informing me of the progress of his attempt to learn the truth as to what had taken place at the Rennes trial. At the end of the month I submitted to Maître Mornard all this correspondence, which disclosed implicitly that the bordereau annoté had exercised an important influence on the judges. Maître Mornard considered the proof not sufficiently decisive to warrant going directly before the Court of Cassation. He was afraid, moreover, that an inadequately prepared inquiry would fail. He preferred to wait for more satisfactory evidence.

He told me of a conversation which he had had some time before with M. Bard, then Justice of the Court of Cassation and later Presiding Justice of the Criminal Division. When Maître Mornard said to him that pardon was no solution and that I did not consider it such, M. Bard replied: "That solution would in fact represent the bankruptcy of justice." Encouraged by this very clear and frank criticism, Maître Mornard spoke to M. Bard of the differences which had arisen between us and certain of our friends, the latter wishing to take action under any circumstances, no matter what the value of the evidence in hand or what the consequences might be. Justice Bard strongly deprecated this attitude and declared that we must not return to the Court of Cassation until we had evidence which might lead to a reversal of the judgment. Maître Mornard then told him of the letter which he had received during the preceding year from Lieutenant-Colonel Picquart, in which the latter had said that we must seize upon any pretext for action, even if we had only one chance in a thousand of success. M. Bard was completely opposed to this point of view, and shared the opinion of Maître Mornard, who considered that the situation in 1902 was not at all the same as that existing prior to the first appeal to the Court. Then, the state of affairs could not have become any worse, and it was necessary to try anything, no matter how slight the chance of success. In 1902, however, the situation was such that every defeat would have meant a step backward.

I replied to Maître Mornard that he knew I shared his views and that, despite the reproof of certain of my friends, I had always refused to act in the dark. At present, however, I believed it was opportune to attempt to clarify the role played at the Rennes trial by the bordereau annoté. And since, with the evidence then at our disposal, much time might pass before we should find decisive proof on this point, it appeared to me to be my duty to request an inquiry. Such an inquiry, if properly conducted, would probably give us the evidence necessary to secure an appeal. I asked Maître Mornard to be good enough to draft in legal form the request for an inquiry. Then I called in succession on M. Trarieux, Ferdinand Buisson, and Jaurès, to inform them of my decision. They all advised me to wait for the end of the senatorial elections before acting. All these discussions could not be carried on without many of my friends being informed of my intentions; and so great numbers of them came to bring me their advice, which I listened to and weighed with the greatest care. Certain of them, however, were offended when they saw that I was not following blindly the plans which they had suggested. . . .

On the evening of November 21, M. Trarieux came to call, accompanied by his son Jean. He read and gave me a letter in which he urged me to request an appeal. He believed that the Committee formed in the Ministry of Justice to examine requests for appeal would itself, through an investigation, find proof for the new evidence whose existence I was to point out. M. Trarieux forgot that this Committee had for its sole function verification of the accuracy of the proofs which I should furnish, and determination as to whether the new evidence presented fell within the prescriptions of the law. In order to induce me to request an appeal, M. Trarieux relied upon a statement to the effect that Major Pauffin de Saint-Morel had informed Rochefort of the existence of the bordereau annoté in 1897. Even if this statement had been established as a fact—which was not the case—it would not have proved that this information had also been given to the judges at

Rennes. M. Trarieux's plan offered no practical solution, but one passage in the letter that he read me was interesting. The fact which he related was confirmed for me a few days later by Lieutenant-Colonel Hartmann, who heard it from General Percin:

GENERAL ANDRÉ, it was said, had on two different occasions examined Major Pauffin de Saint-Morel, and had asked him to tell what had taken place. The Major did not deny, said the Minister, either his visit to Rochefort or his patriotic divulgation, but he refused to talk and took refuge in ambiguities. It was his duty, he said, not to compromise his superiors who had placed their confidence in him.

Meanwhile General de Boisdeffre had written to General André, not for the purpose of enlightening him on the accuracy of the fact, but to tell him that he ought to be indulgent, that he must not punish too severely his former adjutant whose attitude had been prompted by the fear of causing a scandal.

I was very much astonished that General André had not considered himself obliged, under these circumstances, to order Major Pauffin to give full explanations.

.   .   .   .

On November 27, there appeared the second volume of Joseph Reinach's *Histoire de l'Affaire Dreyfus*. The book is admirably written and intensely interesting throughout. It is a distinguished work and one for which I am very grateful to Reinach. My only regret was that he had sometimes been too indulgent toward adversaries who were dishonest and unscrupulous, and a little too severe toward friends who, even if they had committed tactical errors, had revealed admirable traits of courage and of conscience.

The *Gaulois* of December 13 published the following article concerning me:

EVEN if he did not commit the treason for which he was twice condemned, does he not remain, in the eyes of all, the initial cause of the terrible social and political disorganization which we now witness.

This revolution, coldly conceived and methodically executed by his companions, will bear his detested name in history. It is now called, it will always be called, "Dreyfusism."

This reasoning was admirable. It denoted a state of fatuity, not

on the part of the author of the article, who did not believe a
word of it, but on the part of readers accessible to such humbug.
The disturbance within our political and social complex was the
work of those who sought to maintain this injustice. The responsibility was to be charged to their crime, not to my innocence.
The Affair had not been the cause, but the consequence, of weaknesses in the preëxisting social state. The Affair had revealed this
condition, not created it. Since that time two groups had been
formed—on one side were the friends of justice, on the other, the
men of little conscience. This distinction is worth more than all
the others. In a word, the Affair helped to cast a little light into
those political shadows and into that social darkness from which
we were suffering.

CHAPTER IX

I SAW Jaurès, in November, 1902, to tell him of the results obtained on the bordereau annoté, and of my intention to request an investigation. He asked me to come and see him again in the course of the following January, after the senatorial elections. I saw him, with Maître Mornard on January 11. We examined the situation at length. Jaurès told me that if I asked the Government if it were willing to receive my request for an investigation, I should elicit a dilatory response, something on this order: let the request be first submitted, and we will examine it. He explained to us with emphasis that the Government must be made to feel that it had the Republican party solidly behind it. It must also be made to understand the importance of taking away from its adversaries the poisoned weapon of an unresolved case, which the latter used on every occasion. After an exchange of views we agreed on the following plan. Jaurès would seize as a pretext the discussion of the election of Syveton in Paris, where use had been made of the poster on the "Ministère de l'étranger."[1] He would then denounce the crime of 1899 and lay the question before Parliament.

I also called on Clemenceau. He had just arrived by train from the Var but he received me at once. When I informed him of Jaurès' project, he exclaimed: "That's dangerous. The Cabinet will already be discussing the reinstatement of Colonel Picquart. You may hinder that." I replied: "I should be deeply gratified by the reinstatement of Colonel Picquart, which will make only slight and tardy amends. But the discussion of the Syveton election is some time off, and so will not interfere with the discussion of the proposal to reinstate Picquart. On the other hand, do you think that my request for an investigation would be favorably

1. In the general elections of 1902, Gabriel Syveton, one of the leaders of the Ligue de la Patrie Française, a candidate in the Second Arrondissement of Paris, had prepared a poster in which he characterized the Waldeck-Rousseau Government as the "Ministère de l'étranger." Although he was elected on the first ballot by a large majority, a request that his election be invalidated was submitted to the Chamber. The investigation lasted some months, and the committee's report was discussed only on April 6, 1903.

received by the Government, if you made a direct overture to that effect yourself?" "No," he said, "certainly not. Take the initiative yourself." To which I replied: "But I will be taking the initiative in submitting to the Government my request for an investigation, after the intervention of Jaurès. The latter aims simply to oblige the Government to receive it, since you recognize yourself that a direct intervention would not produce this result." In the end, it was decided that Clemenceau should discuss the matter with Jaurès. . . .

I saw Jaurès again some days later. He had won Clemenceau to our plan. He had, moreover, talked with Ranc, who was always ready to give us his complete coöperation, and he was to see Waldeck-Rousseau.

The same evening I saw Maître Demange who had talked with Waldeck-Rousseau. The latter, he told me, understood my very keen desire to secure a judicial review of the Rennes decision, but he considered the request for an investigation dangerous since it might not succeed. Maître Demange went on to say that Waldeck-Rousseau had little confidence in the representatives of the Ministry of War and in the independence of the officers who would be summoned to testify, but knew a very reliable person at Rennes who could give us more complete information than we already possessed concerning what happened at the trial of 1899. I explained to Maître Demange how favorable the situation was for this action, and that it was impossible to wait indefinitely, and then run the chance of uncertain results. For more than two years now we had been making every possible effort. Moreover, there was still sufficient time before the intervention of Jaurès for Waldeck-Rousseau to obtain more precise and positive information.

I also attempted at this time, by going to the sources themselves, to verify all the stories relative to what happened at the time the vote was taken by the Court-Martial at Rennes. After all my investigations, I succeeded only in verifying what Maître Demange had learned directly from Captain Moreau, adjutant to General Chamoin—namely, that when Colonel Jouaust brought the voting to an end by casting his own vote for acquittal, he was dumbfounded by the result his conduct of the proceedings had produced and made a speech which won back two or three judges.

Then they looked about for a solution—which was "extenuating circumstances"! How had he won over these judges? What speech had he delivered to them? Did he, as certain men have claimed, refuse to accept a new vote—for acquittal—under pretext that it was illegal? I was able to get no light on this subject.

During the early part of February I met Maître Leblois at the office of Maître Mornard. The former criticized our plans at length, without, however, offering anything better. His remarks took this line: If I should submit my request for an investigation after the intervention of Jaurès, I should appear to be following in his furrow. I replied that it would be much less natural for Jaurès to follow in mine. He then added that, if I did this, I would let Jaurès capture the Affair as a representative of the Socialist party. I replied that Jaurès was interested in the Affair by conviction and as a public figure, and that it was the place of all Republicans to lend him their support. Furthermore, I defied him to find another deputy in Parliament who dared take such a step. I pass in silence over the other remarks of Leblois, but, since he told me that he was speaking not only for himself but for Colonel Picquart and certain other friends, I promised to submit his ideas to Jaurès.

Jaurès replied that he was taking this step in the interest of the country and not merely in the interest of an individual. Should his intervention take place after the submission of my request for an investigation its effect would be diminished, for he would then appear merely in the guise of my attorney, coming to the tribune to support my request. Moreover, his intervention in the Chamber of Deputies might lead to revelations which none could foresee and which might modify the tenor of my request. Finally, if I asked for an investigation before his intervention, and if, as the result of some incident during the session, the latter were postponed, I should risk finding myself in an embarrassing position. Since I shared Jaurès' opinion, I naturally approved of what he said and urged him to see Leblois and set forth these arguments himself. Leblois came to see me the next day and told me frankly that Jaurès had successfully met all his arguments.

On February 6, Jaurès discussed with me the plan of his speech in the Chamber. It was perfect. He was to develop the occult role which the bordereau annoté had played in the Affair and the way in which it had finally exercised an influence on the minds of certain judges at Rennes. Every time that there had been any danger, the bordereau was stealthily discussed and reasons of state were invoked to convince those who were hesitating. Jaurès was determined to force all of the actors in the drama to appear on the stage. He would tear off every disguise, and would oblige them to explain themselves publicly.

Jaurès told me also of the conversation he had had with Waldeck-Rousseau, who expressed his hearty sympathy for the work of justice which Jaurès was about to undertake, but recommended prudence. He advised Jaurès in relating the history of the bordereau annoté to make use only of public documents and official testimony. Finally, he approved Jaurès' intervention from the tribune of the Chamber but thought that it would be preferable that I should not immediately thereafter submit my request for an investigation. I could thus await revelations the speech might bring forth. This was not my view, but I agreed that I could not make a final decision until the intervention had taken place. . . .

On March 7 I received a visit from M. Semenoff, Paris correspondent of the Russian newspaper, *Novosti,* and deeply devoted to my cause. He told me this story. Mme. Séverine gave him the name of the person who had furnished her with the material for her article on the bordereau annoté, which had appeared in the *Fronde,* December 20, 1900. This was M. Ferlet de Bourbonne, whom M. Semenoff sought out and finally, after several interviews, induced to speak. M. Ferlet de Bourbonne admitted that he had talked to Mme. Séverine about the bordereau annoté, and that he had told her General Mercier had with him at Rennes a photograph of this document. He had not, however, declared that the bordereau had been communicated to the judges but had simply said that in all likelihood it must have been. M. Ferlet de Bourbonne then told M. Semenoff this story of the bordereau annoté. The bordereau and the documents indicated therein arrived in Berlin. The bordereau was then annotated by the Emperor himself as follows: "Send as soon as possible the documents indicated. Make this scoundrel of a Dreyfus hurry. [Signed] : Wilhelm.'' This document, the most colossal forgery of the Affair (in which, moreover, forgeries had sprung up on every side), then came back to Paris. There it was purloined from the German Embassy by an agent of the French Ministry of War. But Herr von Münster, the German Ambassador, threatened M. Casimir-Périer, President of the Republic, who was obliged to return the document and to swear on the Bible that he would never speak of it. However, before returning the document, General Mercier took care to have it photographed. Since they could not show a photograph to the Court-Martial in 1894 as the basis of the accusation brought against me, they had had a tracing of the document, without the annotation, made by Esterhazy who was then in the service of Sandherr. The human mind would indeed need to be credulous to accept such fables, for their improbability is patent. But above all how could Esterhazy, tracing a document said to have been written in my hand, have reproduced not my writing but his own?

. . . .

In February Lieutenant-Colonel Hartmann came to see me on a moving errand. He told me that the Minister of War had in his possession a document which would enable me to reopen my case —that the question of appeal was now up to him. He had not himself seen the document, but General Percin, the Minister's Chef du Cabinet, had talked to him about it. I arranged to have Colonel Hartmann meet Jaurès at my house. He repeated what he had told me, and added that the document had been seen and read by General Percin. General André, the Minister of War, had discovered the document in his drawer when he took over the Ministry. It seemed to me amazing that General André should have kept this document to himself, if it had this importance, and should have failed to submit it officially to the Minister of Justice. In any event it was agreed, some days before the discussion of the Syveton election, that Colonel Hartmann should ask General Percin what this document contained. If he should refuse to reply, Jaurès would precipitate an incident over the question from the tribune.

Some time later in the Senate, Clemenceau interpellated the

Minister of War on sanitary conditions in the Army, apropos the very sad death of Colonel Hartmann's son, who had died quite suddenly while doing his year of military service at Rouen. We all shared his profound grief. He was unable to secure the moral amends which he had a right to expect and was deeply wounded. Henceforth he refused to intervene on my behalf. I told Jaurès of this decision. He quite understood Colonel Hartmann's very natural grief but he deplored his attitude. He agreed to write himself to General Percin for an interview, so that he might ask him the contents of the document in the Minister's hands.

I saw Jaurès again on March 29 and was deeply disappointed. General Percin had revealed the contents of the famous document in question, whose secret had been so closely guarded, the document which by itself was to enable us to reopen the case. This document was none other than the letter which General de Pellieux wrote on August 31, 1898, requesting his retirement, immediately after the Henry forgery was discovered (a forgery of which he had made use at the Zola trial). This letter used unmeasured language concerning those who had deceived him, and was susceptible of producing a great moral effect on the Chamber, but it offered no basis for requesting an appeal. Jaurès agreed that he would try to secure the exact text of the letter. This he did through Brisson, who requested it from the Minister of War. The letter included in particular this sentence: "I have lost confidence in those of my superiors who had given me forgeries with which to work." Brisson was to produce an incident in the Chamber, at the time of Jaurès' intervention, and was to ask Cavaignac how it was that he, Brisson, had not been informed of this letter by his Minister of War when they were in the midst of a crisis.

On the day preceding that on which Jaurès was to speak, M. Ferdinand Buisson, Deputy from the Seine, came to tell me how disturbed many members of the Chamber were concerning Jaurès' intervention. The Left groups were not pleased by the importance which Jaurès was assuming and by the fact that he wished to drag them along after him without consultation. As a safeguard against all danger of an order of the day condemning, as in the last Parliament, "all revival of the Affair," the Radical Socialists had decided on principle (reserving the rights of individuals) to demand an "order of the day pure and simple."[2] This would have meant leaving the question where it was. I said to Buisson that I considered it impossible to foresee what would take place in the Chamber, but that it was wise to come to an agreement on orders of the day, if any should be submitted. At the moment, I said, Jaurès had no intention of asking approval for his speech.

2. Passing to consideration of the next item on the agenda, without comment one way or the other on the Dreyfus Affair or its revival. On orders of the day, see p. 149, note 1.

CHAPTER X

THE discussion of the Syveton election took place on April 6 and 7, 1903. Jaurès began speaking on the first day but finished his discourse only on the day following. The first session was perfect, Jaurès' speech, with its trenchant logic, was admirable. Cavaignac was vigorously taken to task by Brisson in the matter of General de Pellieux' letter, and broke down pitifully. In the following session Jaurès continued his speech which produced a profound impression. As soon as he had finished, General André, Minister of War, came to the tribune, and in the midst of applause from all of the Left made the following declaration:

GENTLEMEN, so far as the case under discussion today is concerned, the Government intends to facilitate in every way the search for the truth and its substantiation.

For my own part, I should like to declare that the honor of the Army is not in any degree involved in this case. I recognize that convictions have been rendered. But at no time have I been happy to see a French officer convicted for the most shameful of crimes.

I will not follow M. Jaurès in the detailed examination which he has made of this Affair. . . . But I believe that the conscience of the country has been disturbed to an unusual degree by the appearance of extenuating circumstances in a crime of this character. While, as a member of the Government, I have respect for the legal truth, I understand perfectly the anxiety and fear entertained by certain ones of you. So that I may at this time make a contribution to the truth, I have brought General de Pellieux' letter, which has been discussed here. . . .

Let me repeat, I am not in any sense examining the question. But the Government is desirous of facilitating the search for the truth in this case, and it would be completely amenable to an order to undertake an administrative investigation. Let me add that, in order to protect my own responsibility, I propose (in accordance with a decision of the Government) to have the assistance of a certain number of judges in the examination of the documents involved.

I was advised immediately of the declaration which General André had just made. I was overjoyed, for the opening of an investigation would necessarily lead to an appeal. But an initial mistake was made when Syveton's election was invalidated, even though he had been elected by a very large majority. It would have sufficed simply to blast the campaign of defamation carried on by the Ligue de la Patrie Française, and by its fitting representative, Syveton, who later resorted to suicide to escape the weight of an ignominious life. Ribot then came to the tribune. Referring to General André's statement concerning the use of judges in his administrative inquiry (a very secondary aspect of his declaration), Ribot gave a Jesuitical speech and shed crocodile tears over the agitation which the case would revive. Jaurès, on the other hand, without waiting to see what orders of the day would be submitted, unfortunately presented the following: "The Chamber, placing on record the declarations of the Government, passes to the order of the day." Jaurès' motion was defeated, 318 to 212. The Chamber then adopted that of M. Chapuis: "The Chamber, confident in the Government and resolved not to permit the Dreyfus Affair to emerge from the judicial sphere, passes to the order of the day." This motion was only unfortunate because it followed that of Jaurès. . . . If Jaurès had rallied to the Chapuis motion without presenting his own order of the day, the former would have been interpreted as favorable, since it expressed confidence in the Government.

My joy of the afternoon (when I heard of General André's declaration) was dashed in the evening and became profound disappointment when I learned of the final results of the Chamber's session. Nonetheless a great step forward had been taken, for the Chapuis motion in no way precluded an appeal. But how were we to attain that object? That was the distracting question. It was my opinion that we should launch the request for an appeal at once. Jaurès, who called on me the next morning, frankly and vigorously opposed such a step. No excitement and no haste, he warned me. The Chamber's vote had left the Government free to undertake the investigation, and it must now be tactfully induced to do so. If I should launch my request now, and if it should be rejected, I could do nothing further during the life of this Parliament. Jaurès was leaving for the South, and was unable to be present at a gathering of friends at my house, which included MM. Buisson, de Pressensé, Reinach, Maître Mornard, and my two brothers, Léon and Mathieu. Clemenceau, whom I had invited, sent me the following letter:

Cher Monsieur:

Thank you for your kind invitation, but I must ask you to excuse me. Since the day when your pardon was accepted, in spite of my vigorous objections, at a meeting at the Ministry of Commerce, I have resumed the position which I intend to maintain. I shall do my duty when that is required, that goes without saying. But you will permit me to remain aloof from "politics" which gave us the amnesty. Thanks to the amnesty, those who will later be denounced will be inaccessible.

The part of the letter referring to the meeting at the Ministry of Commerce was aimed at my brother, Mathieu. The point concerning " 'politics,' which gave us the amnesty" was a shaft at Jaurès. I replied to Clemenceau:

I HAVE just received your letter, and it greatly pains me.

As to that part of it which concerns me personally, I have frequently explained the conditions under which I accepted the pardon. As to the part which concerns my brother, he has told me repeatedly that at the Ministry of Commerce, in the face of your vigorous opposition, he said "that he would not separate himself from you," but that at this very point you rose and after a few moments said: "If I were your brother, I should accept."

You know my opinion concerning the amnesty. I consider it profoundly unfortunate. I protested against it on two different occasions, and if there is anyone whom it has injured it is myself.

But yours is too keen an intelligence not to know that in a battle there are always differences as to tactics, but that they do not prevent all forces from coöperating to attain the common end.

Clemenceau found nothing to reply to my letter. In any event, at the meeting at my house on April 8, 1903, the situation was canvassed, and we agreed that in spite of Jaurès' opinion to the contrary, it was impossible for me to do nothing after his intervention from the tribune—at least within a limited time. Buisson and de Pressensé undertook to call on Combes, the Premier, and point out to him that if the Government did not carry out the investigation made necessary by Jaurès' revelations in the Chamber, it would play into the hands of the Nationalists. In the latter case I would launch my request for an investigation in order to win public opinion. De Pressensé informed me of the result of his step in this telegram:

BUISSON and I have just come from seeing the Premier. Without being able to give you here the details of our conversation, I can say that we received a very strong and well-founded impression that it would be unfortunate and harmful to send your letter at the present moment. If you would be good enough to come to my house tomorrow morning about eleven o'clock, I can tell you certain things which I cannot write.

I called on de Pressensé the next day, and he gave me this account:

AFTER we left your house, Buisson and I went to see the Premier. We had a long conversation. . . . We asked M. Combes if the Government intended to pursue General André's offer of an investigation. M. Combes told us that there had been a Cabinet meeting in the interval between the two sessions of the Chamber at which Jaurès spoke. At this meeting, great resistance had developed on the part of the President of the Republic, M. Loubet, and on the part of several members of the Cabinet, to the declarations that General André proposed to make from the tribune. They had yielded only after a warm discussion. But now, added the Premier, following the session of the Chamber in which the Chapuis motion was voted, if the Cabinet were asked to give concrete form to General André's offer, insurmountable opposition would appear, and the result would be a refusal.

Buisson and I then pointed out to the Premier that to fail to give form to General André's offer would be disastrous, as much from the point of view of Republicans, as from that of the country. We emphasized the fact that this would be a retreat by the Government in the face of the Nationalists. Under these conditions, we could only advise Dreyfus, who was resolved to act, to proceed with his plans. M. Combes threw up his arms and cried: "That would be a disaster, for the request for an investigation would certainly be refused by the Cabinet, just as the Chamber refused General André's offer." Then M. Combes confided in Buisson and myself in the greatest secrecy: "I am hopeful that my Ministry will last until November, so that we may bring the congregations' question to an end. Both General André and I make it a point of honor to terminate the Dreyfus Case. In place of an official investigation, General André will undertake what he has a perfect right to do and what is no affair of any other minister—a personal investigation."

As a result of this interview de Pressensé asked me, in his own name and in that of Buisson, to agree to sacrifice my plans and not send my request for an investigation. I know, he said to me, that you will be criticized, but I also know that you have always been willing to sacrifice your pride, that you have never thought to thrust yourself forward, and that you have never aimed at anything but the end which you wish to attain. You must do as much again today. I agreed to the request of de Pressensé and Buisson.

In the afternoon of the same day, M. Hément of the *Temps* called on me. He had seen the Premier after the morning's Cabinet, and the latter had asked him to tell me what had happened. The attitude of the Cabinet had become more favorable; General André's investigation would take place. An initial note appeared in the *Temps* to this effect: "The Ministers discussed the events and the vote in the Chamber's session of the day before yesterday. The Premier is to confer on this subject with the Minister of War." This note was to have been followed some days later by a second, which would say that General André was authorized to open the dossiers of the Dreyfus case. But this note never appeared.

After a futile wait for this second note, I asked Maître Mornard to send to the Minister of War Dr. Dumas' letters concerning the conversations which he had had with Major Merle, Judge at the Court-Martial at Rennes, so that these might be included in the dossier of the investigation. This was not so much a matter of the letters themselves, which were already known through the speech of Jaurès, as one of affirming my determination to have the investigation. I wished also to determine whether the inquiry was in progress. The Minister of War simply acknowledged the receipt of the letters without intimating whether or not the inquiry had begun.

Days of feverish and distracted hope followed. I learned that nothing had yet been done at the Ministry of War. The note announcing the beginning of the inquiry had not appeared. On the other hand, the *Petite république* published a letter from Ferlet de Bourbonne to Jaurès affirming the existence of the bordereau annoté; and the *Temps* published revelations of the former German Lieutenant Wessel concerning the false testimony of Cernuszki. I thought that I ought now to put these new disclosures on record and squarely pose the question of an investigation before public opinion. Hence I wrote the Minister of War, requesting an investigation of all the new evidence which I had collected up to this time. It was actually this request which, after various alternatives had been considered and numerous attempts made, was the lever which loosed the machinery of the inquiry.

Jaurès was away, and I was unable to submit my request to him or to warn him of my intention of sending it. Before doing so, however, I showed it to de Pressensé, who was favorable. At the same time I asked him to see Combes as soon as my request should arrive. De Pressensé was obliged to leave for Lyons and sent Leblois to inform me of the result of his interview with Combes. The latter wished to submit my request to the Minister of Justice, and thus change it into a request for an appeal. Such a request would be rejected since the facts were not sufficiently well established. That would have been simply to stifle the whole matter.

I asked Hément of the *Temps* to see Combes and learn precisely what his intentions were. Combes told him that: (1) He considered that he was obliged to reply to me at once; (2) he viewed the vote of the Chamber as prohibiting an administrative investigation, at least for the time being; (3) he thought that later, when we were far enough removed from the vote of the Chamber, an administrative inquiry would be possible; (4) under the existing conditions, since he was obliged to reply to me, he was considering submitting my letter to the Minister of Justice, who would reply in turn that there were no grounds for initiating the procedure leading to appeal, the evidence not being sufficiently well established; (5) he would agree to leave the Affair in suspense in order not to prejudice my case through an unfavorable decision by the Minister of Justice. In the latter case, he desired that I write a second letter, asking that the first be withheld at present.

I at once communicated these developments to Jaurès and to Buisson. I asked them to act in accord with the reply I made to the Premier through Hément, and of which I informed them. My reply was:

I WILL never write the letter which M. Combes asks. If the Government

submits my request to the Minister of Justice, that would be a scandal.
I know as well as they that the evidence I presented was not well established. It was precisely for that reason I was asking an investigation.
If I had thought I was in a position to submit the matter to the Minister of Justice, I would have done so. If the present Government acts
in this way, if it submits my request to the Minister of Justice, or if it
refuses the inquiry, it will take a place below that of the Méline Ministry. M. Combes was not obliged to reply at once. If he did not wish to
make the investigation immediately, he had merely to postpone his reply.

Buisson saw Combes on the next day and told me that he hoped
I should obtain satisfaction.

The *Temps* published on April 26 a letter of Reinach to Ferlet
de Bourbonne on the subject of the bordereau annoté. Reinach
included a letter which had been written him by Prince von
Münster on April 20, 1901, in which the traffic of Esterhazy with
Schwartzkoppen was acknowledged for the first time. Reinach
was of the opinion that the publication of this letter constituted
new evidence and that there were now grounds for drawing up
a request for an appeal.

On the morning of April 27 Combes summoned Hément and
asked him to tell me that he was agreeable to making no reply to
my request for an inquiry for the time being. On one hand, it
was thought impossible to make the investigation at this time, in
the light of the vote in the Chamber. On the other, he was absolutely determined to undertake it at an opportune moment and
thus to give me satisfaction. General André wished to do so at
once, but Combes had made him see that from the political point
of view this was impossible. Hence they would leave the public
in ignorance of this situation in order to avoid prejudicing my
case. As for an appeal based on the letter of Prince von Münster,
injected into the discussion by Reinach's letter in the *Temps,*
that did not seem to be promising enough to warrant such a request. One would risk a negative reply from the Committee on
Appeal. Beyond the unfortunate character of such a reply in itself, it would also have the serious disadvantage of impeding the
administrative investigation, which had been decided upon. On
the other hand, if the letters published by Reinach were not followed by an immediate request for an appeal, Combes continued,
they would constitute an important addition to the evidence

which the administrative investigation could produce. They would thus aid in bringing about a request for an appeal, which this time would have more adequate foundations.

I knew that Combes' good faith was unquestionable, and that I could count on his word and on that of General André. Subsequent events, moreover, revealed that he had been perfectly right concerning the letter published by Reinach. I also received the following letter from Buisson, who had seen the Premier:

BEFORE leaving Paris, I had, on Saturday evening, the interview which you asked me to seek in your letter of yesterday. Since the Premier told me that things had been arranged with Hément I thought that there was nothing to write you. It is clear that we ought to let things take their course and let circumstances work for justice. Now that you have said what you had to say it is not for you to press matters, to settle the question of time, or to fix the form which the investigation will take. You have had official cognizance taken of your request, and you can have all the patience which they feel they have a right to ask. Events may even move along to a certain point without your intervention, witness Reinach's letter which adds a document of capital importance to these already available.

It is not to you that one may say, courage! But one may be permitted in any case to add: take hope, reason will triumph in the end.

I saw Clemenceau on May 4. He had talked with the Premier, who seemed to him to be animated by the best intentions. Clemenceau assured me of his coöperation and added that he was ready to do anything I should consider helpful. I likewise asked Maître Demange, immediately after I had dispatched my request, for an investigation, to see Waldeck-Rousseau and induce him to intervene with the Government in support of my request. Waldeck-Rousseau expressed his active sympathy with my cause but replied that this would be impossible. For some time his relations with the Government of M. Combes had been chilly, by reason of the Government's policy which he disapproved, and now these relations had become frigid. When Maître Demange asked Waldeck-Rousseau's opinion concerning a request for an appeal, founded upon the available evidence, the former confirmed his view and that of Maître Mornard that it would mean defeat. On the other hand, Reinach retained his conviction and vigorously urged Jaurès to favor an immediate request for an appeal, based

upon the existing evidence, of which the "new evidence" was
Prince von Münster's letter which he had recently published.
Jaurès, who was then at Villefranche d'Albigeois, wrote me a
long letter on this subject, from which I take this passage:

I HAVE many things to say to you which I can only explain and discuss
orally with our friends. Meanwhile, things are ripening. I think, with
you, that we must push on the investigation concerning Cernuszki. We
will induce the Government to agree. The appeal will then very quickly
mature. I am hopeful that before the end of June everything will be in
readiness, and I beg our friends, for the sake of a few weeks, not to
compromise a success which seems to me certain.

The *Gaulois* of May 23 published a long article by General Zurlinden, who had been Minister of War in 1898 in the Brisson
Cabinet. This article was a reply to articles by Brisson which had
appeared in the *Siècle* and dealt with incidents in my case which
had taken place during his Ministry. General Zurlinden disclosed
the evidence on which he had based his opinion in 1898 and declared that his conviction had not been changed. That same evening I wrote a letter to General Zurlinden, replying to his article. I asked the editor of the *Gaulois* to publish it, in accordance with article 13 of the Press Law of 1881. In the *Gaulois* of
May 25 appeared a note in which the newspaper stated its refusal to publish my letter. I decided to force it to do so. But at
the moment of sending the complaint, Maître Demange showed
it to a colleague, and the latter pointed out that, in accordance
with the law of 1881, I had not the right to force the publication
of a reply that might involve the paper in a suit by a third party.
It is true that the third party was Esterhazy, who was so completely disqualified that none of us—Maître Mornard, nor Maître
Demange, nor my notary—had thought of this limitation, although it is explicit in the law. Hence I was content to publish
my letter in the newspapers friendly to me:

Paris,
May 23, 1903.

To General Zurlinden:
  In your letter published by the *Gaulois* you say that the study which
you made in 1898 of the dossier of 1894 convinced you of my guilt.
  You derive my guilt from alleged confessions which were confuted in

striking fashion by the Court of Cassation in 1899 and subsequently by myself at Rennes. You no longer speak in your article of the bordereau, sole basis of the accusation on which I was condemned. You could not be ignorant of the fact that the bordereau was by Esterhazy.

Nor do you speak of the secret documents. Here again you cannot be ignorant of the fact that they do not apply to me, that the majority of them are forgeries.

On numerous occasions you have said and written that the day when you should learn that I was innocent, you would not hesitate to support an appeal. That is what the Court of Cassation, after a thorough investigation, did declare, by the unanimous vote of its forty-five members.

And yet you continue to declare me guilty of the most terrible of crimes, but without adducing any proof and without daring to use on your own responsibility a single one of the falsehoods or forgeries which have been amassed against me.

Did the bordereau annoté by the Emperor of Germany determine your conviction? If so, why do you not show this document in the full light of day? What kind of a belief is it which is based on documents one dares not produce?

There does not exist a single proof against me which will resist a minute's examination. My entire life, all my suffering, the investigations of the Court of Cassation, the infamy of Esterhazy—all cry aloud my innocence.

In my unmerited disgrace, the cruelest which could exist, it is a pity that you lack the courage to state what you know to be the truth.

.   .   .   .

I wrote to the Prince of Monaco that after the publication of Prince von Münster's letter to Reinach, in which the treasonable relations of Esterhazy with Schwartzkoppen had been publicly admitted by the former German Ambassador to Paris, there were no longer any considerations which should influence Germany not to surrender the documents enumerated in the bordereau. On June 6, I received this reply:

I HAVE reflected on what you wrote me, and I recognize the justice of the conclusions you draw from Prince von Münster's letter to M. Reinach. In official circles, however, men often obey a very different conscience from that which inspires the acts of the average honest man. If this were not true, what you ask would have taken place long ago. It seems to me impossible that General von Schwartzkoppen should now be given the permission which was previously refused. Nevertheless, as soon as I believe that my intervention will have sufficient influence to bring about such a result, rest assured that I will hasten to use it toward this end. You well know that my object in life is before all else to contribute to the progress of justice and humanity.

Paris le 30 octobre 81?

Madame.

Ma voix n'a jamais cessé de défendre
le capitaine Dreyfus contre les lâchetés et
les absurdités. Aujourd'hui que la sagesse
des plus hauts magistrats de la France
fait taire les passions, je vous apporte
à vous que je connais seulement par vos
douleurs, un témoignage par admiration,
et je souhaite à vos enfants l'oubli du
rêve barbare dans lequel ils ont grandi.
Je crois qu'ils ne seront pas résignés
.... quand
ils comprendront qu'aux dernières heures
de ce siècle, les voix de la raison et du
cœur peuvent être couvertes par celle
de l'intolérance; que l'antisémitisme
est contemporain de Pasteur! Et le
martyre de leur père leur causera
le regret d'avoir vécu trop tôt, alors
que la culture des esprits n'a encore

Letter from the Prince of Monaco to Mme. Dreyfus.

ON July 3 I learned from Jaurès that General André, the Minister of War, had decided to begin the investigation as soon as Parliament had recessed. The inquiry was to be carried out by the Minister, assisted by M. Cretin, Controller General and Director of the Legal Department of the Ministry of War, and by Captain Targe, his adjutant. After the end of the session, on July 17, I learned, again through Jaurès, that the examination of the dossier of the case had begun, and that a certain number of forgeries had already been discovered among the secret documents. As a matter of fact, Captain Targe had begun his work as early as June 4. But an article had appeared on June 11 in the *Gaulois,* indicating that the Affair was being revived, and so Premier Combes had asked that, in order to avoid an interpellation, the investigation be interrupted until the end of the Parliamentary session. Even so, the investigation had been continued at the Ministry of War, but this was mentioned to Jaurès only at the beginning of the Parliamentary vacation. . . .

Early in August I heard certain details of the progress of General André's investigation. The latter had proceeded systematically, beginning in 1894, and had then reached the year 1898. He had found in the filing cases of the Ministry documents for the defense which had been very carefully concealed during the trial. General André had questioned Gribelin and Major Pauffin de Saint-Morel. Gribelin declared that he knew nothing of the bordereau annoté. Major Pauffin admitted that in 1897 he had called on Rochefort and Drumont (we had known nothing of this latter move). But he declared he had said to them merely that "an attempt was being made to substitute Esterhazy for Dreyfus, whereas at the Ministry of War, they were certain of Dreyfus' guilt." . . .

Finally, on October 22, Jaurès wrote me that he had received heartening news of what had been accomplished during the Parliamentary vacation. Some days later he told me of the principal results obtained by the investigation of the Minister of War. I then assembled a group of friends at Maître Mornard's in order to consider what should be done. Those present were de Pres-

sensé, Buisson, Reinach, Leblois, and Demange. Jaurès was kept
at the Chamber by his interpellation on the Armentières strike.
After a long discussion, we agreed that the information at hand
was not sufficiently precise to enable us to come to a definite decision. It was decided that de Pressensé should see Jaurès at
once, so that together they might ask the Government to communicate the results of the investigation to Maître Mornard. The
latter could then analyze them from a juridical point of view and
determine whether they presented "new evidence" sufficiently
well defined to permit a request for an appeal. On the next day I
learned from de Pressensé that Jaurès . . . had already asked
General André to transmit the dossier of the investigation to the
Minister of Justice and that he was awaiting a reply.

This reply was slow in coming, and so I saw Jaurès again on
November 17. He told me that two days earlier he had wanted to
renew his request, but that Brisson had urged both him and us to
postpone this action for a few days and to have confidence in him
meanwhile, since there was a matter whose prior solution was essential. According to Leblois, Brisson's motives were these. Mal-
versation of the secret funds of the Intelligence Bureau had been
discovered in the administration. In this connection they wished
to prosecute General Gonse, and a report was to be presented to
the Government. Brisson viewed the prosecution of General
Gonse as a useful preface to our appeal, and for that reason
wished us to await the Government's decision. I considered this to
be a mistake (which, moreover, the Government did not commit),
and that the prosecution of General Gonse could only result from
action on the Affair and could not be its preface. As a matter of
fact, the dossier of the investigation had been sent by the Minister of War to the Premier on October 19, 1903, and at each
Cabinet meeting General André asked without success that it be
sent to the Minister of Justice.

On November 19 I dined with Deputies Etienne and Thomson
and this chance encounter had, thanks to their helpfulness, the
happiest results. I pointed out to them the situation in which the
Government might find itself, if it continued unjustifiably to
vacillate about submitting the results of the Minister of War's
investigation. An interpellation in the Chamber of Deputies
might raise the question as to whether, as rumor had it, General

André had made an investigation of the Affair. The Government might then find itself in an embarrassing situation. Whereas, if the Government took the initiative, it could then maintain that it had kept the question on the judicial plane, and was hence acting in conformity with the Chamber's vote. To accomplish this step would mean merely transmitting the dossier to the Minister of Justice, who, following the normal practice, would communicate its results to Maître Mornard. If the latter then considered that an appeal was warranted, two equally satisfactory solutions were possible: either the Government might itself ask for an appeal, or I might direct such a request to the Minister of Justice. Etienne and Thomson found my attitude reasonable, and Thomson promised to discuss this view with M. Combes.

On November 22 Jaurès told me that the dossier of the investigation had been submitted to the Minister of Justice. Finally the great step had been taken! I was overjoyed, and felt the deepest gratitude to these unselfish men who had given me so generously of their aid in the months just past. . . .

On the afternoon of November 26 I received a carte pneumatique from Maître Mornard asking me to see him at once. He told me that M. Vallée, Minister of Justice, was favorable to an official submission of the case to the Committee on Appeal, since the evidence provided by the Minister of War's investigation seemed to him to justify an appeal. M. Combes, however, in order to protect the Government in case of an interpellation in the Chamber, preferred that I should myself submit the request for an appeal. He urged Thomson to communicate confidentially to Maître Mornard the results of the inquiry. The latter had been obliged, however, to return the dossier as soon as he read it, and now gave me a summary of the essential facts.

We were both deeply indignant as we verified once again all of the crimes against justice which had been committed. Not only had they changed certain documents in order to make them appear incriminating, but they had concealed those which were favorable to me. What a hideous state of mind on the part of those who had shared in the formation of the dossier! We were of the opinion that the evidence warranted the preparation of a request for an appeal[1] and so we drew up a draft of the appeal,

1. For Dreyfus' request for an appeal, in full, see Appendix VI.

which I was to look over quietly at home and return the next day. I could make only vague allusions to the results of the Minister of War's inquiry, since these had been given us in confidence.

When I arrived at Maître Mornard's office on the following morning, November 26, to return to him my request for an appeal so that he might submit it in the afternoon to the Minister of Justice, he told me that he had been summoned to M. Vallée's office at nine o'clock that morning. The latter was prey to new hesitations as to the path to be taken. He was also fearful of an interpellation, wondered how he would explain the Minister of War's inquiry, and so on. . . . In a word, M. Vallée appeared to Maître Mornard to have lost his recent enthusiasm for submitting the request for an appeal himself. Maître Mornard was obliged to point out to him that the path followed had been quite normal and regular, and that, once I had submitted my request for an inquiry to the Minister of War, it was the latter's right and duty to execute it. M. Vallée then asked that the submission of the request be kept secret until we should be faced by the *fait accompli,* i.e., submission of the request to the Committee on Appeal. I saw no objection to this procedure, but, knowing by experience that it was impossible to avoid gossip, I suggested that the Minister hasten to submit the case to the Committee.

Our difficulties on this day of November 26 were not yet at an end. Maître Mornard had an appointment for three o'clock in the afternoon with the Director of the Criminal Division of the Ministry of Justice, to whom he was to submit my request for an appeal. That morning there had been a small Cabinet meeting at which M. Loubet, President of the Republic, was present. He, along with M. Vallée, had wanted immediate initiation of the procedure of appeal. General André had been willing to ask for the appeal himself; but when M. Combes told him that, in case of interpellation, it would be preferable that the initiative come from me, it was decided that he should merely add his report to my request. Furthermore, the Premier feared that an interpellation would cause the overturn of the Ministry before the procedure had been set in motion. The fears of M. Combes were exaggerated, for if there had been an interpellation, it would actually have contributed to the strength of the Government. In any event M. Combes, influenced by this fear, sent Thomson to ask Maître Mornard to defer the submission of my request until the Ministry should be in a stronger position. Maître Mornard replied to Thomson that, since he had been directed by me to submit a request for an appeal, he could not postpone it without more explicit reasons. At five o'clock Thomson returned to tell Maître Mornard that all the difficulties had been smoothed over, and at six-thirty the latter registered my request for an appeal at the Ministry of Justice.

On November 27 I received a message from the Premier that, at the morning's Cabinet meeting it had been decided to return, on the following day, a favorable reply to my request for an appeal, and that the Government would send a note to the press on the subject through the Havas Agency. On the next day, I read with joy the note which the Minister of Justice had had communicated to the press. . . . The newspapers devoted to Esterhazy and the Nationalists were thrown into confusion. They found nothing but insults with which to defend a bad cause.

I waited impatiently for the submission of the report of M. Mercier, rapporteur of the Committee on Appeal. The latter, composed of three justices of the Court of Cassation and three directors of the Ministry of Justice, met on December 24 to hear M. Mercier's report. I learned immediately after the meeting that the Committee had unanimously adopted a motion in favor of appeal of the Rennes judgment.

The year 1903 ended amid happy auspices; at last I could foresee the end of my trials. On this occasion I received from many sources congratulations which deeply touched me. My friend Much, a classmate at the École Polytechnique who was very close to M. Dupré, a member of the Committee on Appeal, sent me the following notes of what happened in the Committee meeting:

GENERAL amazement among its members at the sight of so many forgeries. But for the amnesty, Mercier and Gonse would be arrested to-day. Great impression made by Targe's report; notably striking effect produced by a certain document of 1895, falsely dated 1894.

CHAPTER XII

IN the preparation of the brief which I proposed to present to the Court of Cassation in support of my request for an appeal, I had once again to read the whole of the proceedings at Rennes. Recalling as they did so many sad and trying days, this task was most painful. I was once more struck by the impotence to which the defense had been reduced. It is true that it had been impossible to refute at once, and without research into the documents of the Ministry of War (many of which were still secret), the boldly falsified statements of the witnesses for the prosecution. Furthermore, the judges had not hesitated between the word of the accusing generals and that of the defense witnesses—truth had been determined by the number of stripes. On the other hand, such an investigation as that now being undertaken by the Court of Cassation (based on documents produced on Court order, in which all the statements of witnesses would be verified) ought to bring to light the falsehoods of the accusation. A certain number of these, indeed, I was already in a position to reveal in my brief.

On January 30, 1904, Maître Mornard submitted his argument to the Court. Justice Boyer was named rapporteur in the case before the Criminal Division. I submitted my brief on February 1. Some days later I read the remarkable brief submitted to the Court of Cassation by M. Baudouin, its Procureur Général, which included these recommendations:

In summary, Alfred Dreyfus was condemned on September 9, 1899 by the Court-Martial at Rennes on charges, none of which will, it appears, survive examination (a fact which would not be sufficient to permit an appeal), as well as on the basis of documents which, since the conviction, have been admitted to be forgeries. The falsification of these documents had for its object both the creation of direct charges against the accused and the undermining of the influence of witnesses for the defense. . . .

We are convinced that the Court of Cassation will do justice to our recommendations, which, upon the order of the Minister of Justice, seek appeal of the judgment and a decision that will prepare the triumph of truth and justice—truth and justice, which, although sometimes concealed or disregarded through human weakness, can never die.

Some days later Maître Mornard informed me that Maître Labori had called to tell him this story. Val Carlos, former Attaché of the Spanish Embassy, had made statements which had been the subject of a report of Guénée and Henry in 1894, and which had served as the basis of the theatrical testimony of Henry during the 1894 trial. Val Carlos had called on Maître Labori to employ him as his attorney. Before allowing him to speak, Maître Labori said to him: "You know my differences with the Dreyfus family; but my sentiments about Dreyfus himself have not changed and I will do nothing to hinder an appeal. Now if you wish still to retain me, speak." Val Carlos then told Maître Labori that he had never been in the regular pay of the Intelligence Bureau, that he had merely received money to remunerate a third person, and that—this is the most interesting part of the story—he had never said in 1894, either to Henry or to Guénée: "There is a traitor in the Ministry, on the General Staff, in the Second Bureau, hunt for him." Maître Labori asked Maître Mornard not to summon Val Carlos for the proceedings on the admissibility of my request for an appeal, so that he might ask to be heard during the investigation which would follow.

A few days after this conversation with Maître Mornard I received a note asking me to call at his office. He told me that, as a result of talking to Maître Labori, he had the impression that the latter very much wished to come back into the case. Maître Labori, moreover, had said that if he were not summoned to testify, he would not permit the case to end without explaining, either on the stand or elsewhere, the role of Waldeck-Rousseau and Joseph Reinach. Maître Mornard then asked me if I would reëngage Maître Labori as counsel. I reminded him that after the urgent representations I had made to Maître Labori, as a result of the incident between him and my brother Mathieu (representations which had been fruitless), I wrote him a final letter in which I said that I was ready to resume the old relations whenever he wished. And yet, in spite of my most sincere efforts, during the following autumn Maître Labori wrote in the *Grande revue* two malevolent articles condemning me. Not content with that, he shortly thereafter offered full "explanations" in several articles which appeared in the *Journal*, in which he took me vigorously to task for an incident for which Bernard Lazare was responsible and of which I knew nothing. I did not reply to Maître Labori, at least not publicly, because I could not and would not forget the very great services which he had, with his ability, his magnificent courage, and his devotion, rendered my cause during those tragic years. Nevertheless, I told Maître Mornard that I refused absolutely to retain Maître Labori again as my attorney.

．　　　．　　　．　　　．　　　．　　　．　　　．

On February 27 I received a call from M. Leproust, Police Commissioner at the Prefecture, and Chief of the First Research Section. He had come to warn me on behalf of the Prefect of Police that individuals belonging to the old Guérin gang planned to seize me in the street, put a plug of chloroform under my nose, thrust me into a waiting automobile, and then kidnap me— all this to prevent the appeal! This was a wild story and I wondered how they were going to prevent the appeal by removing me from the scene. I smiled at this plan, but M. Leproust said that it was very serious and that he had been ordered to have me protected. Happily the protection lasted only a few days.

．　　　．　　　．　　　．　　　．　　　．　　　．

The proceedings before the Criminal Division of the Court of Cassation began on March 3, 1904. At last I could see the dawn of the day which I had awaited so impatiently. At last I could see approaching the moment when I should be delivered from this terrible nightmare in which I had lived for ten years. The rapporteur, Justice Boyer, first read his report, which was logically ordered but quite colorless. As I had expected, he recommended that the request for an appeal be allowed. The Procureur Général began his oral charge which he completed on the following day. M. Baudouin was very clear and very firm. He summarized the history of the Affair and concluded by recognizing my innocence. Finally, on the third day, Maître Mornard delivered an admirable plea, at once brilliant and very stirring.

The Criminal Division's inquiry began on March 7, 1904. The Court heard Captain Targe, the Minister of War's adjutant, who presented with penetrating comments the original documents which had been examined in the course of the Minister's inquiry. . . . During the days following, the examination of the dossier containing the secret documents continued. Although the Court was not supposed to concern itself further with the alleged confessions (which it considered to have been disposed of definitively by the decision rendered by the three Divisions of the Court of Cassation on June 3, 1899), a new and interesting document on this subject was nonetheless discovered. Lieutenant-Colonel Guérin had alleged at the Rennes trial that on the morning of the degradation, January 5, 1895, his attention was completely absorbed in listening to these so-called confessions. And yet Colonel Guérin's service report, drawn up after the degradation and found in the offices of the Military Government of Paris, ran thus: "Parade concluded. Dreyfus protested his innocence and shouted: '*Vive la France.*' No other incident." . . .

. . . .

On March 14, I learned to my great sorrow that the noble Trarioux was dead. For the past year I had followed the course of his illness with anxiety. I was disturbed that I could not confide in him my hopes. He was not to witness the triumph of a just cause to which he had given his whole heart. I felt an infinite gratitude toward him, and had a profound respect for this upright and faithful character, so splendidly generous. A great soul had left us.

. . . . . .

I felt that we should take advantage of this opportune moment to ask the Court to send commissions of inquiry to the foreign military attachés of 1894, in order to learn the contents of the documents enumerated in the bordereau. I brought this point to the attention of Maître Mornard. This, I said to him, would furnish the means of crushing all resistance. If the Court hesitated, he had an excellent argument in a recent article by General Zurlinden in the *Gaulois*, which was as dishonest as it was stupid. This venomous article, however, could be of service to us, for one's unscrupulous adversaries are sometimes useful in bringing truth to light. General Zurlinden pointed out, in fact, that the key to the mystery was in Berlin. Hence one had only to ask for it by sending commissions of inquiry. Maître Mornard shared my view and submitted a request that such commissions be sent to the foreign military attachés of 1894—Colonel von Schwartz-koppen and Colonel Panizzardi. When, however, Delcassé, the Minister of Foreign Affairs, was consulted semiofficially by the Procureur Général, his attitude was unfavorable.

Delcassé's attitude surprised me greatly, and I had urgent overtures made to the Government so that it might agree to the sending of commissions of inquiry. I did not succeed, and in this connection I learned the following: "Several Ministers are of the same opinion as Delcassé, notably General André. Their reasons are these: (1) The French public would never accept any testimony whatever coming from Germany, and our adversaries, the Nationalists, would forge themselves a weapon from this evidence; (2) William II is furious and shows it in his speech; he sees Germany isolated in Europe, and might refuse in a categorical and insolent manner to let Schwartzkoppen testify, which would be a humiliation for our country; (3) there is every reason to believe that at the present moment the German Government is not disposed to do a favor for the French Government." Delcassé also succeeded in having the Cabinet adopt an unfavorable attitude by pointing out that there were in the diplomatic dossier documents subsequent to the Rennes trial, which demonstrated Germany's irritation because no attention had been paid to the official note published by the German Government and communicated to the judges at Rennes on September 8, 1899.

.　　.　　.　　.　　.　　.　　.　　.　　.　　.

On March 23 Captain Targe completed his testimony before the Criminal Division and included one new and interesting fact. He had found in the Ministry of War the rough draft of a report by Major Bayle, a document alleged to have disappeared and whose disappearance was imputed to me. In this way a falsehood of General de Boisdeffre was destroyed. The sinister du Paty was then heard. He was malicious and treacherous; his whole argument was based on the Bertillon solution and on the Panizzardi dispatch, the official text of which he denounced as a forgery.

Val Carlos was also heard, and declared that he had never made the statements to Henry or to Guénée which had been repeated during the 1894 trial and which had been the subject of two reports. When du Paty was summoned to sign his deposition he wished to modify his earlier testimony, and had to be sharply called to order. The Procureur Général asked him to turn over to the Court the commentary which he had prepared on the secret documents submitted to the judges in 1894. Du Paty refused. M. Baudouin then read him the article in the Penal Code relating to theft of documents connected with a trial. Du Paty decided to submit the document.

As to General Gonse, he, poor wretch, was pitiful—crushed by the weight of the disgraceful acts he had committed. Maître Mornard questioned him about the document, alleged to be of April, 1894, relative to the organization of the French railroads. When he asked General Gonse why, if the document had actually been of the year 1894, it had not been submitted to the judges of the first Court-Martial, the latter replied : "I knew that you would ask that question." To which Maître Mornard replied in turn. "You must then have prepared an answer to it." "Why no!" exclaimed Gonse, "I have no answer." Despite its normal gravity, the Court nearly burst into laughter.

The chief criminal, General Mercier, was then heard. He was determined not to accept the paternity of the work published by a "Former Student of the École Polytechnique," entitled "A Study of the Testimony of M. Bertillon and Captain Valério at the Rennes Trial," a tissue of lies and errors whose very foundation was forgeries. When he was questioned about the bordereau annoté and the German Emperor's letter, General Mercier replied that he had never heard the bordereau discussed and had never seen the letter. And yet Colonel Stoffel had told him that he had seen a photograph of the latter, and had repeated the text of it to him. General Mercier added that he did not believe that an Emperor would write to his Ambassador in such terms and that if this letter existed it must be apocryphal. What then was the significance of the open letter to General Mercier, published by the *Gaulois* of August 14, 1899? What was the meaning of his concealments at the Rennes trial? It was obvious that General Mercier was seeking to escape once more from one of his lies.

On April 8 my wife was summoned before Justice Petitier. She was questioned about the famous indentation found on my brother Mathieu's letter, confiscated at my house in 1894. Du Paty and others had made this the subject of a charge against me, under the pretext that the difference between this indentation and the edge of the paper was the same as that between an indentation on the bordereau, and the edge of the latter. My wife declared she was certain that this indentation did not exist in my brother's letter when it was seized. Moreover, she explained the mistake committed concerning the designation of this missive, incorrectly known as the *"lettre du buvard."*[1] In this connection, my wife was confronted with du Paty who made her elaborate bows to which she did not deign to respond. Justice Petitier suggested to my wife that she try to find whether we still had the buvard and the papers confiscated in 1894 and returned to her after the trial. Happily we found them again. In the buvard, which was just as it was when it had been returned, we found, in addition to certain other confiscated papers, the envelope of the packet sealed in 1894. All these papers, as well as the envelope bearing the signature of du Paty, of Gribelin, his clerk, and of my wife, had the same indentation as that in my brother's letter. They had all been part of the same sealed packet. This indentation, then, had been made in order to hold the string surrounding the packet. The seal itself, placed there to hold the end of the string, was still on the envelope. What a wretched impostor du Paty was! He had had this indentation made while he looked on at the time the packet was sealed in 1894, and then later he had had the impudence to make it a charge against me.

In his testimony Captain Targe had referred to certain letters of General Chamoin, General de Gallifet's representative at the Rennes trial in 1899. General Chamoin sent a daily report of the sessions of the Court-Martial to the Minister of War. These letters are characteristic of the state of mind which dominated the Rennes trial. On August 7, 1899, General Chamoin wrote: "The first session is over, and it has passed without incident. Dreyfus first protested his innocence loudly, and then discussed the various elements in the accusation coldly and in a voice

1. A *buvard* is a type of folding desk blotter, in which a certain number of letters could be laid flat.

which was often monotonous. He denied everything, both primary and secondary charges. His impressive countenance was often contracted, an indication at once of the great suffering and poignant emotion felt by a man who plays the major role.'' I surely had the right to deny everything, the right to deny all the alleged charges, whether primary or accessory, because I had never failed in my duty at any time. But when I read further on, "He knew no feeling, his heart did not speak," I was dumbfounded and outraged. . . .

The inquiry before the Court of Cassation had already produced interesting results. My opponents, however, continued to form a solid bloc. There was nothing unusual about this, for once steeped in crime, it is difficult, if not impossible, to free oneself. They now abandoned the secret dossier, upon which they had so much relied, and returned almost exclusively to the bordereau, the only genuine basis of the case. But in order to attribute the bordereau to me, in the face of all of the evidence, they relied on technical and cryptographical considerations. The former point of view was absurd, since no one knew what the documents enumerated in the bordereau contained. The cryptographical discussion was based on the Bertillon solution, which was a monstrosity—a mass of errors on a foundation of forgeries. And yet, under the influence of prejudice, the human mind accepts the most extraordinary statements. It was essential that these two arguments be destroyed in lucid and decisive fashion.

On the request of the Procureur Général, whose competence to consider technical questions General Mercier had denied, the Minister of War formed a Committee of Inquiry, composed of General Balaman, former President of the Technical Artillery Committee; General Séard, former Director of the Artillery; General Villien, member of the Technical Artillery Committee; and General Brun, Director of the École Supérieure de Guerre. After a long and detailed study, this Committee submitted a report on the technical aspects of the bordereau, which was in turn presented to the Court of Cassation. The report's conclusions were frankly and categorically favorable to my cause.

The Criminal Division of the Court of Cassation likewise appointed a Committee, composed of MM. Appell, Dean of the Faculty of Sciences and member of the Academy of Sciences; Dar-

boux, Permanent Secretary of the Academy of Sciences; and
Poincaré, who taught the Calculus of Probabilities at the Sorbonne and was also a member of the Academy of Sciences. The
function of this Committee was to examine Bertillon's solution,
as well as that of Major Corps, which differed from the former
but arrived at the same conclusion—that the bordereau was a
forged document written in a geometric hand. These eminent
scientific authorities verified Bertillon's measurements by means
of the precision instruments of the Paris Observatory, and submitted a very complete and much documented report examining
these solutions in all their details. The Committee's conclusions
were explicit: the bordereau was not a forged document, but
was written in a running hand.

Even before this Committee was appointed by the Court, some
extraordinary studies of the same subject had been made. Gabriel Monod produced a penetrating refutation of Major Corps's
system. When the anonymous pamphlet by a "Former Student
of the École Polytechnique" on the Bertillon solution appeared,
MM. Molinier, Professor at the École des Chartes; Bernard, min-
ing engineer and former student at the École Polytechnique;
and Painlevé, member of the Academy of Sciences, published
authoritative disproofs of this solution. . . .

.   .   .   .

Lieutenant-Colonel Picquart was also heard by the Court of
Cassation. He gave luminous testimony on the documents in the
secret dossier, submitted to the judges in 1894, and on du Paty's
commentary. But when he was induced to speak of the Rennes
trial, he declared that Maître Labori had been prevented by his
client from participating in the trial. This was an abysmal error. I had never requested Maître Labori not to participate. Indeed I took no part in the events which led him to make this decision.

I testified before the Criminal Division on June 22, 1904. For
the first time in my life I crossed the threshold of the Palais de
Justice, where my name had so often echoed. I was waiting to
testify in the passage leading to the courtroom, when the Procureur Général passed with M. Melcot, the Avocat Général, to
whom he pointed me out. M. Melcot left M. Baudouin, came

toward me, and said: "I am not a member of the Criminal Division, and will have nothing to do with your case. Permit me to shake your hand and to express my entire sympathy. I have been convinced of your innocence since the day when I heard General Mercier lie." A few moments later I was advised that the session had begun. I testified, and, with documents in hand, offered proof of the audacious falsehoods of my accusers. . . .

At this same period the Rochefort-Val Carlos case was tried before the Tribunal Correctionnel.[2] The case was a result of a controversy arising out of Val Carlos' testimony before the Court of Cassation. Defending Val Carlos, Maître Labori declared that he had been prevented by my family's solicitations from bringing out all the truth at Rennes. And yet my family never at any time interfered with his liberty of action. Furthermore, Maître Labori asked—although the question was in no way concerned with this case—that a Court-Martial be summoned to pass final judgment on my case, following the Court's inquiry. It is permitted to a man in public life to express his opinion on such a question in the press, but Maître Labori ought to have known that such a thing on the part of a former defense attorney was inadmissible in court.

In his testimony before the Court of Cassation, Cuignet spoke at great length on the Panizzardi dispatch of November 2, 1894. He declared that the text in code presented by the Ministry of Foreign Affairs was incorrect, hence the decoding was incorrect also. Cuignet produced another text in code, which he stated to be the authentic one. This text in code, when translated, gave precisely the same version as that of the first draft by the Quai d'Orsay,[3] made when the latter was searching for the key to Panizzardi's code. Cuignet's thesis was conclusively destroyed by the testimony of Paléologue, representing the Minister of Foreign Affairs. The latter stated that there had never been but one text in code (that submitted to the Court of Cassation in 1899) which corresponded to the version finally arrived at in 1894. Paléologue's statement had been corroborated during the

2. Criminal Court of first instance, having jurisdiction over cases involving misdemeanors.

3. The French Foreign Office. For the original and translation of this message, see pp. 50–51.

Court of Cassation's detailed inquiry of 1899, which included an investigation in the relevant departments of the Ministry of Posts and Telegraph.

An interpellation concerning Cuignet took place in the Chamber. Following his testimony before the Court of Cassation, the latter had inundated the Minister of War with letters of an unseemly character. General André, moved by an instinct of charity, determined to find out whether Cuignet was of sound mind. Before proceeding to measures of punishment, he had Cuignet given a medical examination. An outcry arose from the Nationalists who declared that Cuignet was being incarcerated to prevent him from talking. When he was interpellated in the Chamber of Deputies, General André defended himself indifferently. It is clear that the Minister of War would have done better to send Cuignet before a Court-Martial or visit disciplinary punishment upon him, leaving his defenders free to demand a medical examination if they so desired.

The inquiry of the Criminal Division of the Court of Cassation came to an end in July, 1904, but its final decision could not be rendered before the judicial recess. . . .

.   .   .   .

Word reached me on August 11 of the death of Waldeck-Rousseau, who had long been ill. For several months his friends had held out no hope for him. France lost in him one of her best servants. He had been convinced since 1894 of my innocence, for he had been made acquainted with all the facts in the case by his friend and my defender, Maître Demange. And yet for a long time he was silent in his sympathy. He knew the whole truth but he permitted events to take their course. This he did even at the time of the elections of 1898, which were fought over an ambiguity, reflecting in considerable measure his own responsibility. Later he was very courageous. He delivered an admirable speech when the Law of *Dessaisissement*[4] was proposed, and he took office in 1899 when the reaction was unleashed and everyone was trembling with fear. But Waldeck-Rousseau once again manifested great weakness at the time of the Rennes trial, when he was duped by General de Gallifet, who, according to his own ex-

4. *See* p. 129.

pression, was in turn duped by his own entourage. After the trial he failed to seek amends energetically for a decision he knew to be unjust, and his sympathy for my cause became very circumspect.

. . . .

I learned on November 14, 1904, that General André had resigned as Minister of War, or rather that his colleagues had tactfully induced him to retire. This act was hardly commendable. Whatever General André's mistakes may have been, he was animated by the best intentions and had been obliged to face a difficult situation. I retained for him profound gratitude for the courage with which he undertook to right the terrible judicial wrong of which I was still the victim. He was succeeded by M. Berteaux, Deputy for the Seine-et-Oise. . . .

CHAPTER XIII

A T last, on November 28, 1904, the Criminal Division of the Court of Cassation rendered its final decision. It was now necessary to prepare the brief to be presented before the full bench of the Court of Cassation. While in the country during the summer, I had already prepared the section dealing with the technical discussion of the bordereau, and, since my return to Paris, the section relative to the critical examination of the Bertillon solution. Maître Mornard, with his usual capacity, assumed responsibility for the other sections. During December I was informed that M. Ballot-Beaupré, Chief Justice of the Court of Cassation, had directed Procureur Général Baudouin to make his brief very complete and to take his own time. For these gentlemen time did not mean what it meant to me, who for ten years had been living this terrible nightmare. . . .

During the early months of 1905, Maître Mornard pursued with tireless zeal the drafting of the brief which he was to present. The Criminal Division had completely overturned all of the alleged charges against me and had laid bare the criminal acts of my accusers. The behavior of the latter had been instinctive and quite elemental. They had simply suppressed, or hidden from the eyes of the judges, the documents which were favorable to me or which destroyed their arguments. On the other hand, when they had a document, which, by a stroke of the pen (the change of a date, the erasure of an initial and its replacement by a "D") could be made to lend itself to a prejudiced interpretation, they did not hesitate to make such a change—that is, when they did not actually stoop to the forgery of an entire document.

The following is a simple example of their Machiavellian tactics. So that I might verify the dates of certain leaves which I had obtained while I was in the service, I had asked Maître Mornard to have my personal dossier in the Ministry of War turned over to the Court. He found that the Ministry of War had in 1894 submitted to the judicial dossier (where it had since remained unchanged) an extract from my dossier, giving my personal efficiency reports. These reports included, first, those which

I had received before my entry into the General Staff, and, second, those given me by three of my Bureau chiefs in the General Staff. I was astonished not to find the reports which General de Boisdeffre, then Chief of the General Staff, must have given me at the end of my probation. Yet these reports existed, and Maître Mornard found them in my personal dossier at the Ministry of War. They were: "Good officer, facile mind, grasps problems quickly; zealous, industrious, commented upon favorably wherever he goes. Will make a good General Staff officer." Since these reports were good and summarized my stay in the General Staff, it was preferred to pass over them in silence and to turn over to the dossier those which preceded them. Of these, the first two reports had given me an "excellent"; the third was that of Fabre, who, at the suggestion of Roget and of Bertin-Mourot, had given me an ambiguous report.

．　　　．　　　．　　　．　　　．　　　．　　　．　　　．

On March 10, I was told that the Procureur Général, M. Baudouin, had completed his brief and had recommended annulment without remanding. . . . On March 15, the Chief Justice, M. Ballot-Beaupré, appointed as rapporteur for the case before the full bench M. Puech, member of the Division of Requests.[1] M. Puech was also the first justice to be appointed to the Court following the decision of June 3, 1899, which set aside the judgment in my case. The appointment of M. Sarrut, Presiding Justice of the Civil Division, had been expected. M. Sarrut had not sat on the first appeal, and he seemed to be indicated, both by the authority which he enjoyed and by his position as Presiding Justice of the Division, the position held by M. Ballot-Beaupré when he was named rapporteur in 1899. The Nationalist newspapers, however, had carried on a campaign against his eventual selection because he was a member of the committee formed to erect a monument to Scheurer-Kestner. M. Ballot-Beaupré yielded. In this connection, one can only repeat the words of M. Loew, who presided over the Criminal Division during the first appeal: "They accused us of having been partial to Dreyfus, whereas, in order to demonstrate our impartiality, we actually leaned over backwards."

1. On the organization of the Court of Cassation, *see* Appendix II.

The day M. Puech was chosen Maître Mornard met M. Sarrut, who told him of a conversation he had just had with M. Ballot-Beaupré. The latter had said to M. Sarrut, apparently in order to excuse himself for not having appointed him, that it was quite exceptional that, at the time of my first appeal, the Presiding Justice of a Division had been appointed rapporteur. He preferred, moreover, that this practice should not be continued, and for this reason he had appointed Puech. Sarrut answered Ballot-Beaupré: "I would not have asked to prepare the report on the Dreyfus case, but if you had offered me the task I should not have declined it."

M. Puech refused the commission, for reasons of health. M. Delcurrou was next appointed and declined for the same reasons. M. Ballot-Beaupré then chose M. Michel-Jaffard, who was third on the list of judges who had had no connection with the first appeal. M. Michel-Jaffard accepted. I knew nothing of his attitude, but I was convinced that, if he were a judge without preconceived ideas of the case, a study of the dossier would completely convince him of my innocence.

On April 25 Maître Mornard completed the preparation of his brief, a task entailing much work. It was a sound production, adequately reflecting his abilities. It was devoted to an exposition of the decisive results of the investigation undertaken by the Criminal Division of the Court of Cassation. In the first part of the brief Maître Mornard presented a general picture of the successive and contradictory solutions employed by the accusation, solutions which "permit us to account for the fantastic state of mind of certain officers who were guilty of scandalous acts and who yet retained the conviction, repeatedly affirmed, that they were doing a useful and meritorious work."

The second part was concerned with an analytical examination of the Rennes trial and of the accusation in the form which it took before this latter Court-Martial. In the third part, the facts revealed since the Rennes trial and their relation to the statements made to the judges were examined. In the fourth part Maître Mornard studied Esterhazy's role and returned briefly to the elements in the accusation as they affected him. In the fifth and last part he examined the juridical consequences to be drawn from the facts established by the investigation, and enu-

Chère, Chère Madame.

Ne perdez pas courage.

ni patience!

Chaque cœur, avec vous!

Duse.

Septembre 99.

Letter to Mme. Dreyfus from Eleonora Duse at the time of the Rennes trial.

merated the grounds for an appeal, which made it essential that
the judgment of the Rennes Court-Martial be set aside.

Maître Mornard concluded his carefully prepared brief by asking that the judgment be set aside without remanding the case
to another Court-Martial. There were many grounds for this. But
in keeping with my expressed desire, he presented no argument
based on the amount of time that had elapsed, imperfections in
the description of the offense, the existence of a pardon, or the
service of the sentence. I did not wish to have the judgment set
aside, without remand, on any grounds which would reflect my
particular situation. I wanted to rely only on those grounds
which would establish categorically my innocence and Esterhazy's guilt. As a result, Maître Mornard based his argument for
an annulment, without remand, on the following two grounds,
taken from the Code of Criminal Procedure: ''(1) The Court
will pass on the facts, without remand, when it is not possible
again to have recourse to the oral testimony of all the parties
concerned.'' Esterhazy, author of the treasonable bordereau and
Schwartzkoppen's habitual informant, was, as good common
sense would have it, a party to the trial. He had been acquitted
by the Court-Martial of 1898; hence he could not be prosecuted
further, and oral testimony of all the parties concerned was no
longer possible. (2) ''If the annulment of the judgment affecting a living defendant leaves nothing which could be termed a
felony or misdemeanor, the case is not to be remanded.'' The
Court's investigation had left no charge against me.

Word now reached me that Justice Michel-Jaffard, rapporteur
for the case, was in poor health. I was hopeful that this would
not retard the submission of his report, and that the case could
reach the Court before the judicial recess, which would begin on
August 15. But I was doomed to disappointment. On May 10, the
Presiding Justice received a medical certificate stating that Michel-Jaffard had been stricken by double pneumonia, following
grippe, and that his condition made necessary some months of
rest. The illness was genuine, but the impression made on the
Court was that the certificate had been purposely exaggerated.
As a matter of fact, those near Michel-Jaffard had been alarmed

by the responsibility which he had assumed in agreeing to prepare the report on the case and wished to see him freed of it. Fear of attacks by the Nationalist press was the abyss where courage foundered. After the Chief Justice and Procureur Général had examined the question, they decided that to relieve Michel-Jaffard, after the previous refusals of Justices Puech and Delcurrou, would result in accentuating the polemics of the Nationalist newspapers. The latter, at the time of the refusal of these two judges, had declared that neither of them wished to accept the task of preparing the report because neither wished to yield to the pressure which it was alleged would be exercised to produce recommendations favorable to Dreyfus. This argument would be used now with even more force, it was believed, since Michel-Jaffard had already begun the examination of the dossier. Hence, fear of slander induced them to abandon what they would have done in an ordinary case—appointing another rapporteur. The Procureur Général called on the Minister of Justice, who agreed with this reasoning. But on May 15 there followed another shock. Michel-Jaffard had declared that, in his present state of health, the pursuance of his task would be equivalent to a capital sentence. It was now necessary to substitute for him Justice Moras. . . . I was hopeful that a rapporteur had finally been found who would prove adequately robust to withstand the demands of this trying task, and, above all, who possessed sufficient courage to follow his mission to its conclusion. . . .

. . . .

In 1904 Dutrait-Crozon had published in the old *Gazette de France,* a monarchist newspaper, a series of alleged critical studies on Reinach's book, *Histoire de l'Affaire Dreyfus.* These he brought together in a volume which appeared in June, 1905, an admirable work of Jesuitry which travestied the truth with all the art of Loyola's disciples. Dutrait-Crozon was sufficiently lacking in tact to send Reinach his book, in which he referred to the latter as a liar and a forger, with this inscription: "To M. Joseph Reinach, in memory of the delightful hours I have passed in his company." . . .

. . . .

We spent the month of August at Randa, in the Valley of Zermatt, one of the most beautiful in Switzerland, and during a great part of September we were near Geneva. . . . Upon my return to Paris, I learned of the death of Cavaignac, Minister of War in the Brisson Cabinet in 1898. Cavaignac had already passed into oblivion. He came for the last time to the tribune of the Chamber of Deputies in April, 1903, when, during his inter-pellation on the Syveton election, Jaurès exposed the history of the bordereau annoté. Jaurès read General de Pellieux' letter of accusation, directed to Cavaignac, which the latter had concealed from his Premier, Brisson. Cavaignac straightened in terror and asked the floor with the gesture of a drowning man. When his turn came, he spoke in accents which no longer had a human sound. All of the Left, standing in the hemicycle, threw back in his face the memory of the Henry forgery, officially posted in all the communes of France. This was his judgment. The plaything of wretches in the Intelligence Bureau of the Ministry of War, who had contrived the plot against justice, Cavaignac in 1898 was inebriated by the acclamations of the Nationalist and anti-Semitic mob. Henceforth his mind was closed to every glimmer of good sense or reason, he committed himself to the struggle against the truth, and in that struggle he was broken. . . .

.   .   .   .

Following its annual recess the Court of Cassation resumed its sessions on October 16. I had hoped that M. Moras would submit his report when the Court reconvened. This, soon was not the case! In the Cabinet meeting of November 7, 1905, the case was discussed. Chaumié, the Minister of Justice, announced (what did not take place) that Justice Moras would submit his report during the first half of December, and that the case could come before the full bench in January. A discussion followed on this subject, and it was decided that the date of the trial would be made to depend on Moras' recommendations. If he recommended that the case should not be remanded to a Court-Martial, it would come before the full bench as soon as possible after the submission of the report. If, on the contrary, he recommended that the case be remanded, it would then be postponed until after the general elections of April and May, 1906. I viewed the latter decision as a political error which would be exploited by our opponents, and I made every effort to have it reversed. In the *Radical* of November 14 appeared a very sensible article by Ranc, in which he said:

WHY not finish with this matter once and for all? Why postpone a solution which is inevitable? The case is ready. Captain Dreyfus, who immediately after his pardon declared that he was determined to carry on the battle until his complete vindication, has kept his word, as all of those who knew him expected he would do. He has submitted a new request for an appeal. He is free. No one in France any longer doubts his innocence. But he is entitled to something more than this. He is entitled to plenary justice, to the legal establishment of the truth. Hence he has turned once more to the first Court of the land. Without delay, Procureur Général Baudouin has submitted his brief. . . . It is a secret to no one that the great majority, practically all, of the judges of the highest Court, will vote to set aside the unjust judgment of Rennes.

In order, however, that the Court of Cassation may pass on this question, the report must be submitted. Why this delay?

In this connection Sigismond Lacroix has echoed a rather unusual rumor. It is said, he relates, that word will be given from the Ministry of Justice to postpone the report. Sigismond Lacroix does not believe that there is any foundation for this report. Nor do I. Beyond the fact that this would be a criminal abuse of power, of which I know M. Chaumié is incapable, it would be a political mistake which could not escape the sagacity of his colleagues.

Yes, an enormous political mistake! Do they wish that, as a result of this postponement and of these delays, the election should coincide with the renewal of the controversy over the Dreyfus Affair, over the lies of General Mercier, over the forgeries and crimes of the General Staff? Do they wish this? We, the Dreyfusards, are ready. We will not permit it to be said that we are fleeing from a new debate, that it is enough for us to have obtained the pardon of the innocent man, that we retreat in the face of the defenders of Henry and of Esterhazy, that we are afraid of the revelations of the terrible M. Cuignet. We are ready and waiting. Let them begin when they will.

But what has the Government to gain from this renewal of the battle? . . .

In the name of enlightened political interest, as well as in the name of justice, an immediate solution of the case is demanded. Let the first Court of the land say its word, the last word.

On December 14, I was informed that Moras, who had been given leave for the preparation of his report, had resumed his

seat in Court. Maître Mornard and I presumed that his report
was complete and wondered why there was delay in bringing the
case before the full bench.

The year 1905 ended without seeing the last of my adversities.
The Court's delay was absolutely incomprehensible to all of us. I
had made my request for an investigation in April, 1903, my request for an appeal in November of the same year. The Court's
investigation had in fact been terminated since July, 1904, and
its final decision on the inquiry had been rendered in the following November. And the case had yet to be decided!

During the early days of January, 1906, I was told that Justice
Moras, whose report was in substance very favorable, recommended remanding the case to a new Court-Martial. In doing so
he relied upon the precedent of 1899. The juridical situation,
however, was no longer at all the same, since Esterhazy was now
admitted to be the author of the bordereau and of the treason,
both through the documents submitted to the Court and by his
own confession. Hence he was now a party to the case. On the
other hand, the Court's investigation had overturned all the
charges against me. Henceforth, Maître Mornard and I were determined to give battle on this question before the full bench, in
order to fix the entire responsibility on the Court should its decision provide that the case be remanded to a new Court-Martial.
But I was no less determined to carry on with energy the struggle for truth and justice before the Court-Martial itself, if the

CHAPTER XIV

DURING the early days of February the Government finally decided to stir from its apathy. Chaumié, the Minister of Justice, directed the Procureur Général to bring the case before the Court as soon as possible. But the Chief Justice, Ballot-Beaupré, replied that all the sessions of the Civil Division would be absorbed by appeals on the contested eligibility of voters, appeals which must be decided before the general elections. Hence he could convoke the full bench only after the elections. . . . Parliament rose on April 13, and the deputies retired to their constituencies to prepare their election campaigns. . . . The general elections were held on May 7 and 14 and were favorable to the policy of the Republican Bloc. . . .

At the beginning of June, I was told that the hearing before the Court would begin on Friday, the fifteenth of that month. This was a great relief. At last I could see the end of my trials, the end of a situation as trying as it is possible to imagine. Some of my friends at this time were afraid that Baudouin, the Procureur Général, would prove too enterprising, that he would go too far in revealing the truth concerning all the crimes of my opponents. I was greatly angered by this attitude and said to them: "Are we going to repeat the mistake made at Rennes, where everyone was handled with gloves while Mercier and his accomplices shamelessly continued their activity? You do not conciliate dishonest adversaries," I added; "you confront them with their crimes, in order to put them where they can do no harm. It would be a serious blunder to seek to excuse, under pretext of a false pacification, the crimes of our opponents."

The Court sessions of June 15 and 17 were devoted to the examination, *in camera,* of the secret military dossier presented by Major Targe, and the secret diplomatic dossier presented by M. Paléologue, Minister Plenipotentiary. The latter, after submitting the dossier, added that he considered it his duty, as a diplomat and as a representative of the Department of Foreign Affairs (whose view was the same as his own), to explain the reasons which permitted him to testify to the sincerity of the declarations made in my favor by foreign powers. These reasons were connected with the circumstances under which the declarations had been made.

On Monday, June 18, the public hearings opened with the reading of Justice Moras' report, which was continued in the sessions of June 18 to 22. I considered Moras' report very firm, in so far as it dealt with the complete insufficiency of the accusations against me. But it was too indulgent toward my opponents and was inaccurate concerning Henry, the significance of whose criminal acts, dating from 1894, Moras failed to recognize. I agreed with Moras that Esterhazy was in fact the traitor. As early as the drafting of Maître Mornard's brief, I had discussed with him in detail the hypothesis that Esterhazy had been engaged merely in counterespionage with the knowledge of Henry —an hypothesis already examined with even more emphasis by Baudouin in his brief. It took courage to admit that the problem of Henry's complicity with Esterhazy had not yet been solved. Although there was no explanation for Henry's role—his desperation since the day of my arrest, when he made a false report, and his accumulating forgeries—still there was no evidence that he had expenses which were greater than his resources. Hence there seemed to be no motive for any complicity with Esterhazy, and every crime presupposes a motive. In the existing state of the question, it was better to reserve judgment on Henry's criminal role.

Maître Mornard appraised Moras' report in this way:

THERE are some very good things in this report, just as there are some bad features. And there are certain inaccuracies. The dominant note is the obvious intention to spare the accused and excuse their acts. At the same time the report is firm in its statement of the insufficiency of the accusation.

Ranc wrote this moving article:

THUS far I have read only the first part of Justice Moras' lucid report, but that is enough to enable me to repeat that, in the eyes of every man who is not blinded by prejudice, the complete insufficiency of the charges brought against Captain Dreyfus is fully revealed. What is also brought into sharp relief is the crime which has been committed, the shamelessness of those who forced from the military judges a conviction which is injustice itself. Read this apostrophe of the rapporteur to General Mercier: "Let us admit that you were obliged to prosecute for the crime of high treason this officer whose career and promise you knew. It was then your first duty, as Minister, to observe the law which you invoked, to act with prudence, to leave the accused complete freedom in his defense. Respect for justice and the honor of the Army made this your imperative duty." Have there ever been more deadly words than these?

And further on, the rapporteur affirms that even before Captain Dreyfus had been questioned, before he had been able to furnish any explanation, his interrogators had reached their conclusions. Before the investigation had begun, Captain Dreyfus' fate was sealed.

There exist no confessions of Dreyfus. That has now been proved and more than proved. On the other hand, however, we do have, signed and available, confessions of du Paty de Clam, and the rapporteur read these interesting documents.

In one of them, du Paty admits that, as an officer of the judicial police, he did not act independently—that he had superiors, that he had to obey them, that he did nothing but conform to their instructions, nothing but execute the orders which they gave him. Yes, he is right in admitting that he was the executor of the base deeds of the General Staff.

And yet his investigation, all his performances, yielded nothing; he was floundering in the dark. . . .

But General Mercier did not wish to abandon the prosecution. He must have, the General Staff must have, a conviction—a criminal—and this criminal must be Captain Dreyfus, must be a Jew!

It was then that Mercier determined to "thicken" the too-fragile proof by submitting to the military judges those secret documents, some of which were forgeries, and which in any event would have evaporated if the defense had known of their existence and been allowed to dispute them.

There you have the work of Mercier! There you have the crime!

In the conclusion of his report, M. Moras, without making a specific recommendation, revealed that his preference lay with setting aside the verdict and remanding the case. His arguments were weak and contradictory. On one hand, he admitted that there was no longer any charge against me. On the other, he declared that he had found no new evidence relative to the bordereau, despite the fact that he had the lucid and peremptory report of MM. Appell, Poincaré, and Darboux. He lacked the courage to pronounce the decisive word, which should have been the logical conclusion to the very careful examination he had just made of the dossier. Although he admitted the charges were base-less, he did not dare ask the Court itself to declare my inno-cence.

The sessions of June 25, 26, 27, 28 and 30, and those of July 2, 3, and 5 were given over to M. Baudouin's charge. His argu-ment was very clear and forceful, branding forever with the seal of infamy the authors of the crimes against truth and justice. Baudouin called a lie a lie, a forgery a forgery, acts for which he cannot be sufficiently praised. His vehement language, which caused some astonishment in precincts accustomed to tranquil discussion, was nothing more than the indignation of a man of integrity, faced by so many lies and crimes. Baudouin drew a scarcely flattering portrait of me, citing the testimony of cer-tain witnesses for the prosecution. In this connection he might have reflected on the very fitting words of one of my General Staff colleagues of 1894, who became—once he had been enlight-ened—one of my defenders and closest friends: "When, in 1894, the Deputy Chief of the General Staff assembled us to announce that you were guilty and that unquestionable proofs of this ex-isted, we accepted this verdict without discussion because it came from a superior officer. Henceforth, we forgot all your good qualities, all our friendly relations with you. And we ransacked our memories for corroboration of the certitude which had just been impressed upon us. Everything served that end."

The sessions of July 5, 6 and 7 were devoted to the splendid plea of my courageous defender, Maître Mornard. His introduc-tion was lofty and noble; his plea as extraordinary for its logic as it was impressive for its force. In distinguished style and with great nobility of thought, he marshaled all of the arguments in the case he was defending.

In summary, during the trial which had now lasted three weeks, the justices of the Court had manifested admirable calm-ness and sincerity. All of the lies, all of the miserable acts of falsification and of forgery were subjected to a calm and pitiless criticism. The guilty were branded with the seal of infamy by the sure hand of M. Baudouin. The whole truth was brought to light, terrible for the criminals but rich in amends for those who had been slandered and whose rights had been disregarded. It was indeed an impressive and magnificent sight when the Court pronounced, in the name of a great and free people, words of justice awaited for years—words pronounced amidst the respect of the entire nation, excepting only a few wretches—forgers or perjurers—who, along with friends cast in the same mold, the Drumonts and the Charles Maurras's, went on stammering their colossal lies. In a letter to the Presiding Justice of the Court of Cassation, General Mercier dared recur to the alleged "historic night." This man was magnificent in his audacity, infamy, and cynicism.

With its unlimited powers, the Court of Cassation had now completely established my innocence. Henceforth, in my view, if the Court hesitated to proclaim the innocence which it had itself made manifest, it would appear to retreat in the face of the truth. And if, after having proclaimed the truth, the Court should hesitate to conform its sovereign judgment to that truth, it would seem to retreat in the face of justice.

On July 9 the Court began its private deliberations on the final judgment. The first session was devoted to the examination of "new evidence." It was unanimously voted to set aside the Rennes judgment. In the sessions of July 10 and 11 the question as to whether the judgment should be set aside with or without remanding the case was discussed. I learned to my profound joy at six-thirty of the evening of July 11 that the Court had voted, 31 to 18, to set aside the judgment without remanding the case. At last I was at the end of twelve years of affliction, the end of my anguish for the future of my children. I seemed to feel that a tremendous burden, which had so long oppressed my heart, had now been lifted.

At noon on Thursday, July 12, the solemn judgment proclaiming my innocence was read. Our joy knew no limits. In the emotion of the moment, my memory went back to those who were no longer there to rejoice in the triumph of a cause for which they had suffered so much: Bernard Lazare, Zola, Scheurer-Kestner, Trarieux, Grimaux, Giry, Molinier, Zadoc-Kahn, my beloved father-in-law, and so many others too soon taken from us. Relatives and friends came to our house in crowds, all of them overjoyed to see me finally at the end of my trials. There were tender scenes which added to my emotion.

I had never doubted the coming of this triumph of justice and truth over error, falsehood and crime. What had sustained me since the fatal day of my arrest, and all during the most terrible suffering, perhaps, that any man has ever borne, was this unwavering faith that some day, to the whole world, France would proclaim my innocence, and would efface this monstrous wrong to its last vestige. I shall always feel profound gratitude toward all those who contributed with such courage and unselfishness to the triumph of justice.

Messages came in great numbers during this day and I had scarcely time to look at them, since we had visitors until late that evening. Messages continued to arrive on the following days.

As soon as the Court's decision had been rendered, I wrote to Mme. Trarieux, Mme. Zola, and Mme. Bernard Lazare, to send my profound respects and to recall to them my gratitude for their regretted husbands. I also wrote to Lieutenant-Colonel Hartmann and to others. From Colonel Picquart I received this reply:

My dear Dreyfus:

Thank you for your note. I can imagine your joy and that of your family. As you know, I would have preferred the Court-Martial, but I shan't be stubborn. Perhaps it is better this way.

The solution adopted by the Court of Cassation, in accord both with law and good sense, was obviously much preferable to that which would have remanded the case to a Court-Martial. The latter procedure would have been useless and without any object, since everything had been examined and passed upon. Such a step would only have prolonged a sterile agitation.

On Friday, July 13, two sessions glorious for France and the Republic took place in the Senate and Chamber of Deputies. The Government had submitted two bills, one of which named me major, the other giving Lieutenant-Colonel Picquart those amends which he deserved, in the form of a promotion as brigadier general. The bill affecting me was adopted by 432 votes to 32, amidst the applause of all the Left. The President of the Chamber, Brisson, then declared: "Your President registers with pride this vote, which consecrates by law that triumph of justice which for the past two days has won for France the acclamations of the whole world." The law concerning Lieutenant-Colonel Picquart was passed by 449 votes to 26. My bill was passed in the Senate by a vote of 182 to 30, that of Picquart by 184 to 26. I was astonished, however (and many of my friends expressed the same surprise), that my promotion to the rank of major had been dated from the day of the promulgation of this law. In justice the same rule should have been applied to me as to Colonel Picquart. He was placed ahead of all those who, at the time when he left the Army, were his juniors in the rank of lieutenant-colonel.

During the session of the Chamber of Deputies in which the laws of reinstatement were passed, Maurice Barrès took it upon himself to speak. He, who during an entire Parliament came to the tribune only twice, suddenly made himself the spokesman of the thirty-two irreconcilables, those for whom no judgment, no reason, no truth could overcome prejudice. Maurice Barrès now undertook to be the champion of Mercier against me. What melancholy courage to wish to be, at any price, the defender of such a criminal! He lost then an admirable occasion to be silent, the best of all occasions. Unhappy man, possessor of such distinguished talent!

During these days I often thought again of all those who were no longer present to share in the triumph of the cause they had so valiantly defended: Bernard Lazare, young author of ability and of a brilliant future, at once artist, poet and sociologist, who was the first to write a brief in my behalf, in which he set forth in simple style all the facts then known. Zola, who brought his genius to the struggle, and of whom Maurice Bartillat said so well in a speech on October 1, 1905, at the commemorative ceremony at Médan: "It was recently said that in Zola 'lived for a moment the conscience of humanity.' Today he is—by virtue of his work, his thought, his influence—the pure and noble expression of the conscience of his country." Ludovic Trarieux, who remembered that he was a *Girondin* and who hurled himself with passion into the fight for the truth. Scheurer-Kestner, noble and beautiful soul, who died at the oar. And so many others! For all of them, it was France who embodied the very highest ethical principles, and they could not permit her to forget her generous sentiments of human justice.

In the days which followed, telegrams and letters continued to arrive in such numbers that it was impossible for me to reply to them. I was obliged to have recourse to the newspapers to thank my friends, known and unknown, and to say how greatly I had been touched by their expressions of sympathy.

On the morning of July 20, the *Journal officiel*[1] published my appointment as chevalier of the Legion of Honor. It had been the duty of General Mensier, member of the Council of the Order of the Legion of Honor, to present to the Council the report on the proposal made on my behalf by the Minister of War. General Mensier accompanied his recommendations with these noble words:

In view of Major Dreyfus' years of service, I might limit myself to saying that the nomination has been made in conformance with the rules, and that we have only to give it our formal adherence. There is, however, quite another duty incumbent upon us. In the presence of a case which has had such painful repercussions in the entire world, I should like to add that we ought to view our decision as constituting just amends for a soldier who has endured a martyrdom without parallel.

The decision of the Council of the Order was unanimous.

On the afternoon of the same day, my stripes were restored in a ceremony which took place in the court of the artillery quarters at the École Militaire. The setting of the Cour Desjardins, with its grey and ancient walls, had remained unchanged since the time when I was a lieutenant in the mounted battery at the École Militaire. For this act of amends, they did not choose that setting near by, the great court of the École Militaire, where twelve years earlier that first terrible ceremony had taken place. This was at my own request, for I was fearful that the emotion stirred by my own memories would be greater than my strength, and that it would in the end overcome my courage.

At half-past one the troops which were to perform the honors, two mounted batteries and two squadrons of the First Cuirassiers, formed in lines parallel to the three sides of the court. They were under the orders of Lieutenant-Colonel Gaillard-Bournazel of the First Cuirassiers. At five minutes of two came the blast of trumpets. General Gillain, Commander of the First Cavalry Division, a man of martial bearing and white moustache,

1. The official organ of the French State.

entered the court on foot and passed quickly in front of the troops. The silence was heavy and impressive. Amid this silence my thoughts, bewildered, fled back to memories of twelve years ago—the howling of the mob, the terrible ceremony, my stripes unjustly torn from me, my sword broken and lying in pieces at my feet. . . . My heart beat as though it would break, the blood rushed to my temples, and my forehead was bathed in perspiration. . . . I had to make a great effort of will to control myself and not to cry aloud my sufferings of the past.

The command, *"Ouvrez le ban,"*[2] awoke me from my painful reverie and brought me back to the reality of the moment, the ceremony of redress. General Gillain drew his sword with a fine flourish, and first presented the cross of officer of the Legion of Honor to Major Targe. The ceremony was concluded with drum and bugle, which at once sounded again to open the ceremony for me. When General Gillain pronounced the usual words, his voice was shaken with emotion, and, as he pinned the insignia on me, he said in a gentle voice: "Major Dreyfus, I am happy to have the duty of presenting your decoration. I know what fine memories the First Cavalry Division has retained of you." He embraced me with great feeling, and his eyes were moist. The troops then took up a position in close formation at the rear. The command, "Forward, march," rang out. With the Lieutenant-Colonel at their head, and preceded by trumpets, the troops passed in review before General Gillain, Major Targe and myself, the officers saluting with the sabre as they filed by. The brasses sounded high and clear on this joyful day.

The troops were gone. I was at once surrounded, and there were cries of *"Vive Dreyfus!" "Non!"* I exclaimed: *"Vive la République, vive la vérité!"* Eager hands were reached out to me. I took them with a warm clasp, and embraced my friends. The whole scene was so moving that words are powerless to recall it. . . . Anatole France came toward me in his turn, and said: "I am very happy and very much stirred. I don't know how I can adequately praise the constancy you have shown through so many afflictions. Your constancy has enabled us to accomplish the work of justice and of amends, crowned by to-

2. The opening of the ceremony of decoration with drum and bugle; the ceremony is concluded with the command, *"Fermez le ban."*

Paris, 4 juillet 1899.

Capitaine,

souffrez que, sans être connu de vous, je vous salue respectueusement à votre retour en France.

Sachant de quelle effroyable erreur vous avez été la victime, j'accomplis mon devoir d'homme et de français, en vous exprimant et ma douloureuse sympathie pour les souffrances épouvantables qui vous ont assailli et ma haute admiration pour la constance

Letter from Anatole France to Dreyfus on his return from Devil's Island.

inébranlable avec laquelle
vous les avez endurées. Vous
êtes soutenu, je le sais, par
le sentiment de votre
innocence et par l'espoir
de la faire reconnaître
un jour. Cet espoir ne
sera pas trompé.

Recevez, capitaine, l'assurance
de mes sentiments de haute
estime et de profonde
sympathie

Anatole France

day's solemnity. Let me take your hand and say no more.'' I then embraced my son, and in turn my wife and the members of my family. These were happy greetings indeed from all those I loved and for whom I had had the courage to live.

I sought out General Picquart, who had been present at the ceremony, and who shook my hand warmly. I expressed to him my profound gratitude, as I did also to M. Baudouin, who was present. But all of this emotion had been too much for me. I suffered from a cardiac disturbance which brought on a brief fainting spell. When I was restored, I drove off with Georges Bourdon, of the *Figaro*, and my son.

What a splendid day of restitution this had been for France and the Republic! My case was at an end. Lieutenant-Colonel Picquart had been reinstated in the Army with the rank of brigadier general, redress for the persecution he had endured for defending me from the moment he became convinced of my innocence. Although all those who had fought for justice and who were still living had not been equally rewarded for the sufferings they had endured in behalf of the truth, it was clear that they would find reward in the inward satisfaction of conscience and in the merited respect of their contemporaries. And even if they seem to be forgotten, theirs is not a smaller share of happiness. For they fought not merely for the cause of an individual, but contributed largely to one of the most extraordinary revivals the world ever witnessed, a movement which will echo into the most distant future, because it marked a turning point in the history of humanity, a magnificent step forward in an era of progress for the ideas of liberty, of justice, and of social solidarity.

THE LAST YEARS

BY PIERRE DREYFUS

THE LAST YEARS

AFTER both branches of Parliament had, by immense majorities, passed the law which reinstated Major Dreyfus as an Army officer, he was detailed to the Fort of Vincennes. There he resumed his duties on October 15, 1906, twelve years to a day after his tragic arrest. Shortly thereafter, he was appointed to the command of the Arrondissement of St. Denis. In spite of the suffering which he had undergone in the painful years just past, he retained an enthusiastic interest in military affairs. He declined to confuse two separate factors: the opinion of an Army which had been deceived with respect to himself, but was now enlightened; and the misdeeds of a few of its leaders, blinded by anti-Semitic prejudice. Then, too, he remained faithful to his oath of 1870, when, as a mere child, he had seen the victorious German troops march through Mulhouse—an oath "to become a French officer so that he might better serve his country and avenge the honor of Alsatians who had been shorn by force from the *patrie.*" Moreover, Dreyfus' reception by his colleagues left nothing to be desired. On July 28, a banquet was given in his honor at the Army Club by the artillery officers of the First Cavalry Division. He was most heartily welcomed on every hand.

Dreyfus was indeed deeply touched by all the attentions shown him, and would very willingly have continued his career in the Army. Unfortunately, due to an error which could not be corrected in time, the law of July 13, 1906, appointing him major, dated his seniority only from the day of the promulgation of the law. Whereas, if his career had followed its normal course, he would now have been lieutenant-colonel, or, in any case, about to be promoted to that rank. In view of the fact that this situation could not be remedied, Major Dreyfus considered that his dignity demanded that he retire. Not without sadness, he applied for retirement, June 26, 1907. Henceforth he devoted his leisure to studies in history and sociology.

Dreyfus was present at the ceremonies accompanying the moving of the ashes of Zola to the Pantheon, June 4, 1908, when he was wounded in the arm by some journalist who fired two revolver shots at him from behind. He was taken at once to a police station near by to have the wound dressed. There it was happily discovered that the wound was not serious. This stupid attack was the occasion for expression of attentive sympathy by numerous friends—a sympathy admirably expressed in the following letter from her whom the whole world knew as the "divine Sarah":

ONCE again you have suffered; once again we have wept. But you ought no longer to suffer, and we should no longer weep. The flag of truth has been placed in the hands of the distinguished figure who lies dead beneath the vaults of glory. That flag will rise above the baying of the mob.

Suffer no more, beloved martyr. Only gaze about you—near by, then farther, then farther still—and you will see the army of those who love you and who defend you against neglect and cowardice and lies. Among these is your friend

Sarah Bernhardt.
June 6, 1906.

Every summer Major Dreyfus went with his family for a month or two in Switzerland—where he invariably had a warm reception—and he often finished his holiday in Italy. He preferred Florence, and loved to sit in the Piazzale Michelangelo, and, in this ideal environment, to admire the magnificent monuments which surrounded him on every side.

The events of 1914 took Major Dreyfus, then in Switzerland, by surprise. As soon as mobilization seemed probable, he decided to return to Paris to reënter active service. He left with his daughter and had just entered France when he learned, on the station platform at Bellegarde, of the murder of Jaurès, the first great victim of the catastrophe. This terrible news caused him deep grief.

On August 2, 1914, Major Dreyfus went to Vincennes, and was assigned as adjutant to the colonel in command of artillery in the zone north of the Intrenched Camp of Paris. He followed with emotion the progress of the march of the German Armies on the capital. While he was at an observation post with other officers in the Fort of Daumont, he witnessed von Kluck's troops emerge from Luzarches, and, instead of coming directly toward them, turn obliquely eastward in the direction of the Ourcq. It is not without interest that it was from the Fort of Daumont that there came one of the first warnings of this manoeuvre of the enemy, warnings which, thanks to the genius of Gallieni, made it possible to bring on and to win the Battle of the Marne.[1]

After having coöperated in placing the zone north of the Intrenched Camp in a state of defense, and when this task was substantially complete, Dreyfus was detailed, on his own request, to the field army. He was given command of the artillery park[2] of the 158th Division, which formed part of the 20th Corps. He was with this Corps in its various peregrinations, and took part in the great battles at Verdun and the Chemin des Dames. In 1917, the 20th Corps relieved the 7th, which included the artillery regiment of "75's" in which his son commanded a battery. Dreyfus was overjoyed at the opportunity of greeting his son on the field of battle at Verdun, a meeting which gladdened a heart devoted to family and country.

As the result of an order affecting the age limit of officers in combatant units, Major Dreyfus was sent to the rear at the beginning of 1918. He was placed at the disposition of the Minister of Munitions, who appointed him to the command of the artillery park at Orleans. On September 5 of the same year, he was made lieutenant-colonel and then promoted to the rank of officer of the Legion of Honor. Madame Dreyfus had been just as eager to serve her country, and, for the duration of hostilities, she performed with unsparing devotion the duties of a voluntary nurse in the hospitals of Paris. Then came the Armistice and the end of the carnage. . . . Lieutenant-Colonel Dreyfus, his health unfortunately much impaired by past sufferings and by the wastage of the War, returned to his tranquil family life. He

1. Instead of continuing the advance, in order to cross the Seine below Paris, as ordered, General von Kluck (commanding the German First Army, on the extreme west of the line) on August 31 wheeled southeastward past the northern front of Paris, with the object of making contact with Bülow's Second Army and of striking the supposed French flank. General Gallieni, Military Governor of the capital, realizing that the German movement offered an exposed flank, convinced Joffre of the opportuneness of a general counteroffensive.

2. Collective name given to the whole of the guns, carriages, ammunition, etc., of a unit of siege or field artillery.

continued to read a great deal and to interest himself above all in everything which appeared relating to the Affair.

In the course of the month of June, 1930, he received from Madame Schwartzkoppen a copy of her husband's memoirs, which had just been published. It was accompanied by the following letter:

Hanover,
June 1, 1930.

Très honoré Monsieur Dreyfus:

I am sending you today by mail the posthumous memoirs of my husband, Max von Schwartzkoppen, General of Infantry, edited by Colonel Schwertfeger: *The Truth about Dreyfus.*

In doing this, I am conscious of acting as my husband would have wished. It had always been his desire to testify in the outrageous case of which you were the principal figure and the victim. For various reasons, which his memoirs clearly indicate, it was impossible for him to do so during his lifetime.

LOUISE VON SCHWARTZKOPPEN
née BARONESS VON WEDEL.

As he read these memoirs, Colonel Dreyfus lived again, with melancholy intensity, the period of physical and spiritual sufferings through which he had passed, and whose memory time had done nothing to mitigate. He suffered bitter regret that Schwartzkoppen had lacked the courage to intervene when he learned of the judicial wrong which had been committed; that he had not, like Colonel Picquart, been willing to sacrifice a brilliant career in order to reveal the truth, and thus obey the dictates of his conscience.

During the last years of his life, Colonel Dreyfus' strength gradually declined, although his mind remained as active as ever. He was more and more confined to his home, where he was surrounded by the affection of his family. In the course of his daily walk, which became steadily shorter, he was often stopped by passers-by, who greeted him and expressed their sympathy and respect. He had the pleasure of seeing his children married and the parents of numerous children, whose love and respect were his joy.

When the final illness struck him down, he never complained. He knew that he was lost, and sometimes he would say that life,

Lieutenant-Colonel Dreyfus in 1934, at the age of seventy-five.

which still made him endure such suffering, had indeed been cruel. With touching devotion numerous doctors, among whom were the most eminent in the profession, gave freely of their time. And they esteemed it a great privilege to be called to his bedside. During this long year of illness, Colonel Dreyfus was unceasingly sustained by her who bears his name so worthily. After months of superhuman effort, she was still at his bedside, and remained there to the last. She cared for him with maternal patience, and her very presence, so much loved, brought him constant comfort and solace. In his wife's glance, the sick man could read again their whole life together, made up as it had been of mutual confidence and respect, affection, struggles shared, obstacles overcome together, affinities of mind and of heart—in a word, of a love deep, steadfast, and radiant.

In this room where he suffered so much, there was one element which had changed not at all. They remained for each other just what they had been after the ordeal—ennobled, more understanding, more sympathetic. In the eyes of his wife, Dreyfus was always the hero of the most tragic of destinies, a man whose resolution, noble character, and unwavering courage had moved a universe. And in the same way, Mme. Dreyfus had never ceased to seem to him an exceptional being, his guiding star, the light toward which, from the depths of his prison, he turned by day and by night. He was ever grateful for her confidence, her faithfulness, her steadfastness, her motherly virtues, her comforting affection. He felt boundless admiration for her stoic courage during the long and painful struggle when, veiled in mourning, simple and affecting, she rallied about her, as about an eternal flame, such deep feeling and strength.

.   .   .   .

Despite every effort made to save him, the patient steadily lost ground. On July 11, 1935, when his son made his daily visit, Colonel Dreyfus held his hand for a long time without speaking a word, and in this silent gesture conveyed to him his final message. About five o'clock on the afternoon of the following day, with his family present, he closed his eyes and quietly passed away.

APPENDICES

APPENDIX I

LETTERS TO CAPTAIN AND MME. DREYFUS
FROM DISTINGUISHED PERSONS

THERE is nothing calculated to give a more adequate impression of the ideas and emotions of their contemporaries than the letters written in the midst of the battle to Captain and Mme. Dreyfus.[1] Those we have included below will doubtless be read with interest. They are not many, if one reflects that at one time Mme. Dreyfus received more than a thousand letters a day from all parts of the world. But they are among the most typical.

The first to soothe somewhat her aching heart and give her a glimpse of that hesitant but comforting dawn when she might once again leave off her mourning garb (worn during her husband's absence) was the letter in which Joseph Reinach told her that Scheurer-Kestner had become convinced of Captain Dreyfus' innocence and wished to have this made known to him. Others followed, and among them the moving letters which we were induced to publish here.

From PRINCE ALBERT of Monaco:

Paris, October 30, 1898.

Madame:

I have never ceased to defend Captain Dreyfus against acts of cowardice and stupidity. Now that the passions of men have been silenced by the wisdom of the highest court in France, I offer you, whom I know only through your suffering, this token of my admiration, and I hope that your children will live to forget the cruel dream they have known as they grew.

I think that they will take little pride in belonging to the human race, when they come to understand that at the close of this century the voice of reason and of humanity could be dimmed by that of intolerance; that anti-Semitism was contem-

1. This introductory note is by Pierre Dreyfus, as are the comments on the correspondents following.

porary with Pasteur! Their father's martyrdom will make them regret that they have lived too soon, at a time when the cultivation of man's mind has only served to make him aware of the extent of his failings.

But later they will learn to know their father's heart, revealed by a cry of distress unjustly suffered. They will ponder the opinion of those men who, by their character and ability, made the name of France respected, and whose acts accorded with their profound convictions. They will bless their valiant mother who was able to overcome the alliance of weakness and folly. The example of this nobility, on one hand, and this baseness, on the other, will offer them the examples which make fine men.

I ask, Madame, that you regard the sentiments which I have here expressed as those of a true friend of that France which views with joy a better future opening before her.

ALBERT, Prince of Monaco.

From ANDRÉ CHEVRILLON, member of the French Academy, whose extraordinary works on England, Morocco, and India have become classic:

Paris, October 29, 1898.
Madame:

Permit one who has been convinced from the beginning, and who for more than a year has not ceased thinking of your dear martyr, to offer you his warm congratulations on the occasion of the Court of Cassation's decision. This day of rejoicing for you is a day of happiness for the whole country, which has vindicated herself and can once more lift her head before the foreigner. Today France needs rehabilitation more than does Alfred Dreyfus.

Please accept, Madame, the expression of my profound respect.

ANDRÉ CHEVRILLON.

From Count JEAN ZAMOYSKY, descendant of a distinguished Polish family.

Posen, June 8, 1899.
Madame:

Although I am a foreigner and have not the honor of being

known to you, permit me to say that I share your great joy as much as I have shared your great unhappiness.

On January 5, 1895, the day of the degradation ceremony at the Champ de Mars, I exclaimed to myself: "This man must be innocent!" Since that time I have continued to tell others my profound conviction of Captain Alfred Dreyfus' innocence. Hence I should be happy if I could be present at the Court-Martial at Rennes, to witness, not the acquittal of your husband nor the vindication of his honor (of that he has no need), but the recognition of the great, the criminal wrong committed, a recognition which will rehabilitate the honor of the French Army.

I should like to be one of the first to shake Captain Dreyfus' hand when he returns from the Salvation Islands—as well as that of the loyal and courageous Colonel Picquart, who has at once the heart of Bayard and the soul of Turenne.

Please accept, Madame, the expression of my respect.

Count JEAN ZAMOYSKY.

From GABRIEL MONOD, member of the Institute, Professor at the Collège de France:

Versailles, July 2, 1899.

Dear Captain:

Permit one who is unknown to you to bring you a heartfelt salutation of welcome at the moment when you have been returned to your family and your country, after the solemn proceedings at which the truth (so long disregarded and wilfully obscured) has finally been recognized and proclaimed. Our home is one of those—more numerous than you think—where your guilt was always doubted, and where, since the publication of the bordereau, we have been certain of your innocence. My wife, my two sons, and my three daughters have, since the beginning, stood with me wholeheartedly in undertaking your defense against those who shared the error of your first judges—and they encouraged me to take my modest part in the efforts of your family and of certain courageous friends of justice to win from the authorities an appeal of your case. You have already been vindicated by the highest of our courts of justice, and you are about to witness your innocence finally proclaimed by your Army comrades and superiors.

It is not alone your honor, it is the honor of the Army and of the country which lies in the hands of your military judges. I am confident that they will render a judgment of amends which will permit every Frenchman henceforth to walk beside you with head high and conscience clear.

Please believe that our sympathy goes out to you and your family, whose heroism, patience, and discretion during your long trials we have so much admired.

GABRIEL MONOD.

From GIRY, member of the Institute and distinguished student of medieval life, whose honest and courageous testimony at the Zola trial caused a sensation:

Paris, July 3, 1899.

Mon Capitaine:

Permit one of those innumerable unknown friends, who has long hoped for your return, to express to you his feelings of sincere admiration and, allow me to add, of affection—feelings which have come from a close study of your case.

This study was originally rooted in anxiety over the question of legality, at a time when I scarcely believed in anything beyond irregularities in your trial. But my investigation gradually led to doubts, and presently the documents I saw not only persuaded me of your innocence but disclosed in you a man who did honor to mankind. When I was asked to undertake the comparison of handwriting examples, it was with tears in my eyes that I examined your most intimate correspondence, as it had been turned over to the court. It seemed to me that in reading it I was guilty of a profanation.

I hesitated to write you, fearing that I should seem to obtrude. But since circumstances have thrust me into your life at so tragic a juncture, I thought that at the time when you have just been returned to your country, to your family, to your old friends, you would perhaps find some satisfaction in receiving from one of your new friends (for whom you are indebted to your terrible misfortune) the sincere assurances of his sympathy, admiration, and unwavering devotion.

A. GIRY.

From ANATOLE FRANCE:

Paris, July 4, 1899.

Captain:

Although I am not known to you personally, permit me to send you my respectful greetings on your return to France.

Knowing the frightful wrong of which you have been the victim, I am only doing my duty as a man and a Frenchman in expressing my heartfelt sympathy for the terrible sufferings which have beset you, and my profound admiration for the unwavering constancy with which you have endured these afflictions. You have, I know, been sustained by the feeling of your innocence, and by the hope that you would one day have that innocence recognized. That hope will not be disappointed.

Accept, Captain, the assurance of my great esteem and my profound sympathy.

ANATOLE FRANCE.

From JOSEPH REINACH:

Paris, July 5, 1899.

Mon Capitaine:

I was delighted with the news your admirable brother sent me this morning by my friend, Bernard Lazare. This is the first letter you will receive from me to tell you of my profound esteem and my absolute confidence in that justice which is to crown the triumph of truth. This is, however, actually the second letter which I have written you. The first, which I sent on September 15, 1897, in my name and in that of Scheurer Kestner, is in my drawer. I shall give it to you personally at a very early date, I hope, and I shall then tell you of the circumstances in which it was returned to me, accompanied by a refusal to forward it to you. In that letter I advised you of the generous work which my old and excellent friend, Scheurer, proposed to undertake. I also expressed those sentiments which I have had for you personally since the first days of this drama, although I have never had the honor of meeting or seeing you. You have learned perhaps from Demange that since 1894 I have never doubted your innocence. When you read that little pamphlet, *The Curé of Fréjus, or the Moral Proofs,* you will understand, not the sure instinct, but the unanswerable arguments which inspired that faith in me. When I wrote you that first letter in September, 1897, I had on two or three occasions seen Mme. Dreyfus, for whom I had the deepest and most devoted respect. It was only later that I met your brother Mathieu. He has one of the noble hearts, one of the finest minds of our time.

After the terrible trials you have sustained with such heroism, I cannot conceive of its being necessary to say to you: "Have confidence." You are approaching the end, Captain, and your vindication will be a solace to you, not only in itself, but also because it will add to the glory of France—which remains the great land of Right—and of the Army, which will be happy and proud to make amends for the wrong done one of her finest sons. It will have been the honor of my own life to have contributed my share to this patriotic work, above all others.

Let me express here, Captain, my sincere and profound affection.

JOSEPH REINACH.

From SCHEURER-KESTNER:

Biarritz, July 9, 1899.

Mon Capitaine:

In the midst of the many tokens of sympathy which you are receiving, I do not wish my own to be absent.

These I send you with a full heart, for I number myself among those who rejoice most deeply that the hour of justice has finally sounded for you.

I have long been convinced of your innocence, and I have followed in bitter anxiety the events which have finally brought the truth to light.

The hideous martyrdom to which you have been subjected you have endured with a courage only a clear conscience could give. But you have had to sustain you, to uphold your honor and the honor of your children's name, a brother and an admirable wife, who have been worthy of you. I have been in a position to appreciate the courage which they have brought to your aid in your great misfortune.

May this sweet solace be for you the beginning of amends.

Soon complete justice will be yours!

Let me express, Captain, my profound sympathy.

A. SCHEURER-KESTNER.

From ÉMILE ZOLA:

Paris, July 6, 1899.

Captain:

If I was not one of the first to write, expressing my deep sympathy and affection upon your return to France, that was because I feared my letter would be incomprehensible to you. I wanted to wait until your admirable brother should see you, and tell you of our long struggle. He has just brought me the good news of your health, your courage, your faith, and so I can now express to you my feelings, knowing that you will understand.

Ah, that heroic brother, he has been the embodiment of devotion, courage, and wisdom! It is thanks to him that, for the past eighteen months, we have cried aloud your innocence. What joy he brought me when he told me that you had come from the grave alive, that this abominable martyrdom had exalted and ennobled you. For our work is not completed. Your innocence must be openly recognized, and this recognition must save France from the moral abyss in which she has nearly foundered. So long as the innocent man remains in prison, we shall have no standing among peoples who are noble and just. At the present hour your great task is to bring us, along with justice, peace—to bring tranquillity to our sad and noble land by completing this work of amends, by revealing the character of the man for whom we have fought and in whom we have incarnated the victory of human solidarity. When the innocent man shall rise, France will become once more the land of fraternity and of justice.

You will also save the honor of the Army, of that Army which you have so loved and in which you place your highest ideal. Do not listen to those who utter blasphemy, who would exalt the Army through lies and injustice. It is we who are its true defenders. It is we who will acclaim the Army on that day when your comrades in arms acquit you and provide for the world that most holy and most sublime of all spectacles, the confession of an error. On that day the Army will represent not only force but justice.

My heart is full. I can do no more than send you all my sympathy for what you have suffered, and for what your valiant wife has suffered. My own wife joins me; all that is best in us, all that is tenderest and most noble, I want to put in this letter, so that you may know that all good people are on your side. *Je vous embrasse affectueusement.*

                                        É. ZOLA.

From the Abbé BRUGERETTE, Professor at the École Ozanam at Lyons:

                                        Lyons, July 18, 1899.

Mon Capitaine:

The homage which this letter brings is that of a Catholic priest who wishes to convey to you the expression of his sympathy and admiration.

My sympathy goes to the innocent man who has suffered all the worst that social injustice could invent. And my admiration goes to the heroic man, whose courage has never been conquered by misfortune. In your person, Monsieur, justice was cynically violated. It will soon be nobly honored, and that is what has consecrated your cause, so that it has taken profound hold of all generous hearts, so that it has bound all men of sincerity to you and your family. Here the words of the Apostle Paul are fitting, words pronounced in times which understood them better than do ours: "There are no longer either Greeks or Jews, circumcised or uncircumcised, barbarians or slaves or freemen. But the spirit of Christ is in us all." That is the spirit of Him who said: *"The truth shall make you free,"* and *"Seek ye first justice."* And truth will make you free, Monsieur. This is the hope of all those who have made it a point of honor to defend your cause, and who have been unafraid (that is why the truth is still dearer to us) to suffer something for her! Courage, Monsieur, you are approaching the end of your ordeal. All the good wishes of those hearts partisan to truth and justice are with you. Their sympathies will be your attendants before the Court-Martial at Rennes.

Please accept, Monsieur, the assurance of my deep respect.

                                        Abbé J. BRUGERETTE.

From HYACINTHE LOYSON, Rector of the Gallican Catholic Church:

                                        Neuilly, July 20, 1899.

Cher et grand compatriote:

I am one of the first who believed in your innocence and who pleaded your cause before men. And I also pleaded it before God.

The thought of you has filled my mind during long days and long nights, and I prayed to God—not the stupid and ferocious idol that has been substituted for Him, but the true and living God, the God of justice and of love.

I asked that He grant you nobility and strength and tranquillity in your martyrdom, and later in your apostolate. For, now that you have returned like a prodigy from the grave and the infernal regions, you no longer belong only to your family and your friends. You belong to a France of freedom and brotherhood, whose cause you have unknowingly personified against scoundrels and madmen, as well as against the irresponsible whom they have deceived.

You belong to a race, that of Israel, which has suffered much, and which has suffered for humanity. That race has in you been hated and persecuted. For your part, you will accomplish your race's high vocation.

I hope that I shall some day meet you. Meanwhile I send you my deeply respectful and Christian sympathy.

HYACINTHE LOYSON.

From M. RAOUL ALLIER, Professor in the Protestant Faculty of Theology in Paris:

La Bourboule, Puy de Dôme,
August 8, 1899.

I know very well, Madame, and I have repeatedly said to myself during the weeks past, that you have other things to do than read letters. That is why I have denied myself the pleasure of writing you and your heroic husband since the day when he set foot on French soil. It is my feeling that in hours like these you are entitled to the use of every instant of your time—and yet—and yet, in the end I have done just what so many others have done. I am no longer of the same mind. I am writing these lines as a comfort to my conscience. May you read them when you have the time.

You know, Madame, the profound respect we have all had for you—all of us who, even from a distance, have followed with deep feeling your tireless efforts for the vindication of your dear martyr. But if your bravery often stirred us, there was something else which drew from us a cry of admiration. That was the courage of him who so long suffered upon his rock of torment. There is only one name with which we can worthily greet him, that of hero.

Yes, I feel small beside this man, who has lived because he willed to live; who kept his faith in justice and in truth; whose confidence in France and love for her has never for an instant faltered. . . .

Allow me, Madame, to follow my thought to its conclusion. I am a Christian, and a Christian by profound conviction. It was my sentiments as a Christian which from the first day, as in the case of so many of our pastors, influenced me to take my place at the side of you, the oppressed. Why should I not tell you of what has been one of my greatest joys?

When I decided to fight in my capacity, a very modest capacity, I knew only one thing: Captain Dreyfus was innocent. He must be freed. Of what he was himself, I knew nothing, and there was nothing I needed to know. He was one who suffered unjustly, and who must be rescued from his torment. The rest did not concern me.

Then when I read his letters, when I learned during the past months what his life had been on that infernal island, and how he had endured all these horrors, a likeness gradually formed in my mind, and I felt that I was going to greet again a friend who was very dear to me. Every morning I gather my children about our old Bible, and read them as much of the Old Testament as of the New. Almost every day we live with the Israel of ancient times, and we pray that something of the soul of these men shall descend to us. In truth, this soul of Israel, with its unshaken faith in the coming of justice, I have felt made manifest in your husband! Across the distance of the centuries I have recognized it again. It is indeed that which my two old grandmothers, descendants of the Huguenots of the Desert,[2] taught me to love and admire. I will say to you frankly what my conscience obliges me to bring you: it is the homage of a Christian soul to a true spirit of Israel. Why did I not do this sooner? I feared, and I still fear,

2. The "Huguenots of the Desert" were those who held the "Synods of the Desert," a series of prayer meetings in remote parts of the South of France in the early years of the eighteenth century. Their object was to revive Protestantism in France, rudely shaken by the revocation of the Edict of Nantes, 1685.

that I am intruding. But now my conscience is at rest, and I am content. And if ever you have the leisure to read these lines, you and Captain Dreyfus will find there only the very imperfect expression of the sentiments which I deeply feel.

Please be good enough, Madame, to pardon the freedom of this letter and believe always in my devoted respect.

R. ALLIER.

M. LOUIS HAVET, distinguished philologist, member of the Institute, Professor at the Collège de France, describing the emotion felt by the spectators at the trial when Captain Dreyfus' testimony was taken, told him of it in these lines:

Mon Capitaine: Rennes, August 21, 1899.

Your words this morning, so firm, so dignified, so clear, and so temperate, produced a great effect, a profound effect, of which I myself was deeply aware, and of which I was happy to tell Mme. Dreyfus at once. The friends of justice were not permitted to applaud you, but they have the right to express to you as individuals the warm sympathy with which they silently listened.

Earlier it was your letters which sustained their courage, and now it is you, yourself, who keep alive their confidence and their eagerness. My wife asks that I tell you how much joy my report has brought her, and to say that our letters will carry this report to others.   L. HAVET.

The great RÉJANE³ wrote on the eve of the judgment:

Trouville, September 8, 1800.

It is impossible for me today, dear Madame, not to write, so that I may be with you and yours. In our present agitation I know not what to say to you, and you have not the heart to read.

When you receive this letter, you will doubtless be very happy! Allow me to take your dear children in my arms and to hope that their dear absent one will arrive at the same time as this letter.

You know how much you can depend on me!

RÉJANE.

3. Stage name of Gabrielle Charlotte, née Réju (1857–1920), French actress.

Learning of the condemnation, Maître LABORI, who had been the admirable attorney for Zola and for Picquart, and whom a coward had some days earlier wounded with a shot in the back, wrote to his client:

Rennes, September 9, 1899.

My dear Captain:

I am much annoyed that the police have forbidden me to go out. I wished at all costs to greet you again. But that is impossible, since *they are having me leave* at midnight. M. Hild has been good enough to carry you the expression of my profound affection.

This condemnation is odious. But thank God the whole world is with you. You have been admirable in your suffering, worthy of the great cause of humanity which you represent.

This cruel hour is only a last ephemeral ordeal, I am certain. I do not speak to you of courage; you are equal to your terrible task.

Au revoir, à bientôt, laissez-moi vous embrasser de toutes mes forces.

LABORI.

From ELEONORA DUSE:

September, 1899.

Dear, dear Madame:

Lose not courage, or patience! Every heart is with you!

E. DUSE.

M. ÉMILE DUCLAUX, director of the Institut Pasteur, conveyed his indignation in these words:

Vic sur Cère, September 10, 1899.

Mon Capitaine:

You have won the first round, half lost the second. You will win the third, if you agree to live. But there are a certain number of beliefs by which you set great store; and these the judgment against you has irrevocably destroyed. If this means one more sorrow in the midst of your grief (as I believe it does), say to yourself as compensation that you have been the moving spirit in the awakening of the conscience of men; that you were the first soldier to cause a common thrill of sympathy and fraternity to pass through the hearts of nations unknown to one another; and that, while we in France were torn by internecine strife, there arose a kind of communion of hearts throughout the civilized world, a communion rising round your name and your innocence.

This conception may add to your courage. Your renewed suffering will help to strengthen the common faith. On the day of your victory there will be great joy, and I have a feeling that that day is not far off.

Meanwhile, please believe in my respectful sympathy for you and your family.

É. DUCLAUX.

From the Abbé J. VIOLLET:

September 10, 1899.

Monsieur:

Permit me to send you the expression of my heartfelt sympathy. Yesterday's judgment is an outrage at once on reason and on justice. It does not affect your honor as a Frenchman and a soldier; it makes you a martyr and a hero. You are aware that the whole world proclaims your innocence, and that even in our unfortunate country, blinded by passion and hatred, all men of honor know you to be innocent.

Divine justice will be rendered each man according to his works. This is the only thought that can sustain you at this time of injustice and despotism.

I pray God that he will make manifest his justice, and that he will give back to our wretched country its sense of justice and charity.

Please accept, Monsieur, the expression of my very deep respect.

Abbé J. VIOLLET.

From the philosopher, ÉMILE BOUTROUX, of the French Academy, Director of the Thiers Foundation:

Meran (Tyrol), September 10, 1899.

Mon Capitaine:

Your calamity is a national calamity.

You will bear it with your usual heroism, calm and respectful of your duty, but also with hope, with confidence, for the sake of your splendid wife, your children, your country, whose honor henceforth is synonymous with yours.

Please accept, *mon Capitaine,* my greetings, my sympathy, and my best wishes.

ÉMILE BOUTROUX.

From Mme. LINA SAND, daughter of George Sand:

Chateau de Nohant, Nohant-Vic (Indre),
September 12, 1899.

Madame:

It is with a heart filled with grief that I send you this word of sympathy. For two years I have followed this sinister battle with undivided attention. Truth is on the march, but what efforts are being made to defeat her!

I want you to have from the house of George Sand an expression of my admiration for your character and of my belief in the innocence of your husband.

Were our beloved Mother alive, her voice would be raised among those of the defenders of justice.

Let me express once again, Madame, my profound sadness and my unwavering hope.

LINA SAND.

From the wife of Jules Claretie, novelist and dramatist, member of the French Academy, who directed the "House of Molière"[4] for nearly thirty years:

Viroflay, September 13, 1899.

Madame:

After that frightful day, I have nothing to say to you. I have prayed, and I pray still. My husband asks me to send to Captain Dreyfus these words, which embody all our thoughts and convictions:

Captain: From the bottom of my heart I am with you. I will

4. The Comédie Française, center of French classical drama today, was founded in 1680, after Molière's death but with his company. The term "House of Molière" can refer either to Molière's troupe or to the Comédie Française itself.

not say to you, as they shouted to you before the judgment: Courage! You have that. I shall say to you: *Hope. We have that.*

Everything that good people can do for a just cause, we will do. More than ever, Madame, I am with you with all my heart and in all my thoughts. I ask you to believe in my deep feelings of devoted friendship.

EUGÉNIE CLARETIE.

From GASTON PARIS of the French Academy, Administrator of the Collège de France:

Cerisy-la-Salle (Manche),
September 15, 1899.

Madame:

If I have not written sooner to express to you and Captain Dreyfus my deep and respectful sympathy, that is because I had sent to the *Journal des débats* a letter which, if it had appeared, would have given public expression to my sentiments. In it I proposed an address to the President of the Republic, asking the pardon of Captain Dreyfus, based not upon the pity which his situation inspires (pity to which neither he, nor you, nor the friends of justice have ever wished to appeal) but on the *moral acquittal* which is implicit in the judgment of the Court-Martial. In my view, such a decision was only the prelude to a rehabilitation which must inevitably follow.

Will you be good enough, Madame, to convey to your husband the expression of my profound esteem, heightened yet more by the unfailing dignity of his bearing during the cruel ordeal of the trial, and to accept for yourself the expression of my most sympathetic respect.

GASTON PARIS.

A moving message from England from Lady STANLEY, wife of the explorer, whose intrepid expedition in search of Livingstone made his name famous throughout the world:[5]

Furze Hill, September 22, 1899.

Cher Monsieur le capitaine Dreyfus:

My husband, the African explorer, Stanley, wishes to join me

5. The original of this letter is in French.

in expressing to you all our sympathy and admiration; our sympathy for your cruel suffering, our admiration for your heroic courage. The whole of England shares our feelings. Here you have none but friends. When you come to England one day, you will see that this is so. I hope that for the present you will devote yourself to the restoration of your health and the enjoyment of life with your dear family. Your suffering has not been in vain. Thanks to your martyrdom, many reforms will be made in your Army and in your Courts-Martial. Your example of dignity, calm, and patience will aid those who suffer unmerited punishment.

My husband wishes me to say that he hopes that during the coming summer you will come with Madame Dreyfus and your two children to stay with us. We have an attractive country place: woods, lake, and meadows, where the children would be very happy, and where you and Madame Dreyfus could enjoy their pleasure. Our town house is in London, but we go to the country only in the middle of July. So you could, if you preferred, have our country house to yourselves during the months of June and July, and we should come down to make you a visit from time to time. We have cows and chickens, so that you would have the purest milk and fresh eggs.

I am hopeful that M. Trarieux, Mme. Trarieux, and Colonel Picquart will also come to us. All this is very much in the future, but it is so pleasant to make plans which seem very simple to carry out, if you are willing.

We English are happy to think that you plan to fight on for the vindication, not of Dreyfus, but of France. The judgment of the Court-Martial is a blot on France, which will be cleansed only on the day when the Court of Cassation shall resolutely declare that the Court-Martial was mistaken. Only then will the bad feeling against France be dissipated. Europe and America cannot entertain sentiments of friendship for France, so long as justice is not done you. Hence, in working for this vindication, you work also for the honor of France. As for your own name and your own honor, they shine forth pure and blameless, illumined by the martyr's aureole.

As you see, God has never abandoned you. He has chosen you as He did the chosen of the past, bound to Him by suffering.

My mother, Mrs. Tennant, has written to Mme. Dreyfus. And so it is our whole family which extends its hands to you.

Please accept, dear Captain Dreyfus, the expression of our sentiments of admiration and friendship.

DOROTHY STANLEY (Lady Stanley).

From NELLIE MELBA:[6]

Hotel Ritz, September 23, 1899.

Dear Madam:

I feel the impulse to address a few words to you to be quite irresistible. I am sharing with you so deeply the joy of the freedom of your beloved husband that I find my eyes continually filling with tears. For many months, nay years, I have followed your fortunes and his with the same intensity of emotion. This is needless to say—I have but shared the sympathetic interest of many millions. But I often wonder if any of the others shared the experience which I am about to relate to you. It was this: When in 1894 I read, with horror, the details of the degradation the thought came to me *What if he be innocent?* That thought came to stay—to remain in my mind with a strange insistence which grew into a positive, but purely instinctive belief, that a hideous blunder, or a hideous crime, had been committed. With a mind so possessed, you will well imagine, dear Madame, with what a passionate interest I have followed the later developments of your husband's case; have hoped and despaired with you, have wept and prayed with you. And now that an end is reached—an end which although legally unsatisfying, is rich with consolation in that you and your children have the beloved sufferer once more with you; that he is free to God's sky and air, and that in the hearts of the righteous and the womb of history, he is pure and great because of a martyrdom *nobly borne*— I ask you to accept the kiss of felicitation and to forgive me for unburdening to you my overcharged heart. I have said there are millions who feel as I do. One meets them everywhere; and their eyes will once more have been dim with tears as mine were this morning when I read an article describing the family group at Carpentras, in which was said "Every face is serene; in every

6. The original of this letter is in English.

eye at last a gleam of happiness; the mouths do not cease smiling'' and again these quite simple, but how pregnant words ''the children will be there tomorrow with their grandparents.'' When a great trouble comes to us in our lives we ask ''Why was it sent?'' You Madam need not ask that question. Your affliction was sent to prove the eternal truth of Shakespeare's words ''There is some soul of goodness in things evil.'' The dew of a universal sympathy had not fallen upon the earth for very long. Human love seemed dead. It only slept! It awoke with a great cry at the spectacle of your husband's unmerited sufferings; his dauntless endurance; the tenacious persistency and titanic championship of truth of those friends whose self-sacrifice and heroism will never be blotted from the pages of history, and of your own unexampled devotion, patience and dignity; and it hovers reverently around you even now that your Beloved is at last at rest in the arms of unfathomable love.

With many tender sentiments

Believe me dear Madam

Yours sincerely, NELLIE MELBA.

From MARK TWAIN :[7]

Sanna, Sept. 24/99.

Dear Mr. Chatto,

Many people will write Madame Dreyfus and tell her of many sure ways to bring back health and strength to her husband. The good will that is at the back of the act saves it from being an unjustifiable intrusion. I wish to add myself to that list of unknown well-wishers, and ask you if you cannot, through M. Zola, get Madame Dreyfus to consider the idea of entrusting to Mr. Kellgreu (49, Eaton Square, S.W.) the restoration of Captain Dreyfus's health.

I have now spent twenty minutes every morning for the past ten weeks in Kellgreu's work-room (here) watching him perform upon his patients; experimenting with the treatment myself; observing the effects of the treatment upon my wife and two daughters; talking with the patients; asking questions of Kellgreu and his assistants,—and making written notes (to the ex-

7. The original of this letter is in English.

tent of 7,000 words) ; and as a result I am now satisfied that Kell-greu can cure any disease that any physician can cure, and that in many desperate cases he can restore health where no physician can do it, and where no physician will claim to be able to do it. He does not profess to do miracles, and the things he does are not miracles—they only seem so, until one has familiarised himself with the principles upon which his method is based; then they are recognisable as the logical and arbitrary outcome of natural laws, with no taint of miracle about them. He does not make extravagant promises, but he *makes* promises, and if the patient stays the allotted time, he makes the promise good. Years ago, when Nathaniel Rothschild of Vienna came to him after vainly submitting his shattered nervous system to the baths and specialists for years, he presently got tired and was going to leave, and Kellgreu said, ''Then you will waste years again, and not get cured; if you stay here I will cure you; if you go un-cured, it can bring an unmerited discredit upon my system, through the authority of your name; therefore, I say to you this, and it is worth considering : that if you go I will never touch your case again, for any money.'' Rothschild remained and was cured.

Then Rothschild said, ''But now that I have been made well without medicines, I shall never be willing to have a doctor again, and what shall I do? I cannot cross Europe to come to you every time there is something the matter with me; since you will not leave London, you must give me one of your assistants.''

It is what happens to Kellgreu—that kind of ill-luck : the rich man takes his pupils away (as Rothschild did) and leaves him short handed. Four or five members of the Rothschild family have been patients of Kellgreu—two London ones and a Frank-fort one among the number—and if Madame Dreyfus should wish to apply to them for testimony, I will furnish you their names and addresses. Also, the London address of Mr. Cohen, whose daughter has been under treatment here these past ten weeks. Also the addresses of the other patients here if desired : they all want to testify—among them Miss Schuhmann (bad heart disease) ; she is the daughter of *the* Schuhmann; among them also, Frau von Kopff of Bremen (bad heart disease) given up by the Berlin physicians 12 years ago, and set on her feet by

Kellgreu, and kept in good condition ever since. He cannot *cure* her, but with two months treatment per year he enables her to climb mountains. I have climbed them with her. Also the address of an English clergyman whose daughter (dying of galloping consumption 9 years ago and given up by the physicians) Kellgreu saved, and she has been strong and well ever since. Also my wife can testify, and you know that she is not a flighty person, but has a thoughtful and well balanced head. (She will edit this letter, and see that it has no exaggerations in it: the one I wrote last night she edited into the fire)

Sincerely Yours,

(*Signed*) S. L. CLEMENS.

P.S. It was Frau von Kopff (mentioned above) who put this fortunate (as I regard it) idea into my head. Her heart, like the hearts of all the world, is with that wronged man and his heroic wife, and she came to me with the tears in her eyes and asked if there was no way to get this message to Madame Dreyfus. ''She should know about Kellgreu,'' she said; ''You know, twelve years ago he raised me from the dead.'' Those were her words. Do you know that old American friend of the German Emperor's and mine—Poultney Bigelow, 5 Oakley Street, Chelsea, and Reform Club? He can tell you what Kellgreu did for him when he was dying of dysentery and had been given up by the physicians; also, he can explain the Kellgreu system to you. The Prince of Wales wanted to call Kellgreu when he burst his knee in Rothschild's house—the doctors defeated it.

Truly Yours,

(*Signed*) MARK TWAIN.

Cannot you and M. Zola get this conveyed to Madame Dreyfus, by translation or otherwise?

From a distinguished prelate to His Holiness Leo XIII:

Stuttgart, September 24, 1899.

Monsieur:

At the time when a kind fate has ended the martyrdom of a brave soldier and patriot, I have the honor to share in those good wishes and that sympathy, which the whole civilized world is hastening to express to you. As a former soldier and jurist, I cannot understand the intrigues and the cowardice of that military justice of which a French court has given so sad a display. I hope, Monsieur, that God in his goodness will complete and multiply a thousand times the pardon granted you by the President of the Republic, and will leave you to rest and to forget your suffering in the bosom of your family. I do not know if it be true or whether it be a chauvinist and anticlerical innuendo that suggests that the clergy and Catholics in France are on the side of your adversaries. As a member of the pontifical family, I assure you, Monsieur, that in Germany the Catholic world has always been on your side.

Happy to contribute in these modest lines to the widespread manifestations of sympathy for you, I am, Monsieur, with the assurance of my profound esteem,

Your very devoted,

Von Schad,

Privy Chamberlain of
His Holiness.

From Yves Guyot, editor of the *Siècle,* former Minister of Public Works, one of the founders of the League of the Rights of Man:

Paris, September 27, 1899.

Cher Monsieur:

Without knowing you, I undertook your defense from the very day on which the Court-Martial of 1894 was constituted. When I witnessed the activities of the former Boulangist newspapers, the interview with Mercier, the brutal fashion in which the colonel presiding over the Court-Martial declared the sessions would be *in camera,* I felt that there were other interests at stake than those of the country and of truth, and I said so.

Since that time the facts have demonstrated that you were the victim of the most abominable judicial crime ever committed.

I did not wish to intrude myself upon you in any way by a profession of sympathy for your suffering, but I am taking the occasion offered today to tell you of the profound admiration which your character inspires in me.

Please remember my wife and my daughters to Mme. Dreyfus and present to her my profound respects; and accept for yourself the expression of my warm regard.

YVES GUYOT.

From AUGUSTE LALANCE, former "Protesting Deputy"[8] for Alsace in the Reichstag:

Pfastatt (Haut-Rhin),
September 27, 1899.

My dear Captain:

Yesterday I read your beautiful letter. It moved me deeply, and I shed many tears.

Merci!

And now let my age and my sympathy justify my offering you one counsel, which is one that would be offered you as well by him who is no longer.[9]

It is in your interest, and above all in the higher interest of France, that there should be an end to the agitation centering about your name, that there should be a year's truce, during which silence would be preserved. We must wait for the end of the Exposition[10] before it will be practicable to begin the campaign for your rehabilitation.

Be patient until then. Concern yourself only with the recovery of your health and the care of that admirable wife who has fulfilled all her duties so completely.

The rest will come in due time.

If you attempt to foretell what history will say of you, you will be proud of the splendid place you will occupy.

It will be said that the enemies of the Republic and of liberty, after having attempted to overturn the Republic through Pan-

8. When Bismarck dissolved the Reichstag in January, 1887, and used official pressure to secure deputies who would indorse the Septennate Law (voting appropriations for the Army for seven years), Alsace elected fifteen *députés protestataires*. Lalance, as one of these, was shortly forced out of the Reichstag.

9. Scheurer-Kestner [note of Pierre Dreyfus].

10. The International Exposition of 1900 in Paris.

ama and the Boulangist movement,[11] provoked the Dreyfus Affair and sought to exploit patriotism and religious faith to murder a wretched man and to deceive the people.

But how many good people there were who discerned the danger and rallied about your name, as about a flag, to defend the inheritance left us by our fathers.

Here is fame worthy of a battle won!

You will realize also that, since the world has existed, no one has been more widely known, or excited more feeling. In all the world your name will be immortal.

That is something. And it is glory, even more than one's own gain, that is the principal aim of men of distinction.

That you have! In the hour of your death you will forget your suffering so nobly borne, and you will say: "Mine was a rich life, for I did service to humanity, and I was an honor to my country."

I send Mme. Dreyfus the expression of my profound respect and deep sympathy, and to you I say with the blunt frankness of Sundgau:

"Eat, sleep, embrace your children, and think of nothing in the past. The future belongs to you!"

Your affectionate compatriot,

Aug. Lalance.

From Georges Clemenceau·

Paris, October 15, 1899.

Cher Monsieur;

I hasten to thank you very warmly for your good letter. To fight for you was to fight for France. The good people who have supported your cause have thus won in advance, no matter what happens to them, the most precious recompense, in the feeling that they have accomplished a duty. May we complete the work begun and deliver our unfortunate country from the madmen who bewitch her and lead her to her ruin.

In this terrible drama you will have taken a most cruel share.

11. Referring to the agitations of the adversaries of the Republic at the time of the manoeuvres centering about General Boulanger, the "man on horseback" (1886–89), and those connected with the financial scandals associated with the construction of the Panama Canal (1889–93).

I hope with all my heart that life will provide those compensations which are your due. Your noble brother Mathieu and your admirable wife will contrive them for you. You are still young. Work for those great ideals which, whatever the brutes may say, are the best part of the French *patrie*.

Very cordially yours,

G. CLEMENCEAU.

Conveying his gratification at seeing Dreyfus free and with his family (gratification which was at that time unanimous among the supporters of Dreyfus), the heroic Colonel PICQUART expressed himself in these words:

Paris, October 20, 1899.

My dear Dreyfus:

I am happy to learn that you are with your family, and to think that this frightful nightmare has finally been ended.

Until that was accomplished, it seemed to me that I was associated with your persecutors in a kind of complicity, and I did not rest easy until I saw you free.

What remains to be done is only a formality, for you have been vindicated as no one ever has; you have been vindicated by the voice of the entire world.

Tous mes respects à Mme. Dreyfus et bien à vous.

G. PICQUART.

APPENDIX II

NOTE ON FRENCH COURTS-MARTIAL AND THE FRENCH JUDICIAL SYSTEM

IN the establishment of a case against a person suspected of treason, the Army authorities had at their disposal the assistance of the Judicial Police, a national bureau of detectives whose function it was to apprehend criminals (civil and military), assemble proofs of their guilt, and present them for trial by the relevant courts. In cases involving military justice the Judicial Police acted under the authority of the Commanding General of the Army Corps District. If the evidence appeared to warrant this step, the Commanding General might, following the arrest, order an investigation and appoint a rapporteur. The Dreyfus Case came within the jurisdiction of General Saussier, Military Governor of Paris, who appointed Major Bexon d'Ormescheville as rapporteur.

The rapporteur undertook an investigation of the case, including examination of the accused. When he completed his investigation, he submitted his report to the Commanding General of the Corps District, who then determined whether the prosecution should proceed or the case be dismissed. If he decided for prosecution, the General then convoked the Court-Martial and set the day of its meeting. It was only now (at least three days before the Court-Martial met) that the accused was notified of the charges and permitted to appoint counsel.

There was a permanent Court-Martial at the headquarters of every Army Corps District in France, with two for the Military Government of Paris. Each Court-Martial was composed of a President and six judges named by the Commanding General from a list of eligibles who served in turn. The rank of the members varied according to the rank of the accused, and in the case of a captain consisted of one colonel (president), one lieutenant-colonel, three majors and two captains. Attached to each Court-Martial were a government commissioner (an officer appointed by the Minister of War to serve as prosecuting attorney) and a rapporteur. The sessions of the Court-Martial were regularly public, but if this were deemed dangerous for "public order or morals," the sessions might be held *in camera* (as was done in the Dreyfus Case). The judgment was reached by majority vote, and was always pronounced in a public session.

Appeal from the judgment of the Court-Martial lay either to the Military Court of Appeal or to the Court of Cassation. The Military Court of Appeal could take cognizance only of questions of law and not of questions of fact. It could address itself only to the question as to whether the procedure had been regular and whether the law had been respected by the judges. On the other hand, the Court of Cassation had a special procedure for such appeals.

The Court of Cassation, sitting in Paris, is the highest court of appeal in France. It is composed of three Divisions, each with fifteen justices and a presiding justice, with a chief justice for the Court as a whole. The Division of Requests and the Civil Division are concerned with appeals in civil suits. The Criminal Division has jurisdiction over criminal appeals, hence over those coming up from Courts-Martial. In these cases, where sentence has presumably been pronounced on an innocent person as the result of false testimony, the Court does not merely consider errors of law but enters into an examination of the facts, holds an inquiry, hears witnesses, and may set aside the judgment of the Court-Martial.

In the period of the Dreyfus Case, the procedure of appeal of a decision by a Court-Martial was initiated by submitting a request for an appeal, setting forth the "new evidence" which had been discovered since the original judgment, the evidence in support of false testimony, and so on (Dreyfus' second request for an appeal appears in Appendix VI). This request was first scrutinized by the Committee on Appeal of the Ministry of Justice, which verified the accuracy of the proofs furnished and determined whether the new evidence fell within the prescriptions of the law. If the Committee's decision was favorable, the request was then submitted to the Criminal Division of the Court of Cassation. The Criminal Division then proceeded to an intensive inquiry. It heard the report of its own rapporteur (one of the justices appointed for this purpose), the charge of its prosecuting attorney (procureur général), the plea of counsel for the condemned, the evidence of witnesses purporting to establish perjury, forgery, etc., in the original trial. The purpose of this inquiry was to determine whether the Criminal Division should allow the request for an appeal. If the request were allowed, then the appeal was argued before the full bench (the Criminal Division, Civil Division, and Division of Requests),[1] which might (1) uphold the original decision; (2) set aside the original decision and remand the case to a new Court-Martial (as the Court did in the Dreyfus appeal in 1899); or, (3) in certain instances,[2] set aside the decision without remand. In the latter case the decision of the Court of Cassation was final. It was this last-named alternative which the Court used in the final decision of 1906 in the Dreyfus Case.

1. Appeals from decisions of Courts-Martial were decided by the Criminal Division alone until the Law of *Dessaisissement* (March 1899), which required decisions by the full bench. This law resulted from the outcry against alleged ''partiality'' of the justices at the time of the first Dreyfus appeal (*see* p. 129). It was abrogated in 1909.

2. *See* p. 227.

APPENDIX III

DEVIL'S ISLAND

FRENCH GUIANA, the seat of the French penal settlement, is situated between Dutch Guiana and Brazil, with an area of about 51,000 square miles and a population of approximately 30,000 inhabitants. Off the coast are the three Salvation Islands, Île Royale, Saint Joseph, and Devil's Island, which make up the special penal colony, primarily for insane and dangerous criminals, and traitors. French Guiana was first made a penal colony by a decree of 1852, and received some 18,000 convicts up to 1867, when New Caledonia superseded it as the chief penal settlement in the French colonies. In 1885, however, French Guiana was appointed as a place of banishment for confirmed criminals and for convicts sentenced to more than eight years' hard labor. Ten years later, exceptional legislation,[1] inspired by General Mercier with Dreyfus in mind, was passed, which set aside the Salvation Islands, in addition to Ducos Island (New Caledonia), for prisoners who were to be deported oversea for confinement within a "fortified inclosure."[2] During the past fifty years some 75,000 prisoners have been sent to the penal settlement in French Guiana.

The rainy season begins in November or December and lasts until the latter part of June. The remainder of the year is practically rainless, but the air is always very humid. During the warmer part of the year, August through October, the temperature frequently rises to 86 degrees, but it rarely exceeds 88. In the cooler season the range varies between 70 and 79 degrees. Although the islands lie just south of the equator, the climate is not oppressive. There is usually a fresh trade wind blowing from the southeast.

Île Royale is the largest of the three islands. It is slightly less than a mile in length, and rises about 200 feet above the sea. The most dangerous prisoners are kept on Île Royale, as they were in

1. Passed by Parliament on February 9, 1895.
2. See p. 72.

Dreyfus' day. On Saint Joseph, which is very small, is the mental institution and the house of correction. The crime for which a man is sent to Devil's Island is usually treason. Alone of the three, it maintains a small, well-kept cemetery: on the other islands, the practice is to cast deceased convicts into the shark-infested waters surrounding the islands. No one has ever escaped from Devil's Island itself. Captain Dreyfus was the first and the best known of all its prisoners. Before he was sent there, the island had served for a leper colony, whose huts had been destroyed shortly before his arrival. After his return to France, no prisoner arrived on Devil's Island until 1909.

APPENDIX IV

"THE FIRST PLEA FOR DREYFUS"

At the end of the month of May, 1900, there was placed in my hands a pamphlet entitled, *The First Plea for Dreyfus*, the text of a letter written from London on January 7, 1895, by the distinguished Brazilian statesman, Ruy Barbosa, and published on the following third of February in the newspaper, *Do Commercio de Rio de Janeiro*. This letter is very curious and interesting by reason of the date at which it was written. Some extracts from it follow:[1]

Here is an event of seemingly tragic character, differently viewed through the eyes of two nations which, although they are separated only by the waters of the Channel, have been summoned to pass judgment on it simultaneously, one of them to find for it a practical solution, the other to examine it solely from an ethical point of view . . .

All that is known of the causes leading to this terrible judgment is to be found in the interrupted sentence of Maître Demange, who declared at the beginning of the Court sessions that the whole accusation rested exclusively upon a document whose authenticity was disputed. The officer presiding over the Court interrupted the lawyer's revelation; it was voted that the trial should be held *in camera;* and the proceedings entered upon the mysterious road which was to lead to the condemnation of the accused . . .

It is not my function to describe in all its details the frightful ceremony accompanying the military degradation, terrible prelude to the superhuman atonement which began yesterday for this wretched man. This cruel spectacle has made all Europe shiver with horror . . .

What divine power could endow this man with the strength to survive the strain attending such an ordeal? Except when one has to do with a wretch of hardened countenance, of heart made

1. The introductory note is by Alfred Dreyfus.

callous by the habitual practice of those vices which destroy strength of character and render the basest villains shameless, there are only two forces capable of protecting the spirit against the shock of so terrible a fall, against the despair caused by so extraordinary a fate: insanity or innocence. But let us not forget that upon Dreyfus' past there is no stain; not the shadow of a suspicion hovers over it. Fifteen years of blameless service, and the position of importance and confidence which he occupies in one of the most delicate branches of the military administration testify to his official reputation. A private fortune assured him not only the necessities but the luxuries of life. A wealthy family, simple habits, a hatred of gambling, a private life bounded by the narrow limits of family affection exclude the hypothesis of one of those mysterious situations which are often the key to clandestine calamities to men's honor. To what unexplained temptation then would this man have suddenly succumbed, proud as he was of the profession to which he belonged, and which his fellow citizens view as an object of the most noble hopes?

Observing witnesses of the degradation declare that the face of the condemned man did not once pale. He held his head high throughout. His step did not falter . . .

When, under the heavy hand of the officer in charge, his *képi* slid down over his eyes,[2] Dreyfus raised his hand with a gesture of entreaty: "By my wife and my children," he cried, "I swear that I am innocent! *Vive la France!*" To the hoots of a group of officers, he replied in tones of sincerity: "Kill me, but do not insult me. I am innocent!" . . .

These persistent protestations of innocence, given the preceding and accompanying circumstances, have no equal . . . Their effect was tremendous.

And yet among Frenchmen it is not even permitted to doubt Dreyfus' crime for an instant . . .

Guilty of what, this criminal? No one knew, and today among the public no one knows.

Nevertheless the existence of the treason has crystallized into an indisputable fact, having all the force of a *chose jugée*.

Where is the *corpus delicti?*

2. As the officer, perhaps roughly, pulled the gold cord from the *képi* (the French military cap).

Where is the proof which links it with the accused?

No one can put his finger on it. No one has seen the dossier. No one is acquainted with the documents, or the testimony of the witnesses. They talk of a paper whose handwriting is attributed to the condemned man, but the only thing that is known about this subject with anything approaching certainty—thanks to the observations echoed in the *Figaro*—is that, of the five experts intrusted with the examination of this document, three declared it to be by Dreyfus, and two supported the contrary view.

As he meditates on these facts, the foreign observer will with difficulty escape an impression of doubt concerning the Dreyfus affair.

This man was condemned in the minds of his compatriots before he was convicted by the secret Court which passed judgment on him. Several weeks before the decision, the Minister of War declared himself convinced of the guilt of the accused. . . .

APPENDIX V

THE ATTEMPT OF SCHEURER-KESTNER TO
INFORM DREYFUS OF HIS INTEREST

JOSEPH REINACH spoke to me of a letter which he had asked Lebon, the Colonial Minister, to forward to me at Devil's Island in September, 1897.[1] Lebon, however, had refused. I asked Reinach to give me the letter, and I also looked up the letters he had written my wife concerning Scheurer-Kestner at this same period. I should like to quote here the principal ones of these, which explain more adequately than any words can the splendid role played by Scheurer-Kestner and by Reinach, and which reveal their generosity and their courage.

On July 17, 1897, my wife received the first letter from Reinach, advising her that Scheurer-Kestner had become convinced of my innocence. She was also informed that, to provide for the eventuality of his death, Scheurer-Kestner was bequeathing to a certain person the responsibility for continuing his work. This was his letter:

Madame:

I have been authorized by my friend, Scheurer-Kestner, Vice-President of the Senate, to tell you that, after the long and painstaking inquiry he has made, he has become convinced of Captain Dreyfus' innocence. You must have been told by Bernard Lazare why I submitted to Scheurer-Kestner this case, which has interested me so deeply and so long. For his part, Scheurer-Kestner had been busy (how, is his own secret), but since July 13 he has been satisfied, and he has said openly to his fellow officers of the Senate and to numerous friends that he is convinced of the Captain's innocence. And he doesn't at all mind saying so to anyone who will listen. What he intends to do henceforth is also his secret. In addition to this message, which he asked me to give you, however, and which I do with deep gratification, I am commissioned to give you two others.

The first is that Scheurer-Kestner, who never ceases thinking with poignant emotion of the martyrdom Captain Dreyfus endures, would be happy if you should find a way to inform him that one of the most

1. The explanatory remarks in this section are by Alfred Dreyfus.

important personages in the Senate (do not name him at this time) has become convinced of his innocence, and will labor henceforth to accomplish what he considers to be an imperative duty. This news will perhaps be, will certainly be, of a nature to mitigate in a measure your husband's cruel torture, and to arm his spirit with the will to live, with joyous hope. The Captain must have no illusions about an early victory. There are still difficulties everywhere. But it is right and desirable that he should know that a powerful and effective step is about to be taken on his behalf. May each of your letters henceforth bring him this assurance: this is Scheurer-Kestner's wish, as it is mine. This is the dawn which reveals the horizon.

How Scheurer-Kestner became convinced is a matter of knowledge. Maître Leblois sought out Scheurer, who was already devoured by doubt, and repeated to him the confidences of his friend, Lieutenant-Colonel Picquart, who had become convinced of my innocence and of Esterhazy's guilt.

My wife was delighted to comply with Scheurer's wish. She wrote to me at Devil's Island that an important personage in the Senate had taken up my case. But this passage was suppressed in the letters I received from my wife, letters which at this time reached me only abridged and as copies.

On August 18, 1897, Joseph Reinach sent my wife this letter:

I should like to convey to you the two following extracts from letters I have received from Scheurer-Kestner:

Under the date of August 7: "I am not at the end of my difficulties, far from it, but I have without reservation let my head surrender to my heart, and I shall win out in the end. I have taken a new step in the past week. It is impossible to describe to you my joy when I think of the happiness which is to be restored. I am like a child thinking of his Christmas toys. And my heart leaps."

Under date of August 11: "This case is becoming an obsession with me. I am waiting impatiently for the day when I can make a public declaration."

On September 10, 1897, Joseph Reinach wrote my wife these lines:

I have received a splendid letter from Scheurer-Kestner, who asks that I cry more loudly than ever that he, Scheurer-Kestner, is convinced. He tells me that he is continuing his campaign of propaganda . . . Here is the end of his letter: "We must continue to have Dreyfus informed that someone is active on his behalf; this must be repeated, if it is feared that one letter has been withheld . . . If, however, contrary to all likelihood, all those letters in which my intervention is mentioned are withheld, then I will write him myself. For the information which I have gathered since my departure only strengthens my conviction. Justice must be done. Justice will be done, or I will perish in the attempt."

When my letters continued to arrive with their same melancholy burden and brimming with impatience, Joseph Reinach understood that the news of Scheurer-Kestner's intervention must not have reached me. He then decided to write himself, and sought an interview with Lebon, the Colonial Minister, in order to submit to him his message and ask him to forward it.

This is the text of the letter intended for me:

Paris, September 12, 1897.

Monsieur:

Perhaps we have never seen each other, we have certainly never exchanged a word. Yet almost immediately following your accusation, I had the feeling that you had not committed the abominable crime with which you were charged, that you were the victim of a terrible judicial blunder. A crime without a motive seemed to me a material impossibility. That a French officer, young, eager, ambitious, assured of a brilliant future, should commit treason for the mere pleasure of committing treason—that seemed to me a moral impossibility. Your attitude on the day of the terrible degradation ceremony, your obvious determination to remain a soldier to the end, completed my conviction.

Last winter a valiant writer of great talent, Bernard Lazare, was the first to have the courage to declare your innocence, which he did in a pamphlet signed with his own name. However, since he had been able to assemble only proofs of a negative character, his immediate success was not what he or your family or your unknown friends had hoped. We were obliged again to be silent, and to wait. You were our perennial scourge. Silence weighed heavily upon us. Then the thought of the injustice to redress, of your sufferings so heroically endured, of the affecting grief of your family, urged us on, and we set ourselves again to the task. In the past few months above all, we have made important converts—officers, writers, savants, historians, public men—whose names you will learn later. With indescribable persistence, Bernard Lazare has never ceased his work of propaganda and the gathering of new proofs.

On July 13 last, definitive conviction was formed in the mind of a man who, by his political position, his high moral character, and his Alsatian origin, seems predestined to be the victorious advocate of your just cause. He has authorized me to give you his name, and it is with his permission that I am writing you. He is Scheurer-Kestner, former Deputy from Upper Alsace and from the Seine in the National Assembly, Senator for life, First Vice-President of the Senate, one of Gambetta's most devoted friends. It is not for me to tell you how he became convinced of your innocence. I must content myself with telling you that on July 14 he confided his conviction to his fellow officers in the Senate, and then asked his friends to cry *urbi et orbi* that he, Scheurer-Kestner, was convinced that you were the victim of a judicial wrong. M. Scheurer-Kestner asked me to advise Mme. Dreyfus so that she might inform you at once of this important and happy news. Need I describe for you the joy of this splendid woman? She wrote you by the first mail, but did her letter reach you? Did it reach you in its complete form? She has had some reason to doubt that. The last letter she received from you, which she sent me and which I communicated to Scheurer-Kestner, was so melancholy and so painful, in spite of the undiminished confidence which you expressed in the future, and it affected us so deeply, that I decided, in agreement with Scheurer, to write you myself. In the letter I received from him this morning, Scheurer declared to me more explicitly than ever his deep and unshaken conviction. He will take action before the end of the year. He has put his whole heart in this work of justice. He writes me: "Justice will be done, or I will perish in the attempt."

At present Scheurer-Kestner is above all desirous that you should be informed. He thinks, he knows that the certainty that your cause, far from being abandoned, has just found the most resolute of defenders, will give you in the long and terrible torment to which you are subjected the strength to live—both the spiritual and the physical strength. It is not enough for us that your memory should be vindicated; justice must be done while you live. Let us hope that the prospect of aid which this patriot brings you will sustain you in your trials, during the last hours of an ordeal so courageously endured. Live! Live for your noble wife! Live for your children, for your brothers, whose devotion has never wearied! Live, Monsieur—I say it with confidence—for France and for the Army!

The interview of Joseph Reinach with Lebon, the Colonial Minister, took place on September 15, 1897. Lebon refused to forward the letter. Reinach reported the results of his interview to Scheurer-Kestner in these words:

September 15, 1897.

My dear Friend:

This morning I went to see Lebon, who had given me an appointment. After a few introductory remarks, I showed him, or rather I read him, the frank letter you had written me. He listened with his usual immobility, smoking a cigarette meanwhile. I then asked him to be good enough to forward to its destination an unsealed letter, which quite naturally he would read. Indeed I offered to read him the letter, in which I informed Dreyfus of your conviction of his innocence and your determination to have justice done. Immediately, and with the same immobility, Lebon declared that he would not forward my letter. I pointed out to him how deep your conviction was, that you were determined to act, how much you desired that this unfortunate man should be informed that his ordeal was approaching its end, and that devoted, resolute, and powerful support was assured him. Fresh refusal. Lebon explained to me, with more embarrassment, that he read all of Dreyfus' correspondence, but that he was not the only one who read it, that it was subsequently read by members of the penitentiary administration in Guiana, of which he was yet more suspicious. As a result my letter would run the risk of becoming known, and for me, as a Jew, this might be a cause of annoyance. I thanked him for concerning himself with my interests, but I told him that I was in the habit of assuming my own responsibilities, and that I was ready to take that of informing a martyr that the First Vice-President of the Senate believed him innocent and was taking an interest in his case. Fresh refusal, always very gentle, but always explicit. "Since you yourself read all the correspondence," I then said to Lebon, "you must have read the postscript of a letter of about July 20, in which Mme. Dreyfus informed her husband that an important personage in the Senate had taken up his case?" "Quite," replied Lebon, "I read it, and I did not let it pass. I did not know that it concerned Scheurer-Kestner, but if his name had appeared in the letter, I should have withheld it just the same . . ." I replied: "Then it is useless to try to inform this wretched and despairing man, who is dying, that aid is on the way." Lebon replied calmly that, if he had been in Dreyfus' place, he would have been dead long ago. I: "But that would have been a confession of guilt." Lebon continued: "That's one way of looking at the matter . . . Then, too, his wife writes him regularly that efforts are being made in his behalf, and I permit the letters to be forwarded so long as no details are given." I tried to make Lebon understand that for three years the wretched man had been surfeited with vague formulas; that the force of a letter which should speak out, which should "name you," would be very different; that if Dreyfus should die before you had been able to act, he, Lebon, would assume a terrible responsibility. He replied that his profession as jailor disgusted him, that it was in fact an abomination to him, but that he could do nothing but repeat to me what he had already said: he would not forward my letter. He added, however, that if "you," who are not a Jew and who are First Vice-President of the Senate, should write Dreyfus to tell him of your conviction, he would submit your letter to the Cabinet, which would decide the question on its own responsibility, a responsibility which he did not wish to assume alone.

I see that Lebon is leaving for Senegal, and that the next Cabinet meeting will take place at the end of September. Hence this is a disguised refusal, a new postponement. In short, I said to him all that one could say to a man. Wasted effort. He will not forward my letter; he will eventually submit yours to the Cabinet; he will speak of my visit to Méline. Then he tried to win my pity for the profession which he, Lebon, is condemned to follow. "Reflect," he said to me in these very words, "that last year, when the rumor was spread of his escape, I was obliged to have him put in irons for a month, and yet he had done nothing." At this I jumped up: "What, just because the *Libre parole* published a baseless story, you inflicted a new and unmerited torture on this unfortunate wretch!" With his imperturbable calm he replied: "I had to do it. Ah, how my profession disgusts me . . . !"

The interview, which had lasted an hour, I brought to an end when I told him that I would inform you of our conversation and of his refusal.

The acts and words of Lebon so well describe the man that comment would be superfluous: his heart was in his minister's portfolio. It was not for one month that he made me endure the torture of the double shackle, but for nearly two.

APPENDIX VI

DREYFUS' REQUEST FOR AN APPEAL, 1903

To the Keeper of the Seals, Minister of Justice,
November 25, 1903.

Monsieur le Ministre:

I have the honor to ask of your justice the review of the decision of the Court-Martial at Rennes, which, on September 9, 1899, by a majority of 5 votes to 2, declared me guilty with extenuating circumstances.

This condemnation, inexplicable after the decision of the full bench of the Court of Cassation of June 3, 1899, was pronounced on the basis of forged documents and perjury; and new evidence demonstrates that I was for the second time condemned when manifestly innocent.

During the debates in the Chamber of Deputies on April 6 and 7, 1903, Deputy Jaurès proved that an audacious forgery had weighed on the consciences of certain judges. This forgery is a document attributed to the German Emperor, and it was said to have been used without the knowledge of the defense, which was ignorant of its existence.

On April 21, 1903, I had the honor to direct to the Minister of War, administrative head of the departments concerned with military jurisdiction, a request for an investigation of the serious errors committed at my expense in the departments subject to his direction.

The results of this investigation, to which I cannot be refused access, have not yet been communicated to me, but I have reason to believe that they completely justify the review which I am asking.

The Minister of War, to whom my request will surely be transmitted, will not fail, moreover, to inform you of the results of the investigation which he undertook as a result of my request of April 21, 1903.

In addition to the decisive results of this investigation, a review is also justified by the following considerations:

PERJURY AND FORGERY

Perjury of Cernuszki: One Cernuszki, a new witness summoned to Rennes by the representatives of the prosecution, declared that he had learned from an Austrian Aulic Councilor,[1] Dr. Mosetig, that I was a spy in the pay of Germany. This evidence was untrue. Its falsity is demonstrated by an authentic declaration by Dr. Mosetig, which I appended to my request for an investigation on April 21, 1903.

In that request I mentioned to the Minister of War the important revelations of a certain Wessel with respect to plots in which agents of the Intelligence Bureau and the perjured witness were concerned. These revelations are confirmed in a memorandum by Wessel to his attorney, Raimondo, forwarded to Maître Mornard and appended to this request. They are also confirmed by a letter of Mme. Wessel to M. Gabriel Monod, sent by the latter to the Minister of War.

Perjuries of Savignaud and Gribelin: Savignaud was a witness recruited by the prosecution to destroy the testimony of Lieutenant-Colonel Picquart, who had discovered the blunder committed by the judges in 1894 and the manoeuvres directed against me.

The Archivist Gribelin had been summoned to give testimony in a similar vein.

Savignaud's perjury is established by letters of M. Scheurer-Kestner and Maître Leblois. Gribelin's perjury he has himself admitted.

Forgeries: The secret dossier used against me contained altered documents; moreover, those who made use of them could not have been ignorant of their falsity.

The document attributed to the German Emperor, the existence of which was explicitly recognized in a letter of M. Ferlet de Bourbonne, is a forgery. The letters sent by Dr. Dumas to Maître Mornard, and forwarded by my attorney to the Ministry of War, show what use was made of this document at the Rennes trial.

NEW EVIDENCE

Colonel von Schwartzkoppen and Colonel Panizzardi, who

1. The Aulic Council was the organ which directed the Austrian Army under the Imperial Regime.

were, according to the prosecution, the foreign representatives to whom I was said to have delivered secret documents, have both admitted that they had never had any relations with me.

A letter from Colonel Chauvet of the Swiss Army to Professor Andrade, sent by M. Andrade to the Minister of Justice, Monis, after the Rennes trial, recounts the solemn affirmations of Herr von Schwartzkoppen.

Herr von Schwartzkoppen's word of honor that he had never had any traffic with me, direct or indirect, was likewise known to the prosecution, which concealed it from my judges. The Minister of War has proofs of it in his archives.

A letter from Prince von Münster to M. Joseph Reinach contains the same affirmations and revealed for the first time that Colonel von Schwartzkoppen had admitted to his Ambassador that the spy who brought him information was Esterhazy, and that their relations went back to 1893. I am appending to my request this letter, which was published by the *Temps* of April 25, 1903, and which the recipient was good enough to give me.

As to Colonel Panizzardi, the telegram so often referred to during the trial would have had a decisive influence on the minds of the judges, if the prosecution had not attempted by illegal means[2] to falsify it in the course of decoding. Moreover, the Minister of War possessed at that moment documents concealed by my accusers and proving that the spy who acted as Colonel Panizzardi's informant continued his relations with the latter after my arrest.

My condemnation, extorted with such difficulty from judges whose doubts were expressed in the form of "extenuating circumstances," was then the product of forgery and falsehood.

I ask the review of my case, because I must have my honor in its integrity, for my children and for myself, and because I have never failed in any of my duties as a soldier and as a Frenchman.

Please accept, *Monsieur le Ministre*, the assurance of my deep respect.

2. *See* pp. 50–51.

INDEX